Leo Strauss on Nietzsche's
Thus Spoke Zarathustra

The Leo Strauss Transcript Series

SERIES EDITORS: NATHAN TARCOV AND GAYLE MCKEEN

 The Leo Strauss Center
The University of Chicago
HTTP://LEOSTRAUSSCENTER.UCHICAGO.EDU/

VOLUMES IN THE SERIES:

Strauss on Nietzsche's Thus Spoke Zarathustra
Edited by Richard L. Velkley

Leo Strauss on Nietzsche's *Thus Spoke Zarathustra*

Edited and with an Introduction by
Richard L. Velkley

THE UNIVERSITY OF CHICAGO PRESS
Chicago and London

The University of Chicago Press, Chicago 60637
The University of Chicago Press, Ltd., London
© 2017 by The University of Chicago
All rights reserved. No part of this book may be used or reproduced in any manner whatsoever
without written permission, except in the case of brief quotations in critical articles and reviews.
For more information, contact the University of Chicago Press, 1427 E. 60th St., Chicago, IL 60637.
Published 2017
Paperback edition 2021
Printed in the United States of America

30 29 28 27 26 25 24 23 22 21   1 2 3 4 5

ISBN-13: 978-0-226-48663-5 (cloth)
ISBN-13: 978-0-226-81679-1 (paper)
ISBN-13: 978-0-226-48677-2 (e-book)
DOI: https://doi.org/10.7208/chicago/9780226486772.001.0001

Scattered excerpts from THE PORTABLE NIETZSCHE by Friedrich Nietzsche, edited by
Walter Kaufmann, translated by Walter Kaufmann, translation copyright 1954, © 1968, renewed
© 1982 by Penguin Random House LLC, used by permission of Viking Books, an imprint of
Penguin Publishing Group, a division of Penguin Random House LLC.

LIBRARY OF CONGRESS CATALOGING-IN-PUBLICATION DATA

Names: Strauss, Leo, author. | Velkley, Richard L., editor.
Title: Leo Strauss on Nietzsche's Thus spoke Zarathustra / edited and with an introduction by
    Richard L. Velkley.
Description: Chicago : The University of Chicago Press, 2017. | Includes index.
Identifiers: LCCN 2017003600 | ISBN 9780226486635 (cloth : alk. paper) | ISBN 9780226486772
    (e-book)
Subjects: LCSH: Nietzsche, Friedrich Wilhelm, 1844–1900. Also sprach Zarathustra. |
    Philosophy, German.
Classification: LCC B3313.A44 S77 2017 | DDC 193—dc23
LC record available at https://lccn.loc.gov/2017003600

♾ This paper meets the requirements of ANSI/NISO Z39.48-1992 (Permanence of Paper).

Contents

The Leo Strauss Transcript Project

Leo Strauss is well known as a thinker and writer, but he also had tremendous impact as a teacher. In the transcripts of his courses one can
see Strauss comment on texts, including many he wrote little or nothing about, and respond generously to student questions and objections.
The transcripts, amounting to more than twice the volume of Strauss's
published work, add immensely to the material available to scholars and
students of Strauss's work.

In the early 1950s mimeographed typescripts of student notes of
Strauss's courses were distributed among his students. In winter 1954,
the first recording, of his course on natural right, was transcribed and
distributed to students. Strauss's colleague Herbert J. Storing obtained a
grant from the Relm Foundation to support the taping and transcription,
which resumed on a regular basis in the winter of 1956 with Strauss's
course "Historicism and Modern Relativism." Of the 39 courses Strauss
taught at the University of Chicago from 1958 until his departure in 1968,
34 were recorded and transcribed. After he retired from Chicago, recording of his courses continued at Claremont Men's College in the spring of
1968 and the fall and spring of 1969 (although the tapes for his last two
courses there have not been located), and at St. John's College for the four
years until his death in October 1973.

The surviving original audio recordings vary widely in quality and
completeness, and after they had been transcribed, the audiotapes were
sometimes reused, leaving the audio record very incomplete. Over time
the audiotape deteriorated. Beginning in the late 1990s, Stephen Gregory,
then administrator of the University's John M. Olin Center for Inquiry
into the Theory and Practice of Democracy funded by the John M. Olin
Foundation, initiated digital remastering of the surviving tapes by Craig
Harding of September Media to ensure their preservation, improve their
audibility, and make possible their eventual publication. This project re-

ceived financial support from the Olin Center and from the Division of
Preservation and Access of the National Endowment for the Humanities.
The remastered audiofiles are available at the Strauss Center website:
https://leostrausscenter.uchicago.edu/courses.

Strauss permitted the taping and transcribing to go forward but did
not check the transcripts or otherwise participate in the project. Accordingly, Strauss's close associate and colleague Joseph Cropsey originally put
the copyright in his own name, though he assigned copyright to the Estate
of Leo Strauss in 2008. Beginning in 1958 a headnote was placed at the
beginning of each transcript: "This transcription is a written record of
essentially oral material, much of which developed spontaneously in the
classroom and none of which was prepared with publication in mind. The
transcription is made available to a limited number of interested persons,
with the understanding that no use will be made of it that is inconsistent
with the private and partly informal origin of the material. Recipients
are emphatically requested not to seek to increase the circulation of the
transcription. This transcription has not been checked, seen, or passed
on by the lecturer." In 2008, Strauss's heir, his daughter Jenny Strauss,
asked Nathan Tarcov to succeed Joseph Cropsey as Strauss's literary executor. They agreed that because of the widespread circulation of the old,
often inaccurate and incomplete transcripts and the continuing interest in
Strauss's thought and teaching, it would be a service to interested scholars
and students to proceed with publication of the remastered audiofiles and
transcripts. They were encouraged by the fact that Strauss himself signed
a contract with Bantam Books to publish four of the transcripts although
in the end none were published.

The University's Leo Strauss Center, established in 2008, launched a
project, presided over by its director, Nathan Tarcov, and managed by
Stephen Gregory, to correct the old transcripts on the basis of the remastered audiofiles as they became available, transcribe those audiofiles
not previously transcribed, and annotate and edit for readability all the
transcripts including those for which no audiofiles survived. This project
was supported by grants from the Winiarski Family Foundation, Mr.
Richard S. Shiffrin and Mrs. Barbara Z. Schiffrin, Earhart Foundation,
and the Hertog Foundation, and contributions from numerous other donors. The Strauss Center was ably assisted in its fundraising efforts by
Nina Botting-Herbst and Patrick McCusker of the Office of the Dean of
the Division of the Social Sciences at the University.

Senior scholars familiar with both Strauss's work and the texts he taught were commissioned as editors, with preliminary work done in most cases by student editorial assistants. The goal in editing the transcripts has been to preserve Strauss's original words as much as possible while making the transcripts easier to read. Strauss's impact (and indeed his charm) as a teacher is revealed in the sometimes informal character of his remarks. Readers should make allowance for the oral character of the transcripts. There are careless phrases, slips of the tongue, repetitions, and possible mistranscriptions. However enlightening the transcripts are, they cannot be regarded as the equivalent of works that Strauss himself wrote for publication.

Nathan Tarcov, Editor-in-Chief
Gayle McKeen, Managing Editor
August 2014

Editor's Introduction

Strauss, Nietzsche, and the History
of Political Philosophy

Leo Strauss had a special relation to Nietzsche's philosophy from his early years. He remarks that being "dominated and charmed" by Nietzsche between the ages of twenty-two and thirty, "I believed literally every word I understood in him."[1] At age thirty he writes that "through Nietzsche tradition has been shaken to its roots. It has completely lost its self-evident truth," an event he finds liberating since it means that one is now free to raise "the question *pos bioteon* [how to live] again."[2] Nietzsche and Heidegger together are the figures that Strauss sees in the early 1930s as exposing "the unradicality of modern philosophy," consisting in its belief that "it can presuppose the fundamental questions as already answered, and that it therefore can 'progress.'"[3] Specific failures in modern philosophy revealed by these two figures are the neglect of the Socratic question about the best life (Nietzsche) and the question about Being (Heidegger). These thinkers complete modern philosophy even as they bring it to an end, and they "lead to the point at which Socrates begins."[4] Yet both also draw on the Christian tradition in different ways. In Nietzsche's case this appears in his account of the "probity" of conscience, a factor in his thought that complicates, if not undermines, his effort to recover the "original ideal" of philosophy in the Greeks. Strauss in 1933 claims that Nietzsche fails to overthrow the powers he struggled against, while Plato enables one to "pose Nietzsche's questions, thus *our* questions, in a simpler, clearer, and more original way."[5] With this insight Strauss begins the return to premodern rationalism, the possibility of which he previously doubted.[6]

In the following decades Strauss develops his understanding of the history of political philosophy and the central problem that underlies the contrast between premodern and modern rationalism: the inherently aporetic relation of the philosophic way of life to its political context. Strauss arrives at the view that modern rationalism, although having "unradical" consequences in cementing the dogma of progress (the belief that philosophy or science is able and required to solve the fundamental human problems), is founded by a radical innovator, Niccolo Machiavelli. Writing of Machiavelli, Strauss states:

> He achieves the decisive turn toward the notion of philosophy according to which its purpose is to relieve man's estate or to increase man's power or to guide man toward the rational society, the bond and the end of which is enlightened self-interest or the comfortable self-preservation of its members. The cave becomes the "substance." By supplying all men with the goods which they desire, by being the obvious benefactress of all men, philosophy (or science) ceases to be suspect or alien.[7]

Strauss proposes that the "realism" of Machiavelli, or his critique of the ideal republics and principalities of premodern philosophy, is adopted by the succeeding tradition of modern philosophy in its project of relieving man's estate, with the intent to overcome the philosopher's ancient plight as outsider and exile. Strauss ascribes to the modern philosopher the primacy of a practical end that is beneficial to all humans, although perhaps above all to the philosopher. The practical end surpasses, if it does not simply replace, contemplative activity as the core of philosophy.

In Strauss's account, philosophy's assumption of the task of mastering nature requires the narrowing of the horizon of philosophical thought to the temporal-historical realm of human projects. In the course of three successive "waves," the enlargement of philosophy's practical responsibility for human welfare is accompanied by the deepening historicization of its theoretical foundations. Nietzsche is the profoundly paradoxical completion of this development, in that his thought presents both a radical critique of modern rationalism and the consummation of the historical turn in modern philosophy. He is thus a crucial figure for Strauss's conception of the history of political philosophy, indeed of the history of philosophy as such. In Strauss's unconventional usage, "political philosophy" is the reflection on the political conditions of philosophy, or on the ineluctable tension between politics and the inquiring mind (thematic throughout Greek poetry, history, and philosophy, but emerging most fully with Socrates), which forms an indispensable (but in the course of modernity, increasingly neglected) starting point of philosophy. In ascribing to Nietzsche a critical-pivotal position as both completing this history and pointing to a new beginning, Strauss gives him a role notably akin to the one he plays in Heidegger's "history of Being." Accordingly, in Strauss's 1959 and 1967 Nietzsche seminars, the reflection on Nietzsche's dual character (as radically modern and as seeking the recovery of Greek wisdom) proceeds as an implicit dialogue with Heidegger's interpretations of Nietzsche. Although this has been little appreciated, Strauss's reading of Nietzsche is one of the major philosophical-historical inquiries of the past century, being not only an original interpretation of this author but also centrally engaged with the foremost reexaminations of the basis and meaning of modernity in recent philosophy. The remarks that follow offer preliminary considerations on Strauss's fascinating friendly agon with the explosive duality of Nietzsche, about which one gains only indications from Strauss's published works.

From his early years onward, Strauss understands that Nietzsche's true concern is with philosophy and not politics. In his later writing and teaching Strauss returns to crediting Nietzsche with rediscovering "the problem of Socrates," thus raising anew the question of the meaning and goodness of the life dedicated to knowledge, even as Nietzsche himself rejects the Socratic alternative as Nietzsche interprets it.[8] But at the time of the 1959 seminar on *Thus Spoke Zarathustra*, Strauss's most prominent published statement on Nietzsche is the concluding paragraph of the lecture "What Is Political Philosophy?" in which the connection between Nietzsche and Socrates is absent.[9] It describes the most widely known perspective of Strauss on Nietzsche as the initiator of the "third wave" of modernity, and it is highly critical in tone. Nevertheless, it sketches some of the most important themes of the contemporary seminar: (1) While retaining the nineteenth-century discovery of the "historical consciousness," Nietzsche rejected the view that the historical process is rational; (2) he rejected the belief that a harmony between the genuine individual and the modern state is possible, thus returning to Rousseau's antinomy from Hegel's reconciliation; (3) he held that all human life and human thought ultimately rest on horizon-forming creations that are not susceptible to rational legitimization; (4) he proposed that the great individuals are creators of horizons, and that the will to power explains their activity; (5) Nietzsche's call to creativity was addressed to individuals who should revolutionize their lives, not to society or the nation, but even so Nietzsche hoped that the genuine creators would form a new nobility able to rule the planet; (6) Nietzsche "used much of his unsurpassable and inexhaustible power" of speech to make his readers loathe all existing political alternatives, without pointing the way to political responsibility, thus helping to prepare the fascist regimes. As an addendum, Strauss alludes to Heidegger, noting that "the difficulty of the philosophy of the will to power led after Nietzsche to the explicit renunciation of eternity."

In the 1959 seminar on *Zarathustra* and the 1967 seminar on *Beyond Good and Evil* and *Genealogy of Morals*, a deeper and more sympathetic account of Nietzsche appears than what the publications before 1960 suggest, and it is further evident in the 1973 essay on *Beyond Good and Evil*.[10] Strauss speaks of learning from Nietzsche in a fashion that is rare for Strauss's treatments of modern philosophers. Nietzsche is a great critic of the progressive and egalitarian ideals of modernity, a stance that Strauss considers seriously. Nietzsche argues that modern scholarship and science cannot give direction to life, that human life at all times needs a hierarchy of ends and goals, that modern secular-atheistic society is confronted with the prospect of spiritual and physical devastation. Strauss claims that the Prologue of *Zarathustra* contains a deep and comprehensive analysis of modern times (chapter 2). Above all, Nietzsche attempts to restore the natural ranking of the philosophic life above the lives of scholars and scientists. It is this that most essentially ties Nietzsche to Plato and Socrates—the bond that Strauss sees already in the early 1930s, but that now becomes a theme of his teaching. Accordingly, Nietzsche in a Platonic mode realizes that profound spirits have need of masks, that philosophy is a mixture of seriousness and play, that the deepest thoughts elude direct communication and logical demonstration. Strauss claims that Nietzsche's dictum that "from now on psychology is again the path to the fundamental problems" is the renewal of Platonic psychology.[11] Such psychology is the exploration of the distinctive nature of the philosophic soul and of the conditions in political-moral life, both favorable and prohibiting, for the turn toward the philosophic life. Rousseau as renewing the problematic relation of the philosopher to politics (the "antinomy" already mentioned) is Nietzsche's modern predecessor in this regard. (Lessing as well earns high praise from Strauss for instructing him in the character of esoteric writing.)

This Platonic concern lies behind Strauss's unusual language of "classic natural right." The 1959 seminar emphasizes the theme that Nietzsche "tried to return from history to nature" and that he was thus on the way to restoring classical natural right (chapter 1). With the term "classic natural right" Strauss refers to the Platonic account of the natural order of society as based on the natural hierarchy of virtues, in which philosophic virtue is the peak.[12] Nietzsche's effort to recover nature in this sense is deeply paradoxical, as he tried to find the way back to nature on the basis of the rejection of nature as a standard (chapter 1). The first use of nature refers to the ranking of lives; the second use of nature refers to nature in a traditional, universalist, nonhistoricized sense. The modern element in the attempt (*Versuch*) is the concept of the unique self as the source of creative interpretation, or as radically anti-universalist "will to power." In other words, Nietzsche assumes the radical particularity of the historical individual, including the great creative spirits, a conception far from the Greek philosophical understanding of nature. On its basis, Nietzsche seeks in *Zarathustra* to achieve the highest unification of creation and contemplation, or of history and nature. Something akin to the Platonic hierarchical ranking of contemplation as the highest good must be achieved by the creative will, which replaces eros for an independent order of being (chapter 8). Nietzsche proposes to attain this in the willing of Eternal Recurrence. The creator who wills his existence eternally engages in a self-knowing or contemplation of what the creative will can achieve (chapter 11). In a pregnant formulation, Strauss states that nature exists through (not as object of) creative contemplation (chapter 13). With this thought Nietzsche seeks to grasp the goodness of nature and the whole in a new way. But the effort raises some unavoidable questions: Is the truth of this creativity an uncreated truth? (chapter 3). Is the will to power grounded in nature in some extrahuman sense or only in human willing? (chapter 14). Even if problematic, Nietzsche's experiment is instructive since "by understanding Nietzsche we shall understand the deepest objections or obstacles to natural right which exist in the modern mind" (chapter 1).

Strikingly, Strauss says that "Nietzsche somehow succeeds, without obvious contradiction, to solve the question of knowledge and the question of nature," and yet "this does not mean that his thought is true" (chapter 8). He avows that Nietzsche's "enigmatic vision," which combines philosophy, poetry, and religion, is "very difficult to understand" (chapter 9). At the same time, Strauss (still commenting on *Zarathustra*) is critical of Nietzsche's disregard for the starting points in ordinary opinion by which philosophy should orient itself, a lack that he relates to the extremism of his rhetoric. Strauss notes that Nietzsche starts from the will to power, "from which I believe one should not start" (chapter 14). In the later essay

xvi EDITOR'S INTRODUCTION

on *Beyond Good and Evil,* however, Strauss suggests a qualification of this criticism, where he declares, as he does in both seminars, his preference for that work as Nietzsche's most beautiful book. He makes his suggestion through restating Nietzsche's self-assessment in *Ecce Homo:* "Beyond *Good and Evil* is the very opposite of the 'inspired' and 'dithyrambic' *Zarathustra* inasmuch as Zarathustra is most far-sighted, whereas in *Beyond Good and Evil* the eye is compelled to grasp clearly the nearest, the timely (the present), the around-us."[13] This change involved the "arbitrary turning away from the instincts out of which Zarathustra had become possible: the graceful subtlety as regards form, as regards intention, as regards the art of silence are in the foreground in *Beyond Good and Evil*" and not in *Zarathustra.*

Further reflection by the reader leads to something as basic as the self or will to power. The 1959 seminar contains the suggestions that the highest reconciliation of concern to Nietzsche is that of Greek and biblical wisdom, and that this is the source of both the depth and the paradoxical structure of Nietzsche's thought (chapters 7, 9). This raises the highly vexed issue of the place of religion in Nietzsche's thought. Strauss holds that Nietzsche is not the founder of a religion but that *Zarathustra* wears the mask of religious teaching (chapter 2). Are the religious elements in Nietzsche then only exoteric? Reverence for the higher human, for human nobility, replaces God, and such reverence is a nontheistic form of the sacred (chapter 3). The highest form of that reverence for self is expressed in the Eternal Recurrence, which is thus akin to religious doctrine (chapter 10). But rather than being theistic, the willing of Eternal Recurrence is the response to the death of God that transforms the nihilistic thought into an affirmation (chapter 11). The higher willing of the creator seeks to overcome the spirit of revenge, or the will to escape time and mortality, which lies behind the project of conquering suffering and the hope of progress in mastering nature (chapters 7, 12). Against that will, the willing of Eternal Recurrence affirms the goodness of nature and the whole.

To this extent the latter willing recalls a classical notion of contemplation that overcomes the fear of mortality. But Nietzsche raises this question: What if the conquest of chance should succeed and the last man, who aspires for nothing but prolonging a comfortable life, becomes the only man, satisfied in his ignoble desire (chapter 10)? Strauss seems to suggest that this is a possibility that classical thought could not foresee, and Nietzsche, seeing that the ranking of forms of life has a contingent basis, must project the continuing existence of the higher life—or nature

as creative contemplation—through an act of will. The higher way of life
is not sustained by an enduring, intelligible order, and its future depends
on the noble benevolence of the creative spirits. As the best in the human
depends on will, the philosopher has the sacred obligation to secure the
future of the best. The existence of the best depends on particular bene-
factions of particular higher beings, whose work therefore is akin to the
work of gods. Strauss indicates that Nietzsche relates this responsibility of the philosopher to his regard for the Hebraic injunction among
the table of values in the section "On the Thousand and One Goals" in
Zarathustra—the injunction that secures the eternity of a people (chapter
4). It is possible that Strauss thinks that Nietzsche hereby has insight into
the deepest issue at stake in the quarrel between Jerusalem and Athens.
The status of the self and individuality in modern philosophy is perhaps
rooted in that quarrel, and Nietzsche may expose the central reason for
the valorization of the modern concepts.[14]

The 1967 seminar presses further this line of inquiry.[15] At the same
time, in both seminars Strauss proceeds with an eye toward Heidegger's
interpretation of Nietzsche, with which he explicitly on several occasions
compares his own reading. In the 1967 seminar he calls Heidegger's two-
volume set of lectures on Nietzsche the best introduction to the earlier
philosopher (session 2).[16] Strauss considers Heidegger the most significant and powerful philosophic successor to Nietzsche,[17] and he finds himself instructed by and in sympathy with Heidegger's critique of Nietzsche's attempt to ground philosophy on the self as will to power. Even so,
Strauss remarks that Nietzsche has motives for his paradoxical highest
thought of Eternal Recurrence that elude Heidegger (chapter 12). The
contrast between Nietzsche's effort to return to nature and the whole-
sale abandonment of nature in Heidegger's "existentialism" is a theme
of both seminars. Strauss weighs whether the difficulties in Nietzsche's
philosophy can be overcome in Heidegger's fashion or whether another,
more classical, alternative is possible. In this reflection Strauss underlines
Nietzsche's attempted unification of Greek philosophy and the Bible as a
crux that Heidegger has missed. In other contexts, Strauss proposes that
both Nietzsche and Heidegger are engaged in forms of this unification.[18]

This state of affairs suggests that Strauss may think that the limitation of Heidegger's reading of Nietzsche is connected to a lapse of
self-knowledge: what Heidegger does not see in Nietzsche may be his
own shadow. With both thinkers Strauss has a keen interest in evaluating their extraordinary undertakings to move beyond modern thought

toward novel interpretations of Greek philosophy—efforts characterized by remarkable learning and penetration. Accordingly, the comprehension of their failures (if they are such) to embrace fully the Socratic way is a grave and inevitable task for the student drawn to Strauss's recovery of Socratic-Platonic philosophy.

Richard L. Velkley
August 2016

Editorial Headnote

The course was taught in a seminar form. Strauss began class with general remarks; a student then read aloud portions of the text, followed by Strauss's comments and responses to student questions and comments. The text assigned for this course was Friedrich Nietzsche, *Thus Spoke Zarathustra*, in *The Portable Nietzsche*, edited and translated by Walter Kaufmann (Viking Penguin, 1954). When the text was read aloud in class, this transcript records the words as they appear in *The Portable Nietzsche*. Original spelling has been retained. Citations are included for all passages.

There are no surviving audiotapes of this course. This transcript is based upon the original transcript, made by persons unknown to us. The quality of the audiotapes was in some cases unreliable. Session 5 was too inaudible for them to transcribe; what appears here as session 5 is a transcript of notes taken by Werner Dannhauser. Sessions 11 and 14 break off with the transcriber's observation that the remainder is inaudible. Sessions 13 and 14 are particularly challenging. The transcriber would in some cases note in parentheses that an airplane flew over or that a student's question or the reader of the text was inaudible. In other cases, he or she would leave a blank space in the transcript. The transcriber also inserted ellipses, which may or may not have meant that the tape was inaudible.

We have dealt with these difficulties in the following way. Ellipses original to the transcript have been retained and are distinguished by a bold typeface. Blank spaces and other indications that the audio was inaudible are rendered by us with ellipses in normal typeface. In some cases, the editor has supplied what he thought was the missing word or phrase. These insertions are in brackets. In cases where the reader was inaudible, the editor has inserted the text.

Minor changes to the transcript are not noted. For example, we have corrected inaccurate noun-verb agreement, rectified peculiar word order, and inserted prepositions or connecting words in the interest of readability. Sentence fragments that might not be appropriate in academic prose have been kept; some long and rambling sentences have been divided; some repeated clauses or words have been deleted. A clause that breaks the syntax or train of thought may have been moved elsewhere in the sentence or paragraph. In rare cases sentences within a paragraph may have been reordered.

Administrative details regarding paper or seminar topics or meeting rooms or times have been deleted without being noted, but reading assignments have been retained. Endnotes have been provided to identify persons, texts, and events to which Strauss refers.

A version of the transcript showing all deletions and insertions will become available on the Leo Strauss Center website two years after print publication of this transcript and can be made available upon request meanwhile for the same price as the printed version. The original transcript may be consulted in the Strauss archive in Special Collections at the University of Chicago Library.

This transcript was edited by Richard Velkley, with assistance from Alex Priou and Gayle McKeen.

1 Introduction

Nietzsche's Philosophy, Existentialism,
and the Problem of Our Age

Leo Strauss: By natural right one understands the right which is by nature, the right which is not made by man, individuals, or society. That there is such a thing, a right by nature, was generally accepted until the early nineteenth century. Today it is generally rejected, and one can say all right is historical: nature has been replaced by history. The natural right doctrine originated in Greece. They were therefore in total ignorance of our experience and our situation, hence it does not seem to be applicable to our situation or to be helpful for the analysis and understanding of our situation. What we need, we are told, are empirical studies of society and proposals of policy based on such studies. But the difficulty arises that the empirical studies as now frequently understood are based on the fundamental distinction between facts and values. Accordingly, the social scientist as social scientist cannot propose policy; he must cease to be a social scientist in order to make value statements for proposals of any kind. Thus we cannot turn to our social scientists for guidance. What shall we do? Shall we turn for guidance to contemporary philosophy? As philosophy, it is not limited by the peculiar relations of science, and by being contemporary philosophy it would be aware of the peculiar character of our situation.

Now this contemporary philosophy is known by the name of existentialism. I am aware of the fact that there is also something called philosophy which is known by the name of positivism, but positivism is admittedly unable to give us any guidance. It cannot do more than clarify values. Existentialism, on the other hand, is a philosophy in the older sense of the term: it claims to be able to give us guidance. Existentialism is often called, and not without reason, the philosophy of our age and our society. Those who are entirely unfamiliar with this phenomenon would profit by Barrett's book *Irrational Man*, which is, I think, the best English introduction to the subject.[1]

Existentialism is surely related to the disillusionment characteristic of the West: the collapse of the belief in progress—that is to say, of the belief in the possibility of democracy as a rational society, a society of free and equals who are in the main rational and public-spirited. The disillusionment is known to all of us. Think of the praise of electoral apathy as a good sign. Think of the talk of elite (elite being in itself a nondemocratic concept), or of the phenomenon called anonymity. I refer only to well-known subjects in social science—*The Lonely Crowd*,[2] the beatnik, or juvenile delinquency—phenomena which can best and most simply be understood by the fact that great public hopes have ceased to determine the present young generation. Other terms are mass society and its mass culture. Whether people claim that these are merely descriptive terms or evaluative terms is a purely verbal affair; to hear these terms and to look at the phenomena designated by them means to evaluate them. There is a connection between this mass society and mass culture and technology, the greatest triumph of which may be said to be the H-bomb, and therewith the whole question whether technology, which promised to be the way toward human happiness on earth, may not be the way toward the extinction of the human race.

All these and an infinite variety of other phenomena are underlying that philosophy called existentialism. Existentialism, however, is not a mere accusation of the present situation or a diagnosis of it. Existentialism attempts to supply us with a profound analysis. We can state its thesis provisionally as follows. The root of all our activities is the belief in reason, the belief in man's ability to master his fate. Existentialism, we may say, makes explicit what is only implied in the general uneasiness of our time and even in the present-day positivism. For present-day positivism, as you all know, denies the power of reason, that reason can establish any value judgments. To repeat, existentialism asserts that the root of the present difficulties is the belief in reason, in man's ability to master his fate, which has given rise to the tremendous modern venture and to the apparently insoluble difficulties which we are confronted with. This is only a reminder of the very common and very popular phenomena with which we have to live.

But we would like to do more than that. We would like to try to understand existentialism and not merely report about it; therefore one must go beyond the popular conflict and turn to its sources. The most important source of existentialism is Nietzsche. In passing, I mention that the understanding of Nietzsche would have the additional advantage for us as social scientists in that it would enable us to understand the deepest roots of fascism. Nietzsche was not a fascist—fascism is only a stupid short-coming of what Nietzsche meant. Still, there is some relation between Nietzsche and fascism, whereas there is no relation between Nietzsche and communism and hardly a relation between Nietzsche and democracy. To that extent, the crude statement that Nietzsche is the father of fascism contains an element of truth.

Now Nietzsche was not an existentialist. Existentialism emerged out of the conflict between Nietzsche and Kierkegaard, the Danish religious writer. Today natural right is generally rejected on the basis of the view that all right is historical. Nature has been replaced by history in the course of the nineteenth century. Nietzsche started from this fundamental change. He started from historicism, the view that all human thought is essentially and radically historical, but he saw in this view (which had become almost trivial by the nineteenth century, at least in Europe) a problem. Therefore, he tried to return from history to nature. To this extent, Nietzsche was on the way to the restoration of natural right as distinguished from mere historicism. By understanding Nietzsche, we shall understand the deepest objections, obstacles to natural right which exist in the modern mind. This is the reason why I plan to give this course in the form of an interpretation of Nietzsche or, more precisely, of Nietzsche's most famous work, the work which he himself regarded as the greatest of his completed works: *Thus Spoke Zarathustra*. There is a translation available in the Viking edition, *The Portable Nietzsche*, by Walter Kaufmann, and I will use this translation.[3]

In order to prepare the discussion, I would like to remind you of certain points which I have made in my book *Natural Right and History*. I will not repeat the argument of that book here—this would be very boring—but I would like to remind you briefly of what I believe I have done in that book. What I tried to do is show that natural right is an open question and not an obsolete issue, as is generally held. I tried to show this by taking issue with the two leading schools of our age, positivism and historicism. Positivism is characterized by the assertion that all value judgments are of a noncognitive nature, that human reason cannot substantiate any value judgment. Historicism is the view that all human thought is radically historical and therefore a natural right is impossible.

After having tried to show that the issue of natural right is not settled, I tried to clarify the whole issue of natural right by the following observation. In the first place, natural right is a very ambiguous term, because it means something very different in premodern thought and in modern thought. I would like to restate this as simply as I can. In premodern thought, the premise of natural right was the end of man as the rational animal, a rational and social animal. On the basis of the understanding of man as a rational and social animal, it is possible to give certain broad indications as to what course of action, what way of life, is conducive to the perfection of man. This, we may broadly say, is the premodern view of natural right. This complete end of man, the perfection of man as a rational and social animal, was also said to be the meaning of the common word happiness. Happiness, a word which we all use and which in a way is used by men of all times, was identified by the classical philosophers, especially Plato and Aristotle, with the complete perfection of man as a rational and social animal. Happiness did not mean mere contentedness but the contentedness of the reasonable human being, contentedness on a certain level. It was implied that a reasonable man cannot be contented unless he has reached perfection as a rational and social animal.

Now what about the modern natural right doctrine? Its starting point is not the end of man but, we may say, man's beginning, his most fundamental, most elementary need: self-preservation. Self-preservation was of course recognized in the older view, but as a lower end. In the modern view, self-preservation became *the* end. But self-preservation can be had on various levels. Merely keeping oneself alive is not very satisfactory for us; therefore it was enlarged to something that was called comfortable self-preservation, and comfortable self-preservation was understood as a mere enlargement of self-preservation. So we can say that in modern thought mere self-preservation on the one hand, and comfortable self-preservation on the other, are the starting point for establishing the meaning of right.

Another formulation of the modern natural right doctrine is to say that the place of happiness was taken by the pursuit of happiness. When the older thinkers spoke of happiness, happiness was meant to possess a clear and universal objective meaning. The claim of modern natural right was that happiness does not possess an objective meaning: everyone understands something else by happiness, and even the same individual understands by happiness very different things in different situations. The pursuit of happiness in the modern interpretation means therefore the pursuit of happiness however happiness may be understood. Therefore, from this point of view, the principle is purely subjective and cannot give birth to a notion of right. The notion of right comes in as follows. In spite of the fact that happiness has no clearly defined meaning, there are certain conditions of happiness which are universal: however you might understand happiness, it was always a unique right to the pursuit of happiness. While happiness itself is purely subjective, the conditions of happiness are universal.

As a consequence of these modern notions, the emphasis shifted entirely from duty to right. In the traditional notion, by virtue of the primacy of the end of man, the rules of life, the rules of action, had the character of duties. Rights were implied and in most cases only implied. In the modern view, however, rights were thought to be the principles from which any possible duties would follow. I mention in a merely enumerative way another characteristic feature of the modern natural right doctrine, the notion of a state of nature. There is a presocial state in which isolated individuals lived but possessed right. The natural rights, we can say, are those which presocial man already possessed, and out of these rights of presocial man these thinkers tried to show what the structure of civil society would be, civil society being nothing but an attempt to safeguard these rights. As a corollary, I add that by virtue of this analysis of modern and premodern natural right, it appears that the difference between Hobbes and Locke is not a fundamental difference, but it is a difference of the utmost practical importance. I would say that Hobbes, Locke, and Rousseau are the greatest representatives of the modern natural right doctrine.

Another point of some importance to clarify the whole issue which I tried to make in that book concerns the difference between Thomas Aquinas and Plato and Aristotle. This is of some importance, because according to the best-known view today, *the* classic of natural right is Thomas Aquinas. The natural right doctrine of Thomas Aquinas is surely much more fully developed than that of Plato and Aristotle. The view is very common that the difference between Thomas Aquinas and Plato and Aristotle is fundamentally that Thomas elaborated the Platonic-Aristotelian teaching, whereas I would say that there is a fundamental difference. I try to explain this as follows: the key term used by Aquinas is natural law; this term, so to speak, does not occur at all in Plato and Aristotle. (This is not literally true: the term occurs twice in Plato, but never in the sense in which it is used by Aquinas, and it does not occur in Aristotle.)[4] What is the significance of this distinction? In the first place, the question concerns the principles of action, the cognitive status of the principles of action. According to the Thomistic teaching, which is not peculiar to Thomas but his is the most famous, these principles are inherent in, or given in, a faculty which we may loosely call conscience. Man possesses a faculty belonging to his nature for knowing the principles of human action. The second point is that in the Thomistic teaching of natural law, there is a reference of that natural law to the giver of that law, to God as the divine legislator. Those fundamental premises of the Thomistic teaching are absent in Plato and Aristotle. The crucial implication of that is that according to the Platonic-Aristotelian teaching there are no universally valid rules of action; there is a universally valid order of the ends of man, a universally valid hierarchy of ends. There is no Platonic-Aristotelian equivalent to the Ten Commandments. To bring out this difference, it is important to consider that the Aristotelian tradition, as long as it was predominant, especially in the Middle Ages, consisted of two branches. The best known is that represented by Thomas Aquinas, but there is also another one which is known to historians of philosophy as the Averroistic tradition, after the Arabic philosopher Averroes. In order to get at the true Aristotelian teaching, it is helpful to make use of the Averroistic teaching as well—not that the Averroistic teaching is necessarily the correct interpretation, but it indicates that we cannot immediately assume that the Thomistic interpretation is correct.

There is a fourth point I would like to refer to, one to which I alluded in that book rather than elaborated it, and that is what I have called the three waves of modernity.[5] Modern thought, which begins in the sixteenth and seventeenth centuries, developed in the seventeenth century this modern natural right doctrine—the doctrine of the rights of man, as it came to be called. This I call the first wave, represented by such people as Hobbes and Locke. This was a radically modified traditional teaching, but it was still a teaching of natural right and even of natural law. The break with this began in Rousseau himself and was carried through by the German philosophers beginning with Kant. We can say that in this second stage, nature disappeared from the thought about right. When Kant speaks of the moral laws, he calls them laws of freedom, in opposition to the laws of nature. The laws of nature are laws like the Newtonian laws; the moral laws have nothing to do with nature. We can perhaps say that in this stage nature is simply replaced by reason, because for Kant the moral law is still the law of reason. This epoch, which begins with Rousseau or Kant, ends with Hegel and certain pupils of Hegel.

In the third wave, not only nature but reason too is abandoned in the moral orientation. This third wave begins most clearly with Nietzsche, and of course we live in that wave. In this stage, universal standards in any sense are abandoned. Both in the premodern sense and in the first and second waves, there was no question that the standards, in order to be true standards, must be universal, but in this last stage the necessity and even possibility of universal standards was denied. This much about what I have been trying to do in my earlier discussion of natural right.

There are a few more things which I have to do in order to prepare the discussion, but first I believe I must explain more fully why a discussion of Nietzsche is of special importance for us.

I begin with the following consideration. If we look at the infinite literature on our subject and see what is really the crux of the problem—why is the very notion of a natural right no longer intelligible or plausible? what is the root of the modern theories of natural right?—we can give this answer: the notion of natural right is based on the assumption that nature supplies us with standards. That implies that nature is good, but how do we know that? The traditional phrase was "The good life is that life according to nature." Why should the life according to nature be the good life? How do we know that nature is good? Could it not be that nature is devilish, that it is the work of a mean demigod as distinguished from a good God, as some rustics formerly held? When people said that nature is good they meant also that nature is intelligent, that there is a fundamental harmony between nature and the human mind. We may begin from this part of the argument. Here again the question arises: How do we know that? It is not sufficient to say that we know natural things to some extent and to try to know them better shows that there must be some natural harmony between nature and the human mind. As a fundamental proposition this is not clear.

Descartes started from this proposition: Perhaps the world is the work of an evil spirit which wishes to deceive us. Perhaps we live in a phantom world which the evil spirit created. Perhaps nature is the work of such an evil spirit and we cannot be sure of our ground if we have not taken seriously this possibility. In other words, let us be much more distrustful than all earlier thinkers have been. Let us be of the utmost distrust, or as Descartes put it, let us engage in a universal doubt, a doubt of every-thing. It may be a mere romantic assumption that nature is good. But then Descartes says: Precisely if we engage in universal doubt, we shall reach absolute certainty and absolute clarity. If that evil spirit wishes to deceive me, I must be a conscious being. This—that I am, as a conscious being, is absolutely certain, under the most unfavorable condition—is the basis of all clarity: *cogito ergo sum*. Descartes made it clear that this hypothetical evil spirit (in which he did not believe, of course) is used only to clarify the whole problem. He said if you replaced the evil spirit by the natural causes—in other words, what we call today science—there would be the same difficulty. Why should mere mechanical causation lie about a mind which is able to see the world as it truly is? There is no necessity of a harmony between what you think and what really is; therefore Descartes tried to solve the problem of knowledge in advance. The answer Descartes gives is that in all circumstances the self-consciousness of the knowing or thinking being is absolutely certain and absolutely clear. In asserting that "I think, I am" as a conscious being, I am not deceived; I await the grip of a deceiver or a deceiving universe. There cannot be an omnipotent deceiver. Even if there is deception—for example, the senses—clear and distinct knowledge is always presupposed in its possibility. Descartes draws this conclusion in his doctrine of error: If I stick to my clear and distinct knowledge, to that kind of knowledge which I have when I say "I think, I am," if I assert only what I clearly and distinctly conceive, if I do not permit my will any influence on my assent, I cannot be deceived. In other words, nature may be bad, reason cannot be bad.

Now this view, that nature *may* be bad or *is* even bad, that reason cannot be bad, is reflected in the modern natural right doctrine which was originated by Hobbes. Hobbes begins with the state of nature, a state of presocial man, a state in which men's lives are nasty, brutish, and short.[6] Man is by nature in an evil condition. As he puts it, nature has dissociated them. Men who cannot live well except in society owe that society entirely to themselves, not to nature. What does this mean? Nature is bad, nature is something to be overcome, or to use the much later phrase, nature must be conquered. Nature is an enemy. Still, Hobbes taught a natural right: he said nature decided the standard. What is the character of that standard? We may say that in Hobbes's view, nature supplies us with a standard which is only negative. It tells us what has to be overcome, and to that extent it gives us direction.

This thesis of Hobbes's was thought through radically and therefore almost destroyed by Rousseau. If natural man is presocial, as Hobbes and quite a few of his pupils have thought, he is prerational. Given the connection between reason, language, and society, man cannot be rational if he is not social. Natural man is presocial, prerational—in a word, as Rousseau himself says, a stupid beast. The consequence which everyone would draw, which Rousseau did not draw: Nature does not supply us with any standard at all. What guidance can we possibly get from a man who is not yet a man? But let us not joke at the expense of Rousseau because we would do it ourselves. The question is: Why did Rousseau not draw this trivial consequence? Because Rousseau was still too certain that if he abandoned natural standards altogether, he would not find any standards. He was still too certain of the traditional view. But let us forget about Rousseau for the present, and let us see how a standard can be found if man is really a stupid animal and nature does not supply the standard.

Now I mentioned before that one can state Descartes's view by saying: nature may be bad, reason cannot be bad. Not nature but reason supplies the standard. Only such knowledge as is purely rational is certainly and evidently true. We possess purely rational knowledge—not of nature, because our knowledge of nature depends on sense perception. Nor do we possess purely rational knowledge of the soul, because what we know of the soul depends very much on internal perception, on what Locke and other men called reflection, and looking back at you. Purely rational knowledge, knowledge depending in no way on events or any other experience, we have only of the moral law, which is to say the law of freedom in opposition to the law of nature. This is the Kantian view: reason takes the place of nature for supplying standards.

The second point I have to make is this. According to Rousseau's analysis, man is not by nature rational. Man is a brute, a stupid animal which has the possibility of becoming a rational being, but what belongs to him by nature is only the possibility. Rousseau called this perfectibility. We might even say malleability: man is the most malleable brute. Because he is so malleable, he can acquire reason. But reason is acquired, it is not a native gift of the human race. There is a genesis of reason. Today these things are very trivial because you are all brought up in the belief in evolution, but you must not forget that this was a hundred years prior to Darwin. The doctrine of evolution as a scientific doctrine came much later than this fundamental consideration. So there is a genesis of reason. This genesis of reason is of course of the utmost importance because somehow the view still prevails that man is characterized by reason, and if reason has a genesis, this is the most important event you can think of. And it did receive a name at about this time: the name is History. So we may say that the original meaning of History with a capital H is the genesis of reason, or the fate of reason. Let me then say this: Rousseau opened up not only the possibility that reason should take the place of nature for supplying the standards, but also that History should take the place for supplying the standards.

I would like to add a piece of information, mere information. In much of the literature, you find of course references to History with a capital H when they speak of Persia, or China, or what have you. The word history is a Greek word, *historia*, and means simply inquiry, but a certain kind of inquiry, namely, that inquiry which proceeds by asking other people. You know of course that quite a few inquiries can be made without asking anyone. For instance, if you inquire about the digestion of a frog, you don't have to ask other people about it. But there are inquiries which can only be made by asking other people, for example, in what room were you born and who was present — to find out, you would have to ask your parents. And what happened in the old days, when there was no writing and no reading, anything of the olden times — i.e., what happened prior to birth — you could know only by asking other people. Therefore, history took on the derivative meaning of inquiry about the past, a record of the past, knowledge of the past, and that is the simple commonsense meaning of history which we still have.

But there is an entirely different meaning of history which is much more recent, according to which history does not mean a way of inquiry or research of knowledge but an *object* of knowledge, a dimension of reality, or however you might call it: the historical process, as it is called. Now a philosophy of history in the more interesting sense of the word was not a philosophy investigating historical inquiry or historical knowledge, but a philosophy regarding the so-called historical process, regarding history as an object, as a dimension of reality. This thing is very recent in these terms. That something like that could have been invented by Augustine in his *City of God* is another matter. But it is important that it is not called that. That is a very long question, a very difficult question, and by imputing the term History with a capital H to any thinker who did not use it, we fail to see the gravity of the premise that there is such a thing as History. One very little illustration: people don't hesitate to speak of the philosophy of history of the Old Testament. It is a very simple observation to say that there is no Hebrew word for history, not even for history in the sense of inquiry. The word used for history today in Hebrew is the Greek word for history. That shows you how problematic this premise is. People did not think at all times in terms of history.

Rousseau plays a great role in the emergence of this concept. But to come back to my general argument, two ways were opened by Rousseau, a thinker of unusual fertility. One doesn't have to like him, and there are many strong reasons for disliking him, I have been told. If you think that this man gave rise not only to idealistic philosophy but also to romanticism in all its forms, a man of such fertility does not exist again prior to Nietzsche. The most fertile thinkers are not necessarily the deepest thinkers—that's another matter, but it is also something of which we have to take cognizance. Rousseau, I would say, is this germinal mind who gave rise to both possibilities: reason taking the place of nature, and history taking the place of nature.

I mention as a third point the way Rousseau himself took. To the extent to which it forgoes another possibility, the way he took officially is a modification of Hobbes's and Locke's doctrine. It is a modern natural right doctrine different from Hobbes and Locke but structurally in its fundamental character of the same kind. But there is something which goes much beyond this, and that is the following point. The natural right doctrine, which Rousseau also accepted, was based on the premise that its basis is self-preservation. Rousseau made this simple reflection: If self-preservation is a fundamental right, we presuppose the goodness of life, the goodness of existence. Why should self-preservation be cherished if the being of the self, the existence of the self, is not cherished? How do we know of the goodness of existence? Rousseau said this goodness is experienced in the sentiment of existence. This sentiment of existence has nothing to do with reason. According to Rousseau, this sentiment can be enlarged to the feeling of communion with nature as a whole. This experience, sentiment of existence, is underlying the concern with preservation of existence. This is perhaps the most fundamental presupposition of Rousseau's thought. Everything is concentrated in this sentence: that the sentiment of existence is derived from the concern with the preservation of existence. So what is the name of that concern with the preservation of existence? Civilization, the whole process of civilization.

Yet we have here this fundamental difficulty: the conflict between the end and the basis. The end is the civilizationary process, which is meant to guarantee the preservation of existence. There is an ineradicable conflict between the primary, the sentiment of existence, and what we do for its sake, the process of civilization. There is an ineradicable conflict between happiness and the effort made for the sake of happiness. Happiness can only be given and not be acquired, and yet by constantly being active, by constantly chasing after self-preservation, we destroy the possibility of ever experiencing that for the sake of which civilization is meant. Happiness and effort are incompatible. The conquest of nature, in other words, is self-defeating. This famous criticism of civilization, of the arts and of the sciences, in Rousseau leads after certain important modifications to present-day existentialism.

I will turn to something I mentioned before: reason and history as substitutes for nature. This thought was fully developed on the way from Kant to Hegel, who in various ways dealt with this question. One can state the result to which these reflections led as follows. The historical process is a rational process. It leads to a peak, the peak being the end of the historical process, where the natural right and all its political implications have come to light. The historical process leads to a point which we can call the absolute moment of universal clarity, at least in the minds of the leading thinkers. The historical process is not controlled by reason, and yet it leads to the triumph of reason—reason, which has a genesis which is not coeval with man, reason has a fate, a fate not controlled by reason and is then subject to history. I hope you see already a very great problem. This in particular was taken care of by the German thinkers, especially by Hegel, by the following assumption, by saying that that fate, to which reason is subject, is secretly controlled by reason. As Hegel calls it, "the ruse of reason in history": apparently only blind action and blind changes, but in these blind changes reason itself is effective. There is teleology of reason in the historical process, but this teleology is radically different from any teleology of nature.

Now Hegel's system meant the triumph of rationalism: everything is rational, even history. All disharmonies have been resolved, there is no longer evil. Surely there are executions and what have you, but they are only illustrations and inordinate elements of the good. The complete rationalism means complete optimism. Now this much is clear: history can only be rational if it is completed, because if it is not completed we cannot possibly see its reasonableness; we don't know what might happen. This thesis of Hegel, that history is completed, naturally aroused the antagonism of quite a few men. The most popular today is probably Marx. The point that Marx and others made is this: there is still so much evil in the world that it does not make sense to say that the completely rational society has been established.

Hegel's opposition demanded an open future. History must be conceived as an unfinished and unfinishable process. This was the pre-Hegelian view. But there is a great difference between, one could say, a sober view of history which regards history as an unfinished and unfinishable process prior to Hegel and after Hegel. The premise was formulated by Hegel as follows: the individual is the son of his time. What is so strange about that? Is it not true that you can recognize the portrait of an individual from his costume? Why is this such an important assertion? Man in his highest and purest thought is the son of his time . . .[7]

What if history is open-ended, as some people call it? What if we live in the midst of this stream radically, meaning regarding the very premises, the very principles of our thought? How can there be truth under these conditions? One can say with some justice that this is the difficulty which was first seen by Nietzsche. Nietzsche accepted this historicist position that man in his highest thought is radically historical. This was more or less common among the intellectual descendants of Hegel at that time, but Nietzsche saw a problem, and for the first time the possibility of truth had become a question and the basis was the so-called historical experience.

Nietzsche develops this difficulty for the first time in an essay called "Advantage and Disadvantage of History."[8] This is the second of four essays entitled *Untimely Meditations*. It is very interesting; when one reads Nietzsche's later prefaces he barely refers to this essay, which is the most famous of all Nietzsche's earlier works. Nietzsche apparently did not see how influential and epoch-making it would prove later. Now what did Nietzsche do in this analysis? He admitted that historical relativism is true. There is no thought which men can ever possess which will not prove to be in need of radical revision. We can never possess a truth. This historical relativism is true. But then he said something which is theoretically[9] not true, but it is a deadly truth: we cannot live on the basis of the purely provisional and relative character of our principles. Nietzsche suggested tentatively and provisionally a solution which reminds us of Plato, namely, let us have nonrelativism as a noble lie. But that is not what Nietzsche said. Nietzsche was too much a modern, honest man. He said we cannot live without a fundamental lie, without a fundamental fiction.

But Nietzsche did not leave it at that, and the other alternative which he developed can be stated as follows: What does it mean to say that historical relativism is true? In a general way, this might be said by someone accepting these premises, but there is one point where he comes to grief, and that is in the case of the man who is really concerned with history: the historian. Now if the historian acts on that historical relativism, he cannot be a historian. How come? The historical relativist, the man who sees the changes of values and principles as a panorama, stands absolutely outside of the historical process and watches it. He is not animated by that which animated the historical actors; he cannot enter into that spirit, he cannot understand it. In other words, the historical relativist's historical representations are untrue, untrue because they are based on a fundamentally false understanding of the actors. A simple example: Can you write a history of music if you are not musical? Of course not. Can you write a history of philosophy if you do not yourself philosophize? Of course not. How can you, if you are not moved by the problems of life, understand people moved by the problems of life? Surely this is not a solution, it is only an indication of the problem.

But if one elaborated on it, which Nietzsche partly did, one arrives at something like this. There is a distinction between two kinds of truth, which was thought of by some followers of Nietzsche some time later as the distinction between objective truth and subjective truth. What science, including history, is concerned with are objective truths, but this objective truth does not give us the real content of history, it gives us only the outside. The true understanding can be acquired only as a subjective truth on the basis of the life experience of the epoch. Now this needs a more precise definition. Even if you speak merely of life experience, we would already indicate one difficulty. Men differ very much in their life experience, and it would follow even on this level that the condition for historical understanding—that means for any understanding of human beings, past or present—is a very broad human experience, much more than statistics of any kind. But this is trivial compared to the following question: What moved the actors, what moved the individuals of the time? In the language of our time: their belief in values. To come a bit closer to what Nietzsche said: their image of a future. To use a term coined after Nietzsche but on the basis of an inspiration by Nietzsche: a "project" which they have formed of their future. Only men guided by such a project and animated by it can understand any other men animated by such projects. Here you see that the subjective truth consists in one's having such a project and one's commitment to it.

This is the existentialist interpretation of Nietzsche, but which does not consider its basis in Nietzsche, and we shall see later on why Nietzsche did not follow in that way. But what is the difficulty here? Obviously this: the objective truth is one. Michelangelo was born on that day, in that town, etc., but that is of absolutely no interest to someone interested in Michelangelo. As for the understanding of Michelangelo's work, there cannot be an objective truth. The understanding of Michelangelo's work is possible for a man only to the extent to which he is animated by something comparable to that which animated Michelangelo, still commitment to a project. But there are of necessity a variety of such projects and therefore commitments to projects. In other words, the subjective truth is necessarily a manifold truth, differing not necessarily from individual to individual but between various possibilities. In other words, the only truth to speak of as far as man is concerned is the subjective truth, but this subjective truth suffers from not being one truth. And we somehow divine that must be one; the other one, which is in fact and by its nature one for all men, is in this sense not truth because it does not say anything about the substance of things. This is the problem as it appears on the basis of Nietzsche's useful essay "Of the Advantage and Disadvantage of History." But in a sense, the problem in Nietzsche remained throughout his life, and we will find in the *Zarathustra* a remarkable passage where an opposition is presented between Zarathustra as the [wooer] of truth and Zarathustra as the madman or poet, meaning the correspondence of one to the objective truth and the other to the subjective.

There is a problem that has never been solved. Nietzsche tried to solve it in the following way. What distinguishes Nietzsche from all existentialists is something very external, and that is his admiration for the Greeks. Nietzsche was by profession a classical scholar. In his admiration for the Greeks he conceived of culture as idealized nature, one is tempted to say perfected nature. The problem then is this: on the one hand, *the* truth — the truth about man, the truth about justice, the truth about right — had to have for him the character of a free project, of a free creation; on the other hand, he held that it is necessary that this goal of man must have its root in nature, nay, that it must be nature. This is Nietzsche's fundamental problem: to find a way back to nature, but on the basis of the modern difficulty of conceiving of nature as the standard. If we enter into the thought of nature and wrestle with this problem, we will understand better what is provisionally expressed in the simple question which I stated earlier: Why should we possibly assume that nature should supply us with a standard? Is it not a mere dogmatic premise of the Greeks and of the heirs to the Greeks, or is there not a necessity in the nature of the very problem which demands a return to nature as the guiding principle? This is the general idea of this course.

2 Restoring Nature as Ethical Principle

Zarathustra, Prologue

Leo Strauss: I would like to repeat something which I tried to convey in the first lecture. Natural right is today generally rejected. The fundamental reason is a belief that nature does not supply us, and cannot supply us, with indications as regards right or wrong. Nature is conceived to be ethically neutral. If we go back to the origin of modern thought, we encounter the hypothetical proposition which can be stated as follows: for all we know, nature may be the work of an evil mind; for all we know, nature is bad. Given this premise, it is impossible to speak of a natural right. This view of a fundamental badness of nature is implied in the common notion of a conquest of nature, because you do not speak of conquest unless you have an enemy in mind. The notion that nature is bad is not merely a fantastic notion which Descartes had hypothetically suggested; it is a very living thought, as indicated in the expression "the conquest of nature."

In the course of modern thought, nature as a key concept was replaced by reason, something radically different from nature and/or history. In Hegel, reason and history had found a perfect union. History is the history of reason, and history is the work of reason. The historical process is rational, and it cannot be recognized as rational if it is not completed. The historical process is completed, that is to say, all theoretical and practical problems are in principle solved. Of course, this is only in principle; every baby growing up has his own problems to solve, but this is not a question of philosophic significance provided the general way in which that problem is to be solved is known.

Hegel's system gave rise to an opposition, the thesis of which can be stated as follows: History is unfinished and unfinishable. That was the older view, the pre-Hegelian view, but now these opponents of Hegel accepted one crucial premise of Hegel, namely, that the individual is the son of his time in every respect, and in the most important respect, that of thought: all thought is radically historical. There cannot be natural standards, that is to say, transhistorical standards, and hence in particular there cannot be natural right.

This view became more and more accepted in the Western world during the nineteenth century, but somewhat earlier in Germany than in the West. In the West, utilitarianism still prevailed until our century, but on the basis of this assumption: that history is unfinished and unfinishable, yet all thought is radically historical. We cannot possibly take a stand outside the historical process, which process will necessarily condemn our highest principles to oblivion sooner or later. Here a great difficulty arises: If all thought is historical or, as some people say, historically relative, how can there be truth? To state it in the simplest way: this very assertion that all thought is historical is of course not meant to be condemned to oblivion in the future. It is meant to be final.

Nietzsche took issue with this problem of historicism in one of his earlier works called "Advantage and Disadvantage of History." It induced him to embark on an enterprise aiming at the restoration of nature as an ethically guiding concept. But this enterprise was beset in Nietzsche with great and perhaps hopeless difficulties. By understanding these difficulties, we will gain a better insight into the problems of natural right, for the difficulties which Nietzsche encountered are due not to any idiosyncrasies of this particular individual (who, as you know, ended in insanity), but the difficulties are due to the modern principles to which Nietzsche adhered. If there should be at any point any inkling of Nietzsche's psychology, then of course we dismiss it as absolutely uninteresting and will not pay any attention to it. The trouble is that this easy explanation does not help.

In "The Advantage and Disadvantage of History," Nietzsche came close to suggesting the following way out of historical relativism, and this way out was epoch-making and underlies what is now called existentialism. The thesis can be stated as follows: There is an objective truth called science, which is ethically neutral; but there is also a subjective truth which is ethically pertinent. This objective truth which is ethically neutral is in itself deadening; the subjective truth is a project, a free project of a man committed to that project, and such a project alone can give meaning to life.

Nietzsche's problem can be formulated provisionally as follows. What is the relation between that free project, which he set forth especially in his *Zarathustra*, and nature? Is Nietzsche's ideal, his project, taken from nature, or is it simply a free project? Is not perhaps nature itself as Nietzsche conceived of it a free project? Now not only the answer to this question but the very understanding of this question depends of course on what Nietzsche himself says. The remarks which I just made, as well as those which I made last time, serve no other purpose than to justify the suggestion that we should study Nietzsche together and therefore the *Zarathustra*, insofar as this is from Nietzsche's own point of view his most important work, in order to gain greater clarity not about Nietzsche in particular but about the problem of natural right.

I turn then without any further ado to the *Zarathustra*, but I have to make one further observation. The *Zarathustra* is not a scientific work, not a philosophic work in the ordinary sense. It would be wrong to say it is a piece of poetry, but we could say, according to what Nietzsche himself says, that it is a work of inspiration and perhaps one could say of inspiration alone. Nietzsche wrote this book, which consists of four parts, in four times ten days, which can only be understood by the fact that some spirit, a good or an evil spirit, came into him. The practical consequence for sober people, as I hope we all are, is that the book is very hard to understand. It is in a way unintelligible without the assistance of Nietzsche's other writings; therefore I will have recourse to his other writings, though they are not of the same level of importance, according to Nietzsche, and therefore I concentrate on *Zarathustra*.

These writings are divided by everyone according to Nietzsche's own suggestions as belonging to three different periods. Nietzsche started out with great hopes of a possible renovation of German culture in the spirit of a man whom he admired throughout his life but whom he almost worshiped in the beginning of his career: Richard Wagner. Nietzsche was a classical scholar, and he would have become the greatest classical scholar of his time if he had not become worried about other questions. In his very first period he tried to connect his admiration for Wagner with his understanding of classical antiquity, and he tried to understand Wagner's operas as a new form of the same phenomenon, which was originally the Greek tragedy. That is his first writing, *The Birth of Tragedy*; and there is another writing called *Untimely Meditations*, which also belongs to this first period of hope. Then there was a disillusionment, and Nietzsche turned to the very opposite of this German romanticism. His next book he dedicated to the memory of Voltaire. He turned to Western positivism. This is a period which is characterized by psychological analysis and a kind of debunking, destructive, analysis more than any other period of his. The most famous writings of this period are *Human, All Too Human*, *The Dawn of Morning*, and *The Gay Science*. Then a third period began with the inspiration of the *Zarathustra*. The writings of the third period are *Thus Spoke Zarathustra*, and the post-Zarathustrean writings, as we can say, are writings which are meant to spell out in a prosaic form what the *Zarathustra* had presented in a higher form. These writings are (I mention only a few of them): *Beyond Good and Evil, The Genealogy of Morals*, the *Twilight of the Idols, Anti-Christ*. In my opinion, *Beyond Good and Evil* is the best and most beautiful writing of Nietzsche, but from his point of view it is on a lower level than *Zarathustra*, meaning only to introduce *Zarathustra*.

First, a world about the title. As you see, it is called *Thus Spoke Zara-thustra: A Book for All and None*. Now Nietzsche teaches through the mouth of Zarathustra. Why did he choose a spokesman at all, and why did he choose Zarathustra? In his later work, *Ecce Homo*, he gives this explanation: Zarathustra, the founder of the old Persian religion, was the originator of moralism, of the view that the conflict between good and evil is the wheel which keeps things going.[1] The moralist *par excellence*, the thinker of the greatest veracity and intellectual honesty, he could be the man who would overcome moralism out of intellectual honesty by seeing thorough the illusory character of moralism.

Now Zarathustra was the founder of a religion. One can say that Nietzsche's Zarathustra is the founder of a new religion beyond Christi-anity, beyond the Bible. This explains the biblical tone in many passages of the book. For example, in the title, "Thus spoke" occurs in Luther's Ger-man translation of the Bible from time to time, but without an equivalent in the Hebrew, nor in the English translation. At any rate, the biblical allusions are intentional throughout the book—a new Bible, one could say, but of course no divine revelation, a merely human teaching. The imi-tation of the Bible is a parody of the Bible, an ironical Bible, an ironical foundation of religion or a preparation for such a foundation. One can also say a faith, with reservation, not quite serious; this might also explain the false tones we find from time to time in that work. This would seem to be inevitable, since Nietzsche was a philosopher and a philosopher as such cannot be the founder of a religion, seriously or half ironically.

But why did Nietzsche choose a spokesman at all? Why did he not present the teaching in his own name? Why did he need a spokesman, a mask? Or, what is the relation between Nietzsche and his Zarathustra? At the end of the Second Treatise of *The Genealogy of Morals*, Nietzsche indicates that he is not Zarathustra: Zarathustra is younger and stronger than Nietzsche.[2] In the *Ecce Homo* he describes Zarathustra as a type, an ideal, Nietzsche's ideal.[3] One could say Zarathustra is meant to be the best in Nietzsche, but by itself. Zarathustra is Nietzsche and he is not Nietzsche. He is described as a superman, a god.

The subtitle: *A Book for All and None*. A book for all is easy to understand; it is not a learned book, not a book only for scholars. This anti-scholarly tendency goes though Nietzsche's writings from the very beginning, and we will find later on some very harsh criticism of scholars as scholars. In his *Untimely Meditations*, he had protested against the gulf between the educated, or scholars, and the uneducated, which according to him was the outcome of the Renaissance and humanism. In opposition to this, he wanted, in the highest sense, popular art—an art for all—and he believed he could find that in Richard Wagner. In the same context he speaks also of the "return to nature." These two things, the return to nature and the return to the people, were of course classically represented by Rousseau, with whom Nietzsche is in a strange way akin throughout his work. A book for all, but in a sense it is a book for no one, for this reason: because it consists of Nietzsche's own thoughts, his own ideas, which as such are not communicable to anyone else and certainly not applicable by everyone else. This, I believe, is the meaning of the subtitle.

If you want some evidence for the latter meaning of Nietzsche, that the truth is a radically individual truth in all important matters and can therefore never be fully communicated, you should read the last aphorism of *Beyond Good and Evil*, in which this is set forth in a very beautiful way.

The bulk of the work consists of "Zarathustra's Speeches." These speeches are preceded by "Zarathustra's Prologue" (*Vorrede*). Let us first consider that Prologue. Zarathustra bids farewell to the solitude in the mountains in which he had lived for ten years together with the animals. On his way to the plain, he meets a friendly hermit. Having arrived in the city of the plain, he addresses the people who had assembled in order to watch a popular spectacle, a tightrope dance.[4] Zarathustra fails completely in his speech to the people: he makes himself ridiculous, like a clown or jester. The people are much more interested in the expected feat of the tightrope dancer than in the moral feat of Zarathustra. The tightrope dancer appears but is teased by the jester, confused by him, and thus he falls down and breaks his neck. Zarathustra comforts the dying man and takes his corpse with him. On his way he meets another hermit, but this time not a friendly hermit but a grumpy one. After he has buried the dead man and has left, he realizes that he needs living companions—living companions as distinguished from the dead corpse, and compan-

ions as distinguished from the people whom he had unsuccessfully tried
to address.

Zarathustra's speeches, as distinguished from his Prologue, are an attempt to find living companions, whereas the Prologue is addressed to
the people. If you look in your translation on page 130, paragraph 8: "and
here ended Zarathustra's first speech, which is also called 'the Prologue.'"[5]
So Zarathustra's Prologue stops here, in the fifth section of the prologue.
Zarathustra's Prologue is not the same as Nietzsche's prologue; Zarathustra's Prologue is only his speech to the people. This speech consists of two
parts dealing with two different subjects: the superman is first, and the
last man is second. Zarathustra is surrounded by two animals. He meets
two hermits and other things; this is an indication and stands here for
either superman or last man. But the first speech is subdivided into two
parts which are not exclusive of one another; and, in addition, Zarathustra and the two hermits, Zarathustra and the two animals, that's always
three.

The first speech proper after the Prologue speaks of the three metamorphoses. What Nietzsche indicates is that there is something beyond
the either/or, beyond the decision and the will. The decision, and the
act of the will, are a part of the larger whole. Zarathustra's Prologue
is preceded by Nietzsche's prologue, which consists of two parts: first,
Zarathustra's allocution of the sun right at the beginning; and then the
conversation with the friendly hermit whom he meets on his way from
the mountain. What does he say? In the conversation with the hermit,
Zarathustra notes that the hermit does not yet know that God is dead.
This terrible proposition expresses *the* premise of the Prologue and of the
work as a whole. We must first try to understand what it means. It comes
to sight as a mere assertion, that is to say, the assertion of an atheistic
creed, which is as much of a creed as any other creed. But this is only true
in a sense. Let us look at a parallel passage—in your translation, page 131,
section 6.

Reader: Zarathustra, however, did not move; and it was right next to him
that the body fell, badly maimed and disfigured, but not yet dead. After
a while the shattered man recovered consciousness and saw Zarathustra
kneeling beside him. "What are you doing here?" he asked at last. "I have
long known that the devil would trip me. Now he will drag me to hell.
Would you prevent him?"

"By my honor, friend," answered Zarathustra, "all that of which you speak does not exist: there is no devil and no hell. Your soul will be dead even before your body: fear nothing further."[6]

LS: You see a parallel case here to the assertion that God is dead. These things, devil and hell, do not exist. Zarathustra makes here an additional remark which throws some light on the basis of the assertion. He says to this dying man: "Upon my honor devil and hell do not exist." Zarathustra does not say: "We do not know of devil and hell" or "We do not know that God exists." He makes these assertions as denials of meaningful assertions. But what is the basis? What he means is: "I could not respect myself if there were devil and hell."

Let us elaborate this a bit more. Devil and hell are possible only in a world created by God. God could not be a most perfect being if he had created or tolerated devil and hell. This is a more discursive statement of what the mere "upon my honor" implies; of course it does not in any way settle the issue. To come back to the first conversation with the hermit, this saintly hermit, a pious man, rebukes Zarathustra for going down to men again: "Why do you go down?" Zarathustra replies: "I love human beings." And then the saint says: "Why did I go into the forest and into the solitude? Was not the reason because I love men all too much? Now I love God, I do not love men. Man is too imperfect a thing for me to love."[7] Now let us try to understand that. What Nietzsche suggests is this: love of God would detract from the love of men. Again, trying to articulate that: the Bible demands of man to love God with all his heart, all his soul, and all his powers, and He demands of man to love his neighbor like himself. Nietzsche, as quite a few modern thinkers before him, revolts against God in the name of love of men. We can say they turn from the love of God to love of men. This was an old story, especially in Germany. Out of the Hegelian school came quite a few men; the best known is probably Feuerbach, who made quite an uproar in the 1830s with books on the essence of religion and on the essence of Christianity. And there, the basis of the revolt was this: in the name of love of men, rebellion against God. And there were other forms of this atheism.

We must first understand what is characteristic of Zarathustra's or Nietzsche's atheism. "God is dead," that is the thesis. That is different from saying "God is not" or "God does not exist." "God is dead" means God once lived. Nietzsche's atheism is a historical atheism. There was a time when the belief in God was good and salutary, but that time is gone. Man's power has increased, man's rank has increased, by virtue of the belief in

God and by virtue of the fight against that belief. Now he has reached the stage where his newly acquired rank is incompatible with the belief in God. This is indicated in the preface to *Beyond Good and Evil*.

The second point we have to consider when speaking of the peculiarities of Nietzsche's atheism is indicated by the allocution to the sun with which the work opens. Zarathustra looks up to the sun and blesses it. The sun is viewed as a beneficent, living being—one could say, although Zarathustra does not say so, as a god. It is blessed by Zarathustra, a poetic conception—an idealized conception, one might say. It is based on the disregard of the lifeless and hurtful character of the sun; the sun as a cause of light and life is viewed with gratitude. Nietzsche's atheism is characterized by an element of gratitude; it is not simply a rebellion.

As a third point, I would mention this. "God is dead" means all our love must be love of men. From this follows a concern with human happiness alone, with perfect satisfaction and contentment of men. That was the first conclusion. What does Zarathustra say to this subject? That is on pages 128 to 130. It is the last part of the speech of Zarathustra. We must read this because it is important from every point of view.

> Reader: When Zarathustra had spoken these words he beheld the people again and was silent. "There they stand," he said to his heart; "there they laugh. They do not understand me; I am not the mouth for these ears. Must one smash their ears before they learn to listen with their eyes? Must one clatter like kettledrums and preachers of repentance? Or do they believe only the stammerer?
>
> "They have something of which they are proud. What do they call that which makes them proud? Education they call it; it distinguished them from goatherds. That is why they do not like to hear the word 'contempt' applied to them. Let me then address their pride. Let me speak to them of what is most contemptible: but that is the *last man*." . . .
>
> "No shepherd and one herd! Everybody wants the same, everybody is the same: whoever feels different goes voluntarily into a madhouse.
>
> "'Formerly, all the world was mad,' say the most refined, and they blink.
>
> "One is clever and knows everything that has ever happened: so there is no end of derision. One still quarrels, but one is soon reconciled—else it might spoil the digestion.
>
> "One has one's little pleasure for the day and one's little pleasure for the night: but one has a regard for health.
>
> "'We have invented happiness,' say the last men, and they blink."[8]

LS: That is Nietzsche's description. I trust that you sense its impressive character, of the atheism of which he knew and which is characterized by the contempt and rejection of the vulgar atheism. If you want to do justice to Nietzsche, we can say that what he has in mind is the atheism characteristic not only of vulgar atheism in the West in general but also of the atheism of communism—although Marx claimed that true creativity will only begin in this final age, when there is only one herd and no shepherd. In fact, we can be sure that that will be the end of all creativity because there will no longer be any necessity, a necessity spurring on to creativity. What Nietzsche says is that this atheism as it exists as an important force in the West—and it was much more of a visible force in continental Europe than in the Anglo-Saxon countries—is much lower than theism has ever been. The death of God makes possible this greatest degradation of man, the last man, and this is the greatest threat now. On the other hand, however, Nietzsche contends that the death of God makes possible a higher form of the superhuman: not the superhuman God, who by his absolute perfection depresses man, but the superhuman man, and that is what he calls the superman.

Now this translator has chosen to translate the term *Übermensch* by "overman," and you can't blame him for that because the superman as a figure of the comic strip has completely changed the word. But on the other hand, I would prefer the literal translation of "superman" because one must forget the other superman when reading Nietzsche, and also because superman reminds us also of superhuman. Nietzsche tries to preserve the connotation of the adjective the superhuman, but somehow he makes the superhuman back into a noble man. The superman is a superhuman man.

The superman is then *the* alternative to the last man. According to Zarathustra's or Nietzsche's contention, modern man stands at the parting of the way, either the way of the last man or the superman. Man as he was hitherto is no longer possible, and we must gradually see the reasons which Nietzsche gives for that. First, we must get the provisional understanding of what Nietzsche means by the superman. Zarathustra's speech on the superman consists of two parts and we have to read a few sections from each part. Let us first take the first part on page 124, section 3.

Reader: When Zarathustra came into the next town, which lies on the edge of the forest, he found many people gathered together in the market place; for it had been promised that there would be a tightrope walker. And Zarathustra spoke thus to the people:

"*I teach you the overman.* Man is something that shall be overcome. What have you done to overcome him?

"All beings so far have created something beyond themselves; and do you want to be the ebb of this great flood and even go back to the beasts rather than overcome man? What is the ape to man? A laughingstock or a painful embarrassment. And man shall be just that for the overman: a laughingstock or a painful embarrassment. You have made your way from worm to man, and much in you is still worm. Once you were apes, and even now, too, man is more ape than any ape."[9]

LS: You see, Nietzsche makes here an allusion to the famous doctrine of evolution, which he takes for granted. The worm, the ape (and the ape is still in man), and a goal of evolution beyond man. But that goal of evolution has the character of an ought: man ought to overcome being merely a human being. Zarathustra's love of man, to which he alluded in his speech with the hermit, is not a love of man as he is, it is a love of man's promise. Man is still too close to the brutes; he must overcome radically his brutishness and brutality. He must move away from the brutes, but where? Toward pure spirituality? Certainly not. The formula which Nietzsche uses in the sequel and which goes throughout the book is "Remain loyal to the earth." No spiritualism, no asceticism, no denial of this world, the earth, or this life. We get then the following provisional understanding: as long as men believe in God, they long for the other world, the other life. Their way of life is fundamentally ascetic. They are filled with a sense of sin and they see goodness in self-denial.

Now let us turn to atheism and consider first the low form which culminates in the last man . . .[10] no self-preservation, but self-realization, a sense of self-dedication. Nietzsche uses the extreme term "to squander oneself." This does not mean what it seems to mean at first glance, but the self-dedication to some task. Now let us look at the second part of that speech, section 4, at the beginning.

Reader: Zarathustra, however, beheld the people and was amazed. Then he spoke thus:

"Man is a rope, tied between beast and overman—a rope over an abyss. A dangerous across, a dangerous on-the-way, a dangerous looking-back, a dangerous shuddering and stopping.

"What is great in man is that he is a bridge and not an end: what can be loved in man is that he is an *overture* and a *going under*."[11]

LS: You see, here in the second speech there is no connection between the doctrine of the superman and evolution, not even an allusion to any ought. Nietzsche speaks here of what would traditionally be called the essence of man, without any regard to the question of the origin, evolutionary or otherwise. Man is the transcending being, the transcending animal, the rope over the abyss. He is not loyal to what he is if he does not follow this way to which his being points, toward the superman. One could say the superman is the end of man, the natural end of man.

I will go on with the interpretation of the Prologue. Zarathustra descends like the philosopher in Plato's *Republic* but, different from the philosopher in the *Republic*, without any compulsion. His descent is entirely voluntary. He is stimulated in that sense not by any need except the need to give, a need caused by abundance and also by his love of man. His responsibility is infinite. Not his fate but the fate of mankind depends on his action. Why is this so? When you read these first speeches on the superman, you must be impressed by the praise of madness, and this is very strange in terms of Nietzsche's fate. That is not quite sufficient, because there has been a perfectly sane man long before Nietzsche who had also written a praise of madness. That was Plato.[12] This praise of madness, the rejection of measure, moderation, and prudence, goes through these first speeches and we must try to understand that.

How is this connected with the essence of man? Man is a rope over an abyss; man has no support to speak of. The starting point of man's motion is the beast, but not the end. Man has no determinate nature; man has no support in his nature. What he is or will become depends entirely on his choice, his will. Given the situation as it exists now, he has a choice between the last man and the superman. As he puts it in the Prologue: human life is still without meaning; its meaning depends on your choice. After you have made your choice, it has meaning, or as he puts it earlier, your will should say that the superman is the meaning of the earth. The superman is not the meaning of the earth in itself, by nature. At the end of the Prologue he speaks of the two animals who are his friends in solitude: eagle and serpent. The eagle is the proudest animal and the serpent the most cunning. We can perhaps say that the eagle and the serpent take the place of the dove and the serpent in the famous New Testament saying.[13] There is a simple formulation of this thought in a remark of Nietzsche's where he describes the superman as Caesar with the soul of Christ.[14]

This much about the Prologue in general. We must now try to link this up with something which is more familiar to us: the social sciences. The social sciences deal with man. What is man, according to the social sciences? Certainly not the rational animal as he was thought to be by Aristotle, because the rational animal as understood by Aristotle possessed a natural perfection and destiny. According to the concept of the social sciences, there is no essential difference between men and brutes. From time to time you hear this formulation: Man is an animal, the animal which uses verbal symbols. This is the whole difference. Clearly there is no connection between this understanding of man and that understanding which we all imply when we use the word "humanity." We have in mind a certain character of man which men can acquire, which we call humanity. This is essentially related to the distinctive character of man to be humane. When you speak only of man as a being which uses verbal symbols, there is no connection between that and humanity.

When Zarathustra brings the corpse of the tightrope dancer out of the city, he buries the corpse in a hollow tree, for he wanted to protect it from the wolves. That is a simple action of humanity. Do we have any possibility of understanding humanity in all its various forms in the light of that conception of man which underlies the social sciences? Needless to say, from the point of view of the social sciences, what Nietzsche calls the last man is not in every way an objectionable thing, for, given the fundamental premises of the social sciences according to which all values are equal, the values of the last man are as defensible or indefensible as any other values. Given this fundamental premise, there seems to be only one fair way of settling conflicts regarding values. I know this is no longer admitted by the social sciences, but it was admitted implicitly a generation ago: the only way of fairly settling conflicts among equals is the will of the majority. You can equally see, if you consider alternatives and take, for example, the will of the minority, that it is not feasible to have the will of the minority decide. In other words, given this principle, the equality of all values, there follows the practical necessity: a bias toward the last man. The gospel of comfortable self-preservation is infinitely more acceptable than any more exacting idea, but these social scientists, for whom comfortable self-preservation is the highest standard, also say: No, we want something else. That other thing they call creativity. By this talk of creativity these social scientists submit to the judgment of those who know what creativity is, because what these social scientists mean by creativity is something which simply does not exhaust the name. One has to look around and see the very rare creative men who have existed or who do exist. Nietzsche was one of those men who, whatever else his defects may have been, knew something about creativity: "One must have chaos within oneself in order to give birth to a star."[15] This is a more meaningful and revealing statement, though very poetic, than what is done in certain departments of education.

One can also put it as follows. The tacit or open premise of social science is that man is indefinitely malleable, and Nietzsche may agree to that. But precisely because this is so, we must wonder what that lowest level is at which man can still be called a human being, and what is the possible maximum. We can provisionally say that the superman and last man are attempts to sketch the minimum and maximum of human malleability.

Also, social science is concerned with the analysis of present-day society for the purpose of prediction. This can be done in narrower and in broader ways: in narrower ways, for example, by discussing the trend of population in the city of Chicago and its suburbs; in broader ways (and this must be done), on the basis of reflection regarding the general character of present-day society compared to the societies of the past. In such an analysis, one cannot be silent about the fact that present-day society is the first secular society that ever existed. There have been men who were secularists in all ages, but the bulk was never secular. This secularism is expressed more shockingly, but also more truthfully, by being called atheistic. If one elaborates this notion of atheism, it is not merely a theoretical assertion but it is also the positive notion of a heaven on earth, which men can establish precisely because they no longer think of a heaven proper: the abolition of suffering. The question becomes inevitable, since this is a very powerful social force and by no means only in the communist creed: How to judge of things, to give them meaning? All these questions cannot be properly elaborated without having some acquaintance with what Nietzsche said, because Nietzsche was the first analyst of this trend after it had come into flower. He is much deeper and comprehensive than, for example, Tocqueville was.

Let us now turn to the first speech, which is of special importance. Never forget one point: Nietzsche's whole argument is based on the premise "God is dead," a premise which is in no way proved but simply assumed. The reasons behind this will appear partly in *Zarathustra* and partly in Nietzsche's other writings. The first speech is called "On the Three Metamorphoses."

I have to make a few introductory remarks. The Prologue had said that, given the premise that God is dead, mankind is confronted with these two alternatives: the last man and the superman. Man can no longer remain merely the human man of the humanistic tradition. Why this is so is a long question which will gradually develop. Now in the first speech, Nietzsche distinguishes three stages: the first is the stage of the living god; the second is the death of god; and the third is the stage of the superman. In other words, Nietzsche gives now more precise indications as to what he means by modern civilization. During the first stage, human morality was characterized by obedience to the "thou shalt." The second stage is characterized by revolt. In the first stage, man knew or believed he knew what was good and bad. The second stage is negative and culminates in simple nihilism. The third stage, the stage of the superman, is beyond revolt and is again positive.

Now this schema has a striking similarity with another three-stage doctrine, the doctrine of Comte, the founder of positivism, whom Nietzsche praised very highly.[16] Comte said that the human mind undergoes three stages of development: the theological, the metaphysical, and the positive or scientific. The theological was that of the Middle Ages, the metaphysical that of the seventeenth and eighteenth centuries, and the positive was ushered in by the nineteenth century. Again, the theological was positive. Men, on the basis of firm beliefs, were capable of deciding. The metaphysical stage was destructive, revolutionary, and therefore culminated in the biggest of all revolutions, the French Revolution. The positive stage, the stage in which the scientific mind is completed, will also enable man to have order: a society as distinguished from revolution. But there is this difference between Nietzsche's and Comte's stages: in Nietzsche, the stages are not different stages of the human intellect as they are in Comte; Nietzsche speaks of a metamorphosis, which is to say a metamorphosis of the mind as distinguished from the intellect. There are three metamorphoses—he does not say three forms—of mind or spirit (*Geist*). Mind antedates the three metamorphoses.

Reader: Of three metamorphoses of the spirit I tell you: how the spirit becomes a camel; and the camel, a lion; and the lion, finally, a child.

There is much that is difficult for the spirit, the strong reverent spirit that would bear much: but the difficult and the most difficult are what its strength demands.

What is difficult? asks the spirit that would bear much, and kneels down like a camel wanting to be well loaded. What is most difficult, O heroes, asks the spirit that would bear much, that I may take it upon myself and exult in my strength? Is it not humbling oneself to wound one's haughtiness? Letting one's folly shine to mock one's wisdom?[17]

LS: The heroic mind antedates the whole development. For some reason, the heroic mind, which is always subject to a god or to a lord, speaks for the most exacting lord, and that is the difficulty. In this speech Nietzsche discusses only the postbiblical metamorphoses. What antedates the Bible and Christianity is below the level of the whole problem because it is prior to the holy God. The pagans did not have holy gods to speak of. The first stage of biblical religion, the most perfect being, all perfection is derivative from God. The first stage he calls the camel, meaning the most obedient; it bows and accepts any burden, and the highest burden is the most exacting: thou shalt. The biblical God demands from man to be loved with all his heart, all his might, all his soul.

The second stage is symbolized by the lion, expressed by the formula "I will" instead of "I shall." This stage is only negative: it is a rejection of the "thou shalt" and does not create any new values. But here a certain difficulty arises. Had Zarathustra not spoken of the will of man? In other words, is not the positive stage, the last stage, which is indicated by the symbol of the child, not also characterized here by the will? This does not find an answer here. What he has in mind here, as the mind as mind is called by him in his prosaic writings "nihilist,"[18] is the willing of nothing, or nothing left to will. According to Nietzsche's analysis, the revolt against the God of the Bible leads eventually to the substitution of nothingness or death. Nietzsche's formula for nihilism is "Nothing is true, everything is permitted." The lion is described here as deserving the delusion and the arbitrariness.

> Reader: But say, my brothers, what can the child do that even the lion could not do? Why must the preying lion still become a child? The child is innocence and forgetting, a new beginning, a game, a self-propelled wheel, a first movement, a sacred "Yes." For the game of creation, my brothers, a sacred "Yes" is needed: the spirit now wills his own will, and he who had been lost to the world now conquers his own world.[19]

LS: At the stage of the lion the mind has lost its work; it has become defective. But you see again in the last stage, the stage of the child, that the mind has will, so that the substitution of the will to the second stage does not exclude the crucial importance of will in the last stage.

I will try to explain this. "Thou shalt" means the transcendent eternal God, the most perfect being. From this follows the imperfection of the world and of man as created beings, as contingent beings, in other words, the imperfection of the world and of man as perishable beings contrasted with the eternal God. From this point of view, man's orientation is other-wordly. Man conceives of himself as a stranger or exile in this world. He rejects this world as evil and sinful. This mind can also be described as the conscience. Conscience is not a Greek term but a biblical, and especially Christian, one. The strict and tender conscience sees the world as evil and sinful. Think of the Tenth Commandment—"Thou shalt not covet"— and the interpretation given in the Sermon on the Mount.[20] According to Nietzsche (and this is not developed here but in his other writings), this strict conscience, which is frustrated by the belief in the biblical God, turns eventually against its basis; it becomes intellectual conscience or in-tellectual honesty, leading to the rejection of the Christian dogma. Chris-tian morality is preferred. The formula for that is "no shepherd and one herd."[21] The shepherd is dropped but the herd remains. Man becomes a mere member of a world. The modern world is characterized after the break with the Christian dogma by moralism, and that leads by neces-sity to the last man. The place of the biblical faith is taken by modern this-worldliness, modern anti-asceticism. The formula is: "Let us make a heaven on earth." But Nietzsche says: You are utterly mistaken, you mod-erns, if you describe yourselves as anti-ascetic, your very this-worldliness is thoroughly ascetic. This seems to us no longer so paradoxical, because it has been popularized by Max Weber in his work on Protestant ethics and the capitalist spirit.[22] The common view was that the capitalist spirit, the opening up of all resources for the pleasure and enjoyment of man, was the process against this otherworldliness of premodern times. Against this Weber contended, on the basis of Nietzsche, that if we look more closely into the spirit of capitalism we find that it is very ascetic. Nietzsche tried to show the same thing by taking the other example of the modern freethinker, namely, modern science, in which he recognizes the medieval monk without the garb of the monk.

But once it becomes clear . . . to give another example of modern mo-rality, and that is the view according to which human goodness consists in compassion, the view of Rousseau and Schopenhauer. Here we find again the biblical mercy without the biblical God. It was Nietzsche's contention that the modern morality is a relic of biblical morality without the support of the biblical God; therefore it is utterly baseless. Once it becomes clear that the modern ideas are baseless, there is no longer any goal. Premodern ideas are completely dead and forgotten. The modern ideas reveal themselves to be illicit spoils from the biblical tradition, and once this is seen man has no longer any goal. Nothing is true and everything is permitted, and that is nihilism. But this nihilism is not limited to morality but extends also to science. Science proves to be based on hypotheses, and not only the hypotheses which are tested and then validated or invalidated, but the fundamental premises of science are tested, for example, the principle of causality, and, in addition, the historical relativity by virtue of which the modern science reveals itself to be less than science and therefore related to a particular historical phenomenon. The result is complete homelessness or worldlessness: the refuge supplied by the biblical God is gone. The lion, according to nihilism, has a passionately destructive character. But what, according to Nietzsche, is motivating the lion? Not viciousness or mere destructiveness; it is the end of conscience generated by biblical faith which takes on the character of intellectual honesty. In this stage, delusion and arbitrariness underlie all known ideas. It is impossible according to Nietzsche to return, say, to classical thought. I quote: "All earlier men had the truth. What is new in our present attitude toward philosophy is the conviction which no epoch ever had," namely, "*that we do not possess the truth*."[23] In other words, all earlier epochs were naïve and this is now gone forever: radical disillusionment, that is to say, radical aimlessness. The alternative is either the complete decay of man—the last man, the satisfaction of bodily needs, and the loss of the possibility of self-contentment or self-respect—or else what Nietzsche calls creation of new values, as indicated by the symbol of the child.

Why a child? There is no revolt anymore. Oblivion—in a sense, no awareness of the past. In the decisive respect, the creation is radically new. The new values are not derivative in any way from the past. The meaning of life must originate in men. The creation of these new values does not serve a preexisting purpose because these values create the purpose. Therefore the creation is purposeless: it is a play or a game, a new beginning, a creation of new values—guided by what? Negative, by the realization of the failure of the old values, and that is reduced by Nietzsche to the formula "God is dead." But the creation of new values is guided also by the awareness of the consequence of that failure, which is the last man.

3 The Creative Self

Zarathustra, Part I, 1–8

Leo Strauss: I would like to develop this notion of the last man still more fully, because without an understanding of the last man it is really impossible to see why Nietzsche is so much concerned with the alternative to the last man. Christian morality without a Christian God, one herd without a shepherd, that is to say, anarchistic self-complacency combined with the abolition of suffering. Heaven on earth, that is to say, social or political hedonism, utilitarianism. As I quoted before from memory: "Just to live, securely and happily, and protected but otherwise unregulated, is man's simple but supreme goal."[1] This is really a good indication of what Nietzsche means by the last man: the withering away of the state, no government of men but only administration of things. The whole human race is a single association of production and consumption in such a way that production and consumption includes the production and consumption of art, for instance. In other words, the so-called creativity of man goes on, but this takes place now in a horizon of production and consumption and therefore art loses its original meaning. The true consequence of the death of God is this: man is radically unprotected or exposed. Suffering remains. There is change through the progress of technical civilization, except to the extent that men become shallower by virtue of the infinite destruction that prevails. Entertainment, exciting and stimulating things every day. Man is radically unprotected: no God tells him any longer what is good and bad, nothing tells him any longer what is good and bad, there is no knowledge whatever of good and bad. Nothing is true, everything is permitted.

The first consequence of the death of God is then the drift toward the last man, and second, nihilism. The nihilists know somehow that contentment on the lowest level is subhuman. But the human, humane values were linked up with the belief in God and therefore they had lost their basis. The alternative to the subhuman is the suprahuman, that is the meaning of the superman. The idea of the superman is the positive guide toward the new values. First, God is dead, that is to say, all traditional values and ideas have ceased to be credible; second, the last man is the most extreme degradation of man. The speeches of Zarathustra do not merely elaborate the meaning of superman, on which of course everything depends; they also in a way justify that premise. In the course of the next meetings, we must see what the more precise meaning of the superman is, simply by illustration, and then also the justification of this idea. We must especially face the question: Why is this necessary? Why is it necessary to transcend the level of the human, the humane, altogether?

The assertion that God is dead is not justified by any reasoning. It is an assertion made, one could say, on Zarathustra's honor, especially a conviction which he could not abandon without losing his self-respect. The alternative which arises from the basis of this premise is either the last man or the superman. The last man is one herd without a shepherd—comfortable self-preservation without the possibility of self-contempt and hence of self-respect, simply the abandonment of anything superhuman. The alternative is the superman, that is to say, a man who embodies the superhuman and does not have to seek it outside of himself. This statement about the last man in the Prologue, which we have read, is generally speaking the most succinct and most comprehensive criticism of our time and its trends. In the first speech of Zarathustra, he discusses what he calls the three metamorphoses of the mind. The forms of the mind discussed there are only post-Christian possibilities, not the pre-Christian ones. This means that Nietzsche has to take up somehow (and we shall see this later in *Zarathustra*) the pre-Christian possibilities such as those presented by classical philosophy.

Now what are these three metamorphoses? The first is indicated by the camel: the belief in the living God as the most perfect being. Men's greatness consists in obedience, in compliance with the "thou shalt," or in surrender to God. The second form is symbolized by the lion: the stage of revolt stimulated by the Christian conscience, which has become intellectual probity and as such turns against the faith—rejection of the belief in God. The danger here is the abandonment of everything superhuman, that is to say, the last man; and on a higher plane, where the last man is an object of disgust, nihilism, no goal at all, or as Nietzsche put it elsewhere: "Men will rather will nothing than not will at all."[2] The nihilist is the man who wills nothingness. The formula for the second stage is "I will." The last is indicated by the symbol of the child, the creation of new values.

These will prove to be the values of the superman. Nietzsche does not use here such a simple formula as "Thou shalt" and "I will," but one could say on the basis of parallels that the formula would be "I am." This is not stated in *Zarathustra*.

The questions which arise here are these. What does the superman mean in more precise terms? Second, why can one not leave it at man and the human as distinguished from the last man, who is clearly understood to be subhuman? This is only another way of saying: Is it true that the basis of all traditional ideas has been destroyed by modern thought, which culminates in atheism? Two radically different reasons are suggested by Nietzsche. One, the cosmic principle applying to all species: evolution. Just as there has been a new possibility beyond every species hitherto, there should be such a possibility beyond man. This cannot be literally true, because the supermen are of course biologically speaking human beings. The more important reason is this, which refers to the specific character of man: man is the rope over an abyss. He must transcend himself.

I turn now to the second speech, which is called "Of the Chairs of Virtue," not, as the translator has it, "Of the Teachers of Virtue," because it is quite clear that Nietzsche has in mind the chair, namely, he does not think of the professors or teachers but the chairs they occupy: lifeless, wooden things. And the interpretation is that these teachers are not distinguishable from the chairs. This speech is merely critical; it is directed against the traditional teaching regarding virtue, a teaching which seems to have almost disappeared.

Now what is the point? The contention of the speech is this: the traditional teaching of virtue regards the end for the sake of which the virtues are required as sleep. Virtues are justified as good by the fact that they are needed for good sleep. Now what is the proof of that? One could say that this is a preposterous attack on the traditional way of teaching virtue, but it must have some meaning. For example, if you look on page 141, paragraphs 3 and 6, you will see quite a few formulae of this nature: "Blessed are the sleepy ones,"[3] blessedness meaning a state of the soul after death. This life has no meaning except as a preparation for the life after death. But the philosophers, whom Nietzsche has here in mind, do not believe in life after death and yet they agree somehow with the Christian view of virtue. They conceive of life as a preparation for something after death. Life is a state in which there is no activity, life is a preparation for sleep, life has no meaning. This is what Nietzsche imputes to the philosophic tradition. Now is there any evidence to support this Nietzschean view? A famous teacher of virtue has said that. In Plato's *Apology*, Socrates makes a remark when discussing what happened to men after death: Either there will be a life after death or there will be a state of dreamless sleep. And then Socrates says how wonderful it would be to be in this condition.[4] This is a historical fact, but it is not to be taken too seriously.

What Nietzsche has in mind can be stated as follows. The view at which he aims says that virtue is happiness, and happiness is peace of the soul. That can be exaggerated to peace of the soul at all cost before one has inquired whether man's situation permits peace of the soul—man's situation, namely, of being a rope above an abyss. Peace of the soul for the sake of contemplation, that was the traditional view. But contemplation traditionally understood is contemplation of already-created values and as such inferior to the creation of new values. The creation of new values requires, as Zarathustra said before, chaos in the soul, i.e., the opposite of peace of the soul.

The second speech contains nothing positive except the remark on page 142 at the end of the second paragraph.

Reader: "His wisdom is: to wake in order to sleep well. And verily, if life had no sense and I had to choose nonsense, then I too should consider this the most sensible nonsense."[5]

LS: "If life had no sense and I had to choose nonsense," which implies life does have a meaning, not with a view to what comes after life, but in itself. How do we know this? What is the origin of that meaning? This is not answered here.

We turn to the third speech, which is "On the Afterworldly." The title of this is partly a pun. In German: "Von den Hinterweltern," "behind the world." But in German it sounds almost like *Hinterwälder*, "behind the forest," "the men from the backwoods"—but literally "afterworld," those who regard the world as God's creation, therefore they say that life has a meaning because they say it is God's creation. Man has been created for the glory of God. The world is the work of the most perfect being, which is in no way in need of the world, and therefore perfection is in no way increased by creation. For if perfection were increased by creation, the good God would be obliged to create the world, and creation would be an act of redress. Therefore the world's perfection is insignificant, and yet God's creation is said to be an act of his love, of his goodness. Hence God became actually perfect by the creation, but the created world is meant to be inferior in perfection to God and in this sense imperfect.

Now all of these points, each of which needs a long commentary, are condensed by Nietzsche into one short paragraph, page 143, paragraph 2: "This world, eternally imperfect, the image of an eternal contradiction, an imperfect image—a drunken joy for its imperfect creator: thus the world once appeared to me."[6]

I indicated before the problem which Nietzsche has in mind: the problem inherent in the assertion that the world is the work of the most perfect being, who is in no way in need of the world. For Nietzsche, this view is to be rejected for being fundamentally self-contradictory. God did not create man: the creator God, the most perfect being, is man's work and man's frenzy or madness, like all gods. Man's suffering from the imperfection dreamt up an absolutely perfect being in heaven. The heavenly world is only a reflection of human life on earth. The incorporeal God is only a reflection of bodily men, of men dissatisfied with the body and earth because of their sickness and decadence. The afterworldly say that God, God's revelation, is the key to the understanding of everything, since if everything is created, to understand something means in the last resort to understand it as created and therefore to understand the process of creation itself. But God does not speak, only man speaks. Speech, understanding, articulation, is possible only as human understanding. The place of God as the key to everything is therefore taken by the ego, which is the measure and value of things, the ego which creates measure and value.

Here Nietzsche telescopes the radical change in modern thought, especially as it occurred in the early nineteenth century in Germany, where they created the ego to take the place of the creator God. But now an important change from the German tradition: the ego belongs to a being which is in a body. It is not pure mind; it belongs altogether to the earth. The ego is the origin of all meaning as a bodily and earthly being as distinguished from a pure mind. The ego thus understood is the origin of all meaning, i.e., of all possible meaning. Therefore, denial of body and earth or ascetic ideals, which regard body and life on earth as preparation for pure spirit in heaven, are destructive of all meaning because meaning can only be as posited by ego, body, and earth. The only consistent alternative to the acceptance of body and earth would be suicide. Nietzsche does not yet establish that life or earth have a meaning; meaning must be created by the ego. He only establishes the condition of all possible meaning, the condition being nonascetic. This much about the third speech, which . . .

no, I think I will go on and speak about the fourth speech, because they form a unity.

The fourth speech is "On the Despisers of the Body." Up to this point, Nietzsche's argument has led from God to the ego, something that imitates the movement from premodern thought to either Descartes or Kant or Fichte. In the next speech, the notion of the ego becomes radically modified. It was already here modified, that is, it was made clear that the ego is not sovereign; it belongs to a being which is in a body and it belongs altogether to the earth . . .

At any rate, the ego includes a thought-content or mind. In other words, the ego is a surface phenomenon. It is controlled by what Nietzsche calls the self; hence the origin of all meaning is not the ego—that was only a provisional stage—but the self. Creation is then not essentially conscious creation because the self is not essentially conscious. Nietzsche makes here the extreme statement that the self is the body. We have to raise two questions: Why is not the ego the self? And secondly: Why is the self body? First, the ego as Nietzsche understands it lives in the world of names, of universals, of roles, of what is common to a man with all men. The ego is not the seat of the uniqueness of individuals and therefore of what can be his best, of his "productive uniqueness."[7] The ego belongs to convention in the widest sense of the term, and is therefore distinguished from something like nature. If Nietzsche had still been free to use these traditional distinctions, he would have stated this proportion: ego to self like convention to nature. The self is essentially elusive, which cannot be said of the ego. In *Beyond Good and Evil*, aphorism 17, he calls that which is deeper than the ego the id. Some of you must have heard that expression, but Nietzsche's understanding of the id is radically different from Freud's. Later on I will make a reflection on the difference between Nietzsche and Freud as far as this is concerned.

The self is the productive core of man and inseparable from the body. There is no human spirituality which is not specific or, rather, individual—-i.e., Goethe's spirituality differs from Shakespeare's spirituality—and no spirituality is possible without a corresponding specific sensuality. For example, the way Shakespeare and Goethe perceived smells corresponds to their difference in the purely intellectual. This productive core in man is inseparable from his core, and Nietzsche goes beyond that and says it *is* his body. This doesn't make sense unless one turns it around. Your body is not a mere body—three-dimensional, organic, studied by anatomy, physiology, etc.—but it is also a self. The body is more than the anatomist and physiologist can say about it. If you read page 146, paragraph 4: "The body is a great reason, a plurality with one sense, a war and a peace, a herd and a shepherd. An instrument of your body is also your little reason, my brother, which you call 'spirit'—a little instrument and toy of your great reason."[8]

You see, the body consists also of a ruling element: a herd and a shepherd. This ruling element is not meant as the brain or the heart or any part of the anatomy of man, so Nietzsche's concept of the body is somewhat different from the superscientific concept of body. The statement "Thyself is thy body" has the same status as another statement of Nietzsche according to which man is the most cunning beast, which implies there is no essential difference between man and beast but only the gradual one, the most cunning.[9] Nietzsche also says that man is a beast which has not yet been delimited—in German, *festgestellt*.[10] Man does not have such a clear essence as other beings have. Man is a rope over an abyss. In his polemics against spiritualism, Nietzsche made too many concessions, we may say, with vulgar naturalism.

But this is not sufficient. Man is not always, nor is he created by God, according to Nietzsche; man is a product of the evolutionary process. Yet as a creator of values, man is also "a first cause"; at the same time, he is a product, an effect. This is not a metaphorical expression; Nietzsche means this very seriously. How can this be? Evolution and similar things are theories, they are applications of the principle of causality, of the categories. These categories of understanding, and not evolution, are the first principles. Nietzsche raises the question of the pure understanding: there is only the understanding of man, and this understanding is in the service of the human organism; hence the human understanding is the product of the process and at the same time it supplies the principle for any possible intellectual constitution of the process. The self, which takes the place of the ego, is a first cause and it cannot be the first cause. As we shall see later, Nietzsche was aware of this difficulty. To summarize, the place of God is taken not by the ego but by the self. The self, not the ego, is the core of man. The self wishes to create beyond itself, not the ego, because the ego is not creative; that is to say, the ego as ego is in itself on its way to the superman, in which human creativity reaches its climax.

This much about the first four speeches, which form a unity. Before I turn to the following speeches I would like to summarize. The phenomenon which Nietzsche has in mind when speaking of the self was traditionally called the soul. Modern philosophy or modern science emerged by the splitting up of the soul into two things: the consciousness or the ego, and body or matter. No soul, strictly speaking. That is the implication of Descartes. Animals are machines, and the principle which was formerly called the soul is purely mechanical. There is no soul. But in the case of some beings, perhaps only of man, these mechanical processes are accompanied by appearances, phantasms, consciousness. There is matter and consciousness, Nietzsche says, and in this respect he only returns to the premodern view that there is soul, there is a subconscious. Because the difference between consciousness and soul is that it is not of the essence of soul to be conscious, Nietzsche goes beyond the tradition by saying that there is a subconscious which can never be made conscious.

And here is the difference between Nietzsche and Freud, for example. Psychoanalysis admits, of course, the subconscious and sets its sphere, but it does not say that it can never be made fully conscious. The argument which is implied against psychoanalysis in Nietzsche tends to be as follows. Psychoanalysis is a science or claims to be a science, but it is of the essence of science to be capable of infinite progress; hence there can never be final knowledge, final scientific knowledge, applied to the subconscious. The subconscious can never be made fully conscious. Furthermore (and this is an equally important difference), the self, and the id as Nietzsche understands it, is creative. The soul, we can say, takes on the character of the creator God, of the essentially mysterious God; thus the soul becomes the self in Nietzsche's sense. The self, we can say, is the abyss of freedom in the soul. Creativity means the ability to produce the wholly unforeseen, the unpredictable. It implies that prediction cannot be simply the goal of human knowledge; otherwise the unpredictable would strictly speaking have only the status of the provisional. The experience we have that men do things which no one has foreseen, this applies to every work of art, obviously, but even to political matters. Who predicted the most important event of our time, or the phenomenon of Titoism,[11] which contains interesting possibilities for the future? No one, until it was there one day.

Above all, discoveries are by their nature not predictable. Generally speaking, "being is elusive." In this statement Nietzsche attacks the traditional statement according to which being is intelligible. This traditional view is of course implied in modern science at its present stage, but here completely modified because being is intelligible only in infinite process and therefore you can say, with equal right, that being is elusive. If something becomes intelligible in infinite process, it never becomes intelligible, because an infinite process by definition cannot be finished. But this is a contradiction in the present-day notion of science, though it is not made clear. Nietzsche says the self is elusive, because for him to be and to live is the same. Therefore, by saying the self is elusive, he is saying in fact that being is elusive. I quote again a statement of Nietzsche: "All earlier men had the truth. What is new in our present attitude toward philosophy is a conviction which no epoch ever had," namely, "*that we do not possess the truth.*"[12] Is this correct? What Nietzsche says is implied in his statement "God is dead." In the traditional theology, God is mysterious, hidden. But the hidden God knows himself fully, that is to say, in himself God is fully intelligible, he is not intelligible to men; therefore the biblical position agrees from this point of view with the position of traditional philosophy. As regards the philosophers, there were at all times skeptics, and skepticism apparently at least implies that we do not possess knowledge. But here there is a subtle difference between Nietzsche and skepticism. Nietzsche does not deny the possibility of knowledge. He doesn't say, as Kant said, that there is an inaccessible thing in itself, and that no knowledge of true reality is possible. What Nietzsche says is that truth is elusive and not simply inaccessible: he implies that there is some awareness of the truth. The only parallel in earlier philosophy to what Nietzsche means is in Plato. The Nietzschean thesis, according to which being is essentially elusive, finds, as I indicated before, its strongest *prima facie* support in modern science. Modern science proved to be, though it wasn't meant to be when it was created by Newton and Descartes, infinitely progressive. It belongs to the idea of science that there can never be a stage where all questions are solved. It proved to be infinitely progressive with the possibility of radical revisions, not merely the infinite process of accumulation, which would be philosophically utterly uninteresting. This, stated metaphysically: Being is elusive, it is accessible but can never be fully controlled.

This much about the first four speeches. I will repeat the thread of the argument. God is replaced first by the ego and eventually by the self. The ego was already implied in modern idealism, but the crucial change is that from the ego to the self, to the whole man with special regard to the core, the productive core of man. This must be the key to the understanding of what Nietzsche means by superman. Nietzsche's notion of the self is the common root of psychoanalysis on the one hand, and existentialism on the other. Both omit something. What is in Nietzsche a unity has been broken up in these incompatible positions.

Student: . . .

LS: In the first place, the mere fact that it was called the soul and not the self is characteristic. In the second place, in the classical notion the highest possibility of soul, which in a way transcends the soul, is the mind, the intellect. The intellect, the highest possibility for man, is characterized by perception of objects belonging to the mind: the highest possibility of man is not creative. For Nietzsche, the highest and deepest in man is creativity. In order to answer your question, one would really have to give an analysis of modern philosophy in every respect. The self is characterized by individuality, by uniqueness, and this uniqueness is the essence of the self. Think of the traditional distinction between the essence and the individual and you see that the argument takes an entirely different course.[13]

. . . What Nietzsche says is this. According to the predominant traditional philosophy, there is no knowledge of God except through demonstration starting from the visible universe. According to a belief which was very common in Nietzsche's time and which is still very common, the traditional arguments have been refuted by Hume or Kant. You start from phenomenon and you will never come to God. The question would then be: What is the chief phenomenon? It is knowledge of consciousness, which takes the place of traditional metaphysics, what became known by epistemology. Nietzsche makes this point. If we analyze our thinking, we see that it is not something ultimate but depends on something which we do not think. We are not in control of our thought. It occurs. The really important things come up by themselves, they are not even self-conscious. "It occurs to you." What does that mean? Thoughts come up from an unconscious ground in man. In the case of the great men, the most creative men, all conscious making succeeds a preceding creative act. What he says is this reasoning follows inference; the insights cannot be produced by reason. This is an old story: the intellect, insight; reason, connection. These insights create ultimately the enormous difficulty: How can there be truth? But the starting point is to say that there is something controlling man lower than his consciousness.

Student: . . .

LS: Let us assume that the self is spiritual and in no way body: the question is whether this is tenable. If you look at a creative man, is there no connection between his highest spirituality and his body? In *Beyond Good and Evil* there is a remark which says that the character of man's sexuality reaches up into his most sublime spirituality.[14] There is something to that; even physiognomy has some of this element in it. We can say that an immaterial substance is dogmatically rejected from the beginning, "upon his honor." What Nietzsche contends is this: If we analyze the phenomenon of the human mind, we are never compelled to assume a purely immaterial act. Whether this is sound, whether a complete analysis of the intellectual act proper would support this, is another matter. To begin with, we must say that we are dealing with certain assertions which have probability given modern opinion. The question must always remain in our mind: What is the true foundation of Nietzsche's doctrine? But we must also see what he is after.

I turn then to the next section, and I believe that speeches 5 to 12 form a unit and that they illustrate what he means by the self. The first section is almost impossible to translate. I translate it "Of Joy and Passion." In German, "Von den Freuden- und Leidenschaften": suffering. The thesis is this: Just as man is radically bodily, his virtue is radically passion. In the traditional understanding, say, in Plato and Aristotle, the virtues are conceived as radically different from the passions. "The passions" means the way in which we are affected, pleased, or pained. Virtue means to take a stand toward the affections. In the Platonic simile, the passions would be like the horses, noble or base, of a chariot; virtue is the character of the charioteer.[15] Virtue is radically different from passions. In the seventeenth century, when this whole doctrine was attacked, it was already stated very clearly that virtue must already itself be a passion. Virtue is the good passion which opposes the bad passion, but the passions can be fought only by passions, reason is too powerless for that. Spinoza, Montesquieu, Rousseau fall into that category. The people who said, for example, that virtue consists in pity or compassion meant by that that pity is the good passion. Fear of violent death is a good passion, and since reason is too powerless, fear of violent death guarantees the possibility of reason being victorious. Nietzsche follows this tradition, but he radicalized it by saying that while virtue is a passion, it is the highest, but there is an inseparable kinship between the highest and the lowest.

Now let us read up on page 148, the first and third paragraph.

Reader: My brother, if you have a virtue and she is your virtue, then you have her in common with nobody. To be sure, you want to call her by name and pet her; you want to pull her ear and have fun with her. And behold, now you have her name in common with the people and have become one of the people and herd with your virtue . . .

May your virtue be too exalted for the familiarity of names: and if you must speak of her, then do not be ashamed to stammer of her. Then speak and stammer, "This is *my* good; this I love; it pleases me wholly; thus alone do *I* want the good. I do not want it as divine law; I do not want it as human statute and need: it shall not be a signpost for me to overearths and paradises. It is an earthly virtue that I love: there is little prudence in it, and least of all the reason of all men. But this bird built its nest with me: therefore I love and caress it; now it dwells with me, sitting on its golden eggs." Thus you shall stammer and praise your virtue.[16]

LS: Nietzsche indicates here in a few words the fundamental difference between his notion of virtue and the traditional notion. Virtue has some character of the self, because if it were merely a character of the ego it would be only a surface phenomenon, but since this self is characterized by uniqueness, the virtues are something different in every different man. While they have the same name, it is hardly more than that. The substance of it is inextricably linked with the character of this or that individual. From the last passage, you see that virtue has very little to do with prudence and reason. There is no universal law, there is no universal end with a view to which certain actions can be recognized as virtuous: "Once you suffered passions and called them evil. But now you have only your virtues left: they grew out of your passions. You commended your highest goal to the heart of these passions: then they become your virtues and passions you enjoyed."[17]

Your highest goal, not *the* highest goal, because the highest goal must be individual. Virtue is sublimated passion. That is what Nietzsche says. Sublimation is Nietzsche's term. Freud took it over from Nietzsche, but there is this difference: when Nietzsche speaks of sublimation, he is always conscious of the connection between sublimation and the sublime, which cannot be said so simply of Freud. Virtues are transfigured passions, the transfiguration of *my* passion to *my* highest good. Passions become virtues by becoming dedicated to a man's highest goal. From this it follows, as Nietzsche makes clear in the sequel, that there can be a conflict between the various virtues. Reason is not here. There is no necessity or even possibility of a moral cosmos. There can and must be conflict between these passions. This conflict, which may lead to the destruction of a man through these conflicting virtues, is infinitely preferable to the satisfaction and complacency of the last man. To repeat the simplest connection of this speech with the preceding one: the substitution of the self for the ego leads to this doctrine of virtue.

In the next speech, "On the Pale Criminal," there is a connection with the preceding speech. We have seen a rehabilitation of the passions as an essential ingredient of anything that can be called virtue. The people attacked in this speech are the judges. By understanding the inseparable connection between good and evil in everyone, one cannot condemn a man. This is addressed to the judges. And again, the analysis of this criminal here shows the difference between the ego and the self. This poor fellow believed he had murdered for the sake of robbing, but in this particular case it was an afterthought by which he tried to justify the murder in the eyes of his poor reason. He must have a purpose, but as a matter of fact, he didn't have any purpose except the act of murder. Nietzsche is concerned here with the difference between the conscious intention and the subconscious and substantive motive.

I will first give my survey of these speeches, and then we will bring up your questions on the basis of your own reading. The seventh speech, "On Reading and Writing," page 152, paragraph 1: "Of all that is written I love only what a man has written with his blood. Write with blood, and you will experience that blood is spirit."[18]

This is of course one of those statements which are so embarrassing to those who admire Nietzsche, and especially when they think of what happened to that blood/spirit thing in Nietzsche's country fifty years later. But we must try to understand this. "Blood is spirit" is absolutely necessary if self is body. One can love only what a man writes with his blood. Nietzsche goes on to make clear what he does not mean: he does not mean a recommendation of heaviness. The thesis of this chapter is the contrary: the highest seriousness and the highest lightness go together necessarily. Blood refers to seriousness. Nothing that is not of the utmost seriousness can be loved and accepted by human beings. There can be something very nice, very charming, but ultimately we despise it if it is not serious. If I may give an example from my own experience, I saw once about twenty or thirty very fine pictures of the English painters of the eighteenth century. The overwhelming impression was that they were not necessary, they could as well not have been there. When I look at a certain portrait of Titian, I know it had to be done, there is no question. What Nietzsche says here is of the utmost seriousness, but this necessarily goes together with the utmost lightness, otherwise there is something wrong with the serious. This is a parallel to this essential connection between the highest and the lowest, as discussed before. You find a peroration of Nietzsche's statement in Machiavelli's writing, which he makes only of certain individuals: that they were characterized by impossible combinations of gravity and levity.[19] Nietzsche says it much more seriously than Machiavelli.

The eighth speech, "On the Tree on the Mountainside": a youth leaves the city seeking solitude. What is the situation? Let us read page 154, paragraph 4.

> Reader: Zarathustra replied: "Why should that frighten you? But it is with man as it is with the tree. The more he aspires to the height and light, the more strongly do his roots strive earthward, downward, into the dark, the deep — into evil."

LS: In other words, there is an essential interconnection between good and evil, and man cannot be supremely good if he is not at the same time supremely evil. In this particular case, the ascent of this young man was induced by his ambition. On this basis he became envious of Zarathustra, and envy is low, corrosive, the destruction of freedom and openness. If a man envies another man, he cannot look into his face, he cannot recognize a thing. Now what happened to this young man? Let us read page 156, paragraphs 2 and 3.

> Reader: "Indeed, I know your danger. But by my love and hope I beseech you: do not throw away your love and hope.
> "You still feel noble, and the others too feel your nobility, though they bear you a grudge and send you evil glances. Know that the noble man stands in everybody's way. The noble man stands in the way of the good too: and even if they call him one of the good, they thus want to do away with him. The noble man wants to create something new and a new virtue. The good want the old, and that the old be preserved. But this is not the danger of the noble man, that he might become one of the good, but a churl, a mocker, a destroyer."[20]

LS: He has broken with the old and respectable. He is in danger of losing his self-respect, and therefore he is in danger of abandoning his highest hope. This danger can be occasioned, as it is here, by his meeting someone whom he cannot possibly equal: Zarathustra. And by the hopelessness of satisfying his own ambition, he knows in advance that he will live in the shadow of Zarathustra, and he rebels against that. He cannot live with that deprivation.

You see here the distinction between the noble and the good. The good ones are those who accept the established on the basis of the established. The noble ones are creative, revolutionaries, and they are superior. This is basically the distinction we have in Plato between those who abide by the *nomos* and those who see the limitations of the *nomos* and therefore transcend it. But what is the difference? Again, there is no connection in Plato between transcending the *nomos* and creativity. On the contrary, those who transcend the *nomos* are those who perceive what is beyond the *nomos*. Let us read paragraph 5 on the same page.

Reader: "Alas, I knew noble men who lost their highest hope. Then they slandered all high hopes. Then they lived impudently in brief pleasures and barely cast their goals beyond the day. Spirit too is lust, so they said. Then the wings of their spirit broke: and now their spirit crawls about and soils what it gnaws. Once they thought of becoming heroes: now they are voluptuaries. The hero is for them an offense and a fright.

"But by my love and hope I beseech you: do not throw away the hero in your soul! Hold holy your highest hope!"[21]

LS: The hero is in the soul: no extraneous standards. Man is the rope over an abyss, that is the essence of man. One can say that Zarathustra appeals only to people who can respect others and themselves. Those who are completely unconcerned with respecting themselves and others cannot be reached by Nietzsche's arguments.

This phenomenon, concern with respect—not only self-respect, but the possibility of respect from others—is something given. But this opinion is derivative from the nature of man, the being which transcends itself. I want to correct my previous statement: these four speeches are really a unity, and they deal with the subject "beyond good and evil" as distinguished from good and bad. Nietzsche rejected the distinction between good and evil, but that does not mean the distinction between good and bad. "Good and bad" means not condemnation but contempt or pity, whereas "good and evil" as Nietzsche understands it means condemnation and, secondly, not guilt but shame.[22]

As for the character of the argument up to this point: in some cases proof of self-contradiction or alleged self-contradiction of the traditional notions; secondly, psychological analysis (for instance, the bodily and terrestrial in the allegedly spiritual and celestial); thirdly, the ... (for example, the self-overcoming of Christianity by intellectual honesty). Do you see the connection between the concept of the self as distinguished from the ego and the doctrine between the highest and lowest of man, and therefore that the virtues can only be transfigured by a noble passion? Nietzsche is not concerned here with the problem of everyday morality but with the highest moral problem, the most delicate moral problem ...

What Nietzsche means by pride must be understood in the light of his specific assertions. Nietzsche's notion of pride is connected with the fact that he conceives of man as creative, and the other side of it is that this human creator is in danger whereas the divine creator is omnipotent. The reverence given to the creator God is now given to the highest in man, but at the same time this reverence must have a delicacy which would be out of place in relation to God. One can say that everything turns, rightly understood, on pride. Wisdom does not consist in contemplation in the Aristotelian sense, where a noncreating being looks at a being which he has not created. But what is contemplation? Contemplation in Nietzsche's sense is compared to a creator looking at his creation. Must not there be behind all creation something uncreated which gives truth to the creation? Is not the statement that truth is creation itself creation? Whatever men assert to be true rests ultimately on the human creation. According to present-day positivism, the principle of causality, for example, is a human hypothesis invented at a certain time. But what about the insight into the fundamental hypothesis: Is this also hypothesis? Must we not fall back in every case on a truth which is not created? That is the problem, and everything turns around it.

Student: Is there an arbitrary quality about the term creation?

LS: It is arbitrary when looked at from without, but not from within. Nietzsche was the one who made the term "value" so popular. For Nietzsche the values are created. For example, in modern-day social science the values are not understood as created—it is at least in no way of their essence to be created. If I say my value is comfortable self-preservation, the value of that value is not bound up with being created: like and dislike establish this value. Nietzsche is much more discriminating.

4 The True Individual as the Highest Goal

Zarathustra, Part 1, 9–15

Leo Strauss: There is no "thou shalt" which precedes the human will. Every law, every notion of just and noble originates in the human will. In the old sophist view, the noble and just are only by convention and not by nature. In the conventional school, that meant a depreciation of the noble and just in favor of the natural. In Nietzsche, it is the opposite: man becomes man by virtue of his subjection to some notion of the noble and the just. But this subjection must be subjection to a law which man imposes upon himself. This law differs and must differ from man to man; it is not a law of reason, a law of universal validity. You may remember Kant's formulation of the categorical imperative: Act in such a way that your maxim can be understood as a universal law. What Kant has in mind is this: in order to see whether a maxim is moral or immoral, we have to subject it to the test of universalization. For example, I act on the principle, I don't want to pay taxes. The universalization is that there ought not to be any taxes, and then I see that this does not work. While for Kant law does originate in the human will—it is one and the same law which will be the outcome of this self-legislation, because the principle is that the law must be universally valid for all men—this is completely dropped by Nietzsche. Reason, consciousness, the ego are surface phenomena concealing the depth of man: that is called by Nietzsche the self, the creative center of man. The self is essentially connected with man's sensuality; therefore Nietzsche can say: "Thyself is thy body." The self is man's whole being, the creative center of man's whole being. All possible meaning of life, and all possible meaning, presupposes the acceptance and affirmation of man's being a bodily and earthly being. Ascetic ideals, living with a view to a life in heaven or a life without a body, are destructive of any possible meaning of life.

The other point which appeared last time was the connection between creativity and nobility. Nietzsche makes the distinction between the noble and the good, the noble man and the good man. The good men are the noncreative who live within an established moral order, but this established order owes its being to a primary creation. So every goodness depends on a primary creativity, and this primary creativity is as it were forgotten. The accepted value system is taken as eternal. The good are the noncreative who live within former creation and absolutize it. They do not know that their principles, too, are of human origin. The basis from which Nietzsche starts is this. Man is an animal, a bodily, terrestrial being which is not guided by instinct as the other animals are, nor by reason, because reason is derivative, but by its own project or creation, that is to say, the ideals. Man does not understand these ideals primarily as his creation, he understands them originally as somehow imposed on him from without. But now we know that all ideals, all values, are creations; that man is not guided by nature, or God, or reason; that he is radically unprotected, a rope over the abyss. All ideals that presuppose that ideals have a foundation independent of man's will are therefore based on error. These ideals are false; they presuppose that man does not face exposedness.

The question which arises is this: Does man's awareness of his fundamental situation, the fact that he is a rope over an abyss, supply him with a standard? In other words, understanding man's fundamental exposedness, does that not already tell us how to live? But if this is so, the right life would be a life according to nature, according to man's fundamental situation; that is to say, it would not be a creation. This is the great criticism of Nietzsche. Mr. Benjamin gave me a statement about this problem in which he elaborates the situation clearly. "What is the standard? How does Nietzsche establish his standard?" That is the question which we must try to answer. Part of the answer is surely Nietzsche's notion of the fundamental situation of man. However this may be, this new understanding of human life will not lead to *the* right life for all men, because there cannot be *the* right life for all men. Different human beings must have different virtues.

I suggest that we now read a few more of Zarathustra's speeches and then turn to a more general discussion. First we have to discuss speeches 9 through 12, which form a unity, and we begin with the speech called "On the Preachers of Death," page 156. One more word about the context. As I said last time, the first four speeches state the problem as the fundamental condition of . . . Then speeches 5 through 8 make clear the most important practical conclusion, namely, that virtue cannot be simply opposed to passion; it can only be transfigured or ennobled passion. There is an inseparable connection between the highest and the lowest of man. One could say this also as follows. Purity of the heart in the biblical sense, "thou shalt not covet," is impossible by nature. Goodness is possible only on the basis of this admitted necessity of the evil, of its transfiguration. Speeches 9 through 12, we can say, are devoted to the most important forms of contemporary badness.

We will read on page 157, paragraph 6.

Reader: "Life is only suffering," others say, and do not lie: see to it, then, that *you* cease! See to it, then, that the life which is only suffering ceases!

And let this be the doctrine of your virtue: "Thou shalt kill thyself! Thou shalt steal away!"

"Lust is sin," says one group that preaches death; "let us step aside and beget no children."

"Giving birth is troublesome," says another group; "why go on giving birth? One bears only unfortunates!"

And they too are preachers of death.

"Pity is needed," says the third group. "Take from me what I have! Take from me what I am! Life will bind me that much less!"

If they were full of pity through and through, they would make life insufferable for their neighbors. To be evil, that would be their real goodness.[1]

LS: Nietzsche is taking issue here with what he calls the preachers of death, with those who malign life. In this connection, he makes this assertion, among others: "for some men virtue consists in committing suicide, for others, virtue consists in being evil." There is not the virtue for all, and there cannot be. We may also take the fourth paragraph on page 158.

Reader: And you, too, for whom life is furious work and unrest—are you not very weary of life? Are you not very ripe for the preaching of death? All of you to whom furious work is dear, and whatever is fast, new, and strange—you find it hard to bear yourselves; your industry is escape and the will to forget yourselves. If you believed more in life you would fling yourselves less to the moment. But you do not have contents enough in yourselves for waiting—and not even for idleness.[2]

LS: That is a further explanation of what it means to believe in life: to believe in life does not mean what is vulgarly considered zest for life. To believe in life is the opposite of forgetting oneself, for life, if it is to be truly human, is to be a rope over an abyss. The general subject of the speech is that the old otherworldliness is very powerful in the modern world and manifests itself precisely in the noisy, worldly activity which is so visible in the foreground of our society. But we must not minimize the implication that for different human beings, different courses of conduct are virtuous. In the next speech, Nietzsche speaks of the other great power in modern life, that is, of late nineteenth-century Germany: there was the monarchy, supported by the altar, and the army. He had spoken of the preachers of death; the starting point was of course the theologians, but enlarged.

In the next speech he speaks of war and the warriors. We will read only one brief passage on page 158.

Reader: I know of the hatred and envy of your hearts. You are not great enough not to know hatred and envy. Be great enough, then, not to be ashamed of them.

And if you cannot be saints of knowledge, at least be its warriors. They are the companions and forerunners of such sainthood.[3]

LS: He here speaks of the warriors because soldiers remind him too much of uniforms. Warriors are superior to the creatures of death but lower than the saints of knowledge. The implication is that the highest human possibility is to be a saint of knowledge. That makes sense only if to live means also to know. In *Beyond Good and Evil*, the supermen are presented as the philosophers of the future; that is how crucial knowledge is in Nietzsche's ideas. The warriors do not preach death but they court death: to love life does not mean in any way to cling to life. Here again, the general observation that it is not a virtue that is universal and is not meant to be universal: this virtue, as appears from the sequel, consists in obedience and not in freedom. Also, it is not free of hatred and envy, which would be absent from the highest human possibility.

The next speech deals with the unity of the two preceding speeches, the state, which is here called the new idol. There is an important point which we must consider. Page 160, bottom.

Reader: State is the name of the coldest of all cold monsters. Coldly it tells lies too; and this lie crawls out of its mouth: "I, the state, am the people." That is a lie! It was creators who created peoples and hung a faith and a love over them: thus they served life.

It is annihilators who set traps for the many and call them "state": they hang a sword and a hundred appetites over them.[4]

LS: Here Nietzsche makes the distinction between the state and the people. The German word is of course *Volk*, which one could translate as nation. These are two radically different phenomena: *Volk* is a fundamental phenomenon; the state is derivative. The relation of *Volk* and state is that of the self to the ego: the state is the surface phenomenon, a merely rational phenomenon, the deeper one is the *Volk*. This surface phenomenon is characterized by reward and punishment and many desires. The *Volk* is characterized by faith and love. This is connected with another point which Nietzsche makes in the sequel: the state is characterized by universality. In principle, what characterizes the modern state, the right of man and the constitutional conclusions from that, is universally applicable and meant to be so. There is a *Volk* and its culture is characterized by uniqueness, so it is strictly the relation between the ego and the self. The state is universal. In its perfected form it treats everyone like everyone else. It levels the differences.

This notion of the state goes through Nietzsche's writings. I refer you to his latest writing, *The Will to Power*, aphorism 717: "The state or organized immorality." What Nietzsche means by that is that the state does for the individuals what individuals do not dare to do, for example, to kill men. Who would wish to be an executioner? But there are quite a few people who are in favor of capital punishment. Or he says, "the state is a machine."[5] We constantly speak of the machinery of government, but one cannot speak of the nation or the *Volk* as a machine, and that indicates the difference. Surely Nietzsche does not oppose the state as such but the idolization of the state, which was particularly powerful in Germany, the country of Hegel.

Then Nietzsche turns to the fourth of these modern forms of badness. The next speech, called "On the Flies of the Market Place"—the subject of that speech can be stated very simply: it is society. The rejection of the modern state and its idolization is common. But Nietzsche's criticism, as distinguished from these ordinary criticisms of the state, is as much directed against society. Let us read on page 163, paragraph 8.

Reader: Flee, my friend, into your solitude! I see you dazed by the noise of the great men and stung all over by the stings of the little men. Woods and crags know how to keep a dignified silence with you. Be like the tree that you love with its wide branches: silently listening, it hangs over the sea.

Where solitude ceases the market place begins; and where the market place begins the noise of the great actors and the buzzing of the poisonous flies begins too.

In the world even the best things amount to nothing without someone to make a show of them: great men the people call these showmen.

Little do the people comprehend the great—that is, the creating. But they have a mind for all showmen and actors of great things.

Around the inventors of new values the world revolves: invisibly it revolves. But around the actors revolve the people and fame: that is "the way of the world."[6]

LS: The great men that are the great actors—that is as great an idol as the state. "The great" has this great moral appeal in the old-fashioned conscience: law, loyalty, etc. Society has the appeal of freedom, which is not so much the characteristic of the state. But here there is also a fundamental danger to the best in man, to his being himself; the solution can only be found by going into solitude, an advice given only to Zarathustra's friend—again, a high form of virtue which can by its nature not be universal. The lack of intellectual honesty, the concern with success and self-assurance through applause, through effect—this is the phenomenon which Nietzsche has in mind.

There are some other points which we have to consider. On page 164, paragraph 3.

Reader: Full of solemn jesters is the market place—and the people pride themselves on their great men, their masters of the hour. But the hour presses them; so they press you. And from you too they want a Yes or No. Alas, do you want to place your chair between pro and con?

Do not be jealous of these unconditional, pressing men, you lover of truth! Never yet has truth hung on the arm of the unconditional.[7]

LS: This market place is, in the first place, characterized by showmanship; the second phenomenon is unconditional partisanship. What is the connection? What Nietzsche has in mind are phenomena which are well known to you, which are stated by critics of our society very frequently and have found their expression even in academic sociology: *The Organization Man*[8]—the celebrities, the book of the month. In modern society, fame is only the proof of worthlessness, which is I think a sound practical rule. Nietzsche characterizes the same society by something entirely different: unconditioned yes or no. Is it not true that our modern society is characterized by liberalism, by the very opposite of the unconditioned yes or no? But that is not quite so simple, because liberalism is the unconditional opposite to the unconditional: nothing may be more illiberal, more opposed to the individual, than liberalism. There is no possibility, for example, of considering the fundamental defects of liberalism. For example, there was an article in the *American Political Science Review* on conservatism[9] which showed on the basis of scientific methods that the majority of conservatives are illiterate psychopaths. The trouble with such an article is not that it was printed in the *APSR*, which is a scandal, but this is not the only place of this kind.

There is one more point which I think we should read on page 166, paragraph 2.

Reader: Indeed, my friend, you are the bad conscience of your neighbors: for they are unworthy of you. They hate you, therefore, and would like to suck your blood. Your neighbors will always be poisonous flies; that which is great in you, just that must make them more poisonous and more like flies.[10]

LS: I think the emphasis should be put on the "must." These low minds cannot help being low. There is no question of sin here, but part of it is the fact that the highest virtue is productive of vice.

We turn now to the next section, which goes to the end of the book, that is, the first part. The first word of the next section is "I love." I don't believe that this is an accident. It seems to me that these ten speeches, 13 to 22, all deal with love. For example, there are "Of Chastity," "Of Child and Marriage," which deal with sexual love; "Of the Friend," "Of the Love of Neighbor," and "Of the Gift-Giving Virtue" deal with love of man or charity. The others too deal with the same subject, even if not as vividly. All these speeches are devoted to the theme of love.

The first theme which Nietzsche discusses is chastity. This speech is slightly nauseating because of the triviality and the unctuous character of the treatment of this important subject. It is certainly not in any way shocking: "Do I counsel you to chastity? Chastity is a virtue in some, but almost a vice in many."[11] Note that it is never a vice, it is almost a vice. Nietzsche does not recommend dissoluteness in any way. I don't doubt that this speech contains very sensible remarks, but in a language which is somehow inappropriate — not because it is indecent but because it has a certain tone of unctuousness. In the third part of the *Genealogy of Morals*, he speaks much more healthily and properly on the same subject.[12]

The next section deals with the friend. It is connected with the preceding one by a remark in this speech to the effect "woman is not yet capable of friendship, woman knows only love." Let us read a few passages, page 168, paragraphs 4 and 5.

> Reader: In a friend one should still honor the enemy. Can you go close to your friend without going over to him?
> In a friend one should have one's best enemy. You should be closest to him with your heart when you resist him.

LS: Do you understand that? Friendship presupposes the deed of the friend; it stands on its own feet.

Student: Doesn't this explain the chastity? Because in lust you give yourself wholly to another person and lose yourself, and that is why he is opposed to lust or sexuality.

LS: He is not simply opposed to sexuality, he is only opposed to a chastity, an abstinence from sexuality which makes a man sicker of life. Mere bodily chastity ruins the soul.

> Reader: You do not want to put on anything for your friend? Should it be an honor for your friend that you give yourself to him as you are? But he sends you to the devil for that. He who makes no secret of himself, enrages: so much reason have you for fearing nakedness.[13]

LS: Friendship excludes close familiarity. There is a kind of sincerity which is very much like one of the boasts of the beatniks, which is absolutely incompatible with self-respect. In the sequel he develops the theme more fully, page 169, paragraphs 2 and 3.

> Reader: A friend should be a master at guessing and keeping still: you must not want to see everything. Your dream should betray to you what your friend does while awake.

LS: Do you understand this? Your dream should not reveal to you what your friend dreams. Not only should you not think of what your friend dreams in a wakened condition, but even in your dreams your friend should be present only in his awakeness. In the famous story, pointed out centuries ago by Plato, we are our lowest in our dreams.[14]

Reader: Your compassion should be a guess—to know first whether your friend wants compassion. Perhaps what he loves in you is the unbroken eye and the glance of eternity.[15]

LS: Friendship is incompatible with pity.[16] The most indiscreet thing is pity, though a man who is incapable of pity is of course a very poor human being. It is one of the most difficult things to be properly compassionate. The indiscretion of pity can be fatal in any friendship. Friendship seems to be higher than love and—that will be made clear in the sequel—higher than a certain kind of love.

In the next speech he begins to discuss this higher kind of love which is perhaps the most important speech in the first book, "On the Thousand and One Goals." This is also more suitable for discussion in the classroom.

Student: What does he mean by friendship?

LS: You would say that friendship necessarily presupposes an agreement. What he has in mind is the relationship between fundamental diversities, and therefore also fundamental diversity of opinion. That is not possible without some agreement. Friendship requires a community of levels rather than content. We cannot help note that Nietzsche did not have friends. Let us take some very simple everyday occurrence. You have not yet written your doctor's thesis. What would you expect a friend to do when you show it to him? You would expect him to be your severest critic. Would not his friendship be dependent on the ruthlessness of his criticism? The question is: How can there be enmity properly, given a certain human level, except by virtue of the inevitable imperfection of all human beings? For example, when Aristotle says friendship is something to be highly respected but truth more so, that doesn't mean he became an enemy of Plato by stating such a doctrine. If Plato had resented it, it would have been merely a weakness on his part, which we can understand but which we cannot respect. The classical view of friendship was based on the view that there is a possible harmony, a cosmos of ideas. If this is denied, if there is deadly conflict, then conflict and the passions that go with conflict, such as jealousy, are condoned. But why not envy and hatred too? These Nietzsche simply rejects. Perhaps we can leave it for the time being at the general formula that Nietzsche's denial of the possibility of a moral cosmos leads to a radically different appreciation of and judgment on higher passions.[17]

In a way, you become yourself only by virtue of this act, and yet friendship is possible only among human beings who impose this law on themselves. From this it follows that since these laws differ radically, there must be conflict. To the degree to which the dedication is full, they cannot but differ in what is for them the most important thing. What Nietzsche says is that in spite or because of it, this alone deserves to be called friendship. Logically it is very easy to say that, but when we try to think of this as a human reality, it becomes hard to understand. What Nietzsche contends is that a general society can only come out of individuals who have spent a very long time in solitude. The character in which the individual becomes the true self culminates, if everything goes well, in a society. That is the essential part of his teaching of the superman. By virtue of the common experience of the radical solitude, the radical "no" to the established and traditional values, there is an understanding which is not possible among those who have not had this experience. There cannot be only the understanding based on community of opinion, there can also be the community of a fundamental experience which is deeper than opinion.

What is the classical notion of friendship and need? There is a need on the part of every individual for friendship. Even Socrates needs people, not for self-assurance but for the exchange without which his pursuit is not possible. The question is: How does Nietzsche understand the need for sociality on the highest level, or does he actually exclude such a thing?

We turn now to the next speech, which is perhaps more accessible, and here Nietzsche turns to things with which everyone today is familiar, on page 171, paragraphs 3 through 5.

> Reader: Verily, men gave themselves all their good and evil. Verily, they did not take it, they did not find it, nor did it come to them as a voice from heaven. Only man placed values in things to preserve himself—he alone created a meaning for things, a human meaning. Therefore he calls himself "man," which means: the esteemer.
>
> To esteem is to create: hear this, you creators! Esteeming itself is of all esteemed things the most estimable treasure. Through esteeming alone is there value: and without esteeming, the nut of existence would be hollow. Hear this, you creators!

Change of values—that is a change of creators. Whoever must be a
creator always annihilates.[18]

LS: The matter is, I believe, clear. There are always given values, and
by creating values he necessarily denies, destroys, the established values.
Life owes all its meaning to creative acts. All values are human creation,
not discovered. Today this seems trivial, you can hear this in every social
science class. The difference is that Nietzsche would never admit as values
what they say are values. A bodily need absolutized would not be a value.
What Nietzsche means becomes clear from his enumeration on page 170.

Reader: "You shall always be the first and excel all others: your jealous
soul shall love no one, unless it be the friend"[19]—that made the soul of the
Greek quiver: thus he walked the path of his greatness.
  "To speak the truth and to handle bow and arrow well"[20]—that seemed
both dear and difficult to the people who gave me my name—the name
which is both dear and difficult to me.
  "To honor father and mother and to follow their will to the root of
one's soul"—this was the tablet of overcoming that another people hung
up over themselves and became more powerful and eternal thereby.
  "To practice loyalty and, for the sake of loyalty, to risk honor and blood
even for evil and dangerous things"—with this teaching another people
conquered themselves; and through this self-conquest they became pregnant and heavy with great hopes.[21]

LS: What Nietzsche has in mind are various kinds of nations, not so
much cultures, of ethnic groups: Greeks, Persians, Jews, Germans. There
is no way of giving a rationale for any of these positions, but one thing
is clear: they are possibilities of dedicating oneself to something higher
than oneself, and that constitutes their dignity. This is the well-known
theory of historicism: the variety of values behind which you cannot go.
"No people could live without first esteeming; but if they want to preserve
themselves, then they must not esteem as the neighbor esteems."[22] This
is an important but strange statement. Why can't all men agree on the
same positings? Why must each nation have values incompatible with
the values of its neighbor? This is a point anticipated by Rousseau in his
writing on the government of Poland,[23] where he speaks of the essential
antagonism of nations regarding their fundamental principles.[24] In other

words, there is a necessity for the antagonism and for the variety of ideas. We should continue this on page 170, paragraph 3.

Reader: A tablet of the good hangs over every people. Behold, it is the tablet of their overcomings; behold, it is the voice of their will to power.

Praiseworthy is whatever seems difficult to a people; whatever seems indispensable and difficult is called good; and whatever liberates even out of the deepest need, the rarest, the most difficult—that they call holy.[25]

LS: So you see there are certain formal principles common to all, but the content differs from nation to nation. If you take the concept of value in current social science, value means something liked by an individual regardless of reason, and the question of hierarchy of values cannot possibly arise. What Nietzsche would say is this: If there is no definite view of good and sacred, then it is not a genuine value system. The fact that there is that triad—the orderly, the good, and the sacred—everywhere there is a nation is of no practical importance insofar as all action depends on what is the law, what is the good, what is the sacred, and that differs from nation to nation.

Reader: Whatever makes them rule and triumph and shine, to the awe and envy of their neighbors, that is to them the high, the first, the measure, the meaning of all things.

Verily, my brother, once you have recognized the need and land and sky and neighbor of a people, you may also guess the law of their overcomings, and why they climb to their hope on this ladder.[26]

LS: Here Nietzsche almost suggests, as did more old-fashioned thought, that the explanation of the value system can be given in terms of, say, the climate, etc. This is still a view of some social scientists: to explain the values of a nation, you can do so in terms of the conditions—economic, climatic, etc. But the more sophisticated social scientists today say that this is not possible. I suppose you understand this part of the argument, which is in a way the beginning of Nietzsche's rational argument.

Don't forget that years before, Nietzsche had written "The Advantages and Disadvantages of History." The fundamental notion underlying this work was the understanding of history as the intercourse and conflict between various nations, each characterized by its own national mind: the denial of universalism. There is no natural law which is the standard. The traditional view of natural law was that variety can occur only on a subordinate level; there is one highest law on which human dignity depends everywhere, and subordinate to this is a variety of positive laws, customs, etc. According to this, there is no natural law and we cannot go beyond these national value systems.

In the sequel we find the most fundamental change. Page 171, paragraph 6.

> Reader: First, peoples were creators; and only in later times, individuals. Verily, the individual himself is still the most recent creation.
>
> Once peoples hung a tablet of the good over themselves. Love which would rule and love which would obey have together created such tablets.
>
> The delight in the herd is more ancient than the delight in the ego; and as long as the good conscience is identified with the herd, only the bad conscience says: I.
>
> Verily, the clever ego, the loveless ego that desires its own profit in the profit of the many—that is not the origin of the herd, but its going under.[27]

LS: In all these old ideas, which are all characteristically pre-Christian—though the German can be said to be medieval, but that is still connected in Nietzsche's view with the pagan German past. Originally, only peoples created values, but the herd or the people at their best are lovers, passionate men. In this stage of human life, the ego was the criminal or, what amounts to the same thing, the bad citizen, the man who thinks only of himself—cunning, calculating. Modern utilitarianism, which conceives of society in terms of the cunning, calculating individual, is only a restatement on the social level of this lowest status in man. The mere self-seeking did not have any respectability in ancient cultures.

Now a fundamental change made itself felt: the recognition of the ego in its moral dignity. This is much younger, Nietzsche says, than the people, the *Volk*, the nation. He goes a bit further: the individual is the youngest creation. The recognition of the moral dignity of the individual is not truly a recognition, a discovery of something preexistent but not previously admitted; it is a certain creation of a certain time. Some loving and passionate men erected this fable of the sovereign individual who is not cunning, calculating, low, but higher than any herd, any *Volk* can be. Originally, morality is herd morality. That means simply that morality has to do with that which preserves the herd. But this is a noble, transfigured—although specific—national morality. In the four nations which he has mentioned, it is not merely the preservation of the herd, but in the spirit of Achillean supremacy or biblical honoring of father and mother. But individualism is still higher.

Student: In a prior passage he said that the individual created the *Volk*; here he says that the *Volk* was the first creation.

LS: But he added in the immediate sequel: "love which wishes to rule and love which wishes to obey together created such fables." Let us speak of primitive people, and then of people with a higher culture like the four mentioned. In this stage some superior individual created such a *nomos*, but they were concerned with the morality for all, the whole society.

Student: The nation seems to create the individual, but on the other hand the nation is itself created by an individual.

LS: Let us say for a moment that every higher nation is created by a superior individual. Then there would still be that difference that he gives the law to the nation as a whole and he is not concerned with the development of individuals as individuals. The moral status of the individual remains the same. The individual is good by complying with the universal law of that society.

Student: You said before that the relation between state and [*Volk* or people] is in a way parallel to the relation between ego and self. But in *Beyond Good and Evil* he says that we cannot know what is best in ourselves.[28] Now with respect to Mr. Dannhauser's question:[29] How does this come about? In light of what motivations does the self, which I take it is the creative self, produce that [*nomos* or law] of which you speak?

LS: The distinction between the collective self and the individual self did not help you? This creation by Zarathustra is not truly a creation by the self, because it did not know itself.

Student: In terms of self-preservation this is very simple, but in terms of the individual creator who does not know the best in himself, who is in a way compelled, does nature not somehow come back in there?

LS: That question will come back in there, but I think we should postpone it. The fact that creation at all stages is not conscious making does not do away with the fact that in some sense the creators did not know that they were creating, and in some stage they know that they were creating. Moses or the old Zarathustra were creators and would have been shocked if they had thought of themselves in that way. Nietzsche's Zarathustra knows that he is a creator. Neither the old nor the new Zara-

ZARATHUSTRA, PART I, 9–15   63

thustra understands the ground of their creativity. The most important point is that for Nietzsche, the moral dignity is not a recognition of the preexisting fact covered over in the past by tradition but is a new positing, a new creation. The things that Nietzsche says are so trivial today that they may not strike you. In the history of civilization, modern individualism is taken for granted.

What is the difficulty, as developed here? In the last two paragraphs of the speech we will see that.

Reader: Verily, a monster is the power of this praising and censuring. Tell me, who will conquer it, O brothers? Tell me, who will throw a yoke over the thousand necks of this beast?

A thousand goals have there been so far, for there have been a thousand peoples. Only the yoke for the thousand necks is still lacking: the one goal is lacking. Humanity still has no goal.

But tell me, my brothers, if humanity still lacks a goal—is humanity itself not still lacking too?

Thus spoke Zarathustra.[30]

LS: This sounds Aristotelian: a being can only be constituted by having an end. But it is not quite meant this way. Now what does he imply? One man has to become aware of this relativity: that no value system has a higher dignity than the creative act by which it came into being. Once this is the case, these value systems lose their convincing power; there can no longer be the nation, the *Volk*, in that old sense. The place can be taken only by a universal society: mankind. That does not say anything about the political organization of the human race. That is not the question here; the question here is only the ideal, the goal. This is surely connected with the preceding creation—the creation of the individual, the different creations of nations, cultures, ideas—then the creation of a being of moral dignity, which came later. They have both destroyed forever the possibility of the nation, the *Volk*, as the highest unit. Here Nietzsche breaks away absolutely with any romantic system of the *Volk* mind. But of course—and that is a tremendous insight—this end, this goal, of the human race must be created. What the book is intended to do is to set forth that ideal, that goal, for the whole human race.

One objection is obvious, and Nietzsche is surely aware of it. There was such a universal ideal, and that was that of Christianity; therefore, the next speech deals with the love of the neighbor. What Nietzsche wants to show is that this ideal too is to be rejected. At a certain time, say, Christianity, universal ideals were developed, but they are the *Volk* ideal. Nietzsche's Zarathustra therefore is the universal ideal, the first ideal altogether which is in a sense consciously created. Nietzsche knows that he creates it although he cannot fully understand his own creation.

Student: . . .

LS: The marketplace is characterized by sheer superficiality. Let us take the distinction between the ego and the self. Both the state and society belong to the ego. The nation belongs to the level of the *Volk*; the market, the exchange of goods and services, including cultural goods, does not. State and society as sketched in these two speeches are the surface phenomena of tremendous power, due to the decay of the nation as well as Christianity. Neither the nation nor Christianity, powers which had formerly molded man, can any longer do it. That is not a mere defect from Nietzsche's point of view. That which will from now on mold man is higher than either the nation or Christianity. Isn't the distinction between state and society an essential modern characteristic? I think this is a fact, and in all reflections which are not quite superficial, where the state is one association among seventy-five, the state is here, society is there.

Student: Somehow it seems that the self has to be a prior phenomenon, and then again it seems that the goal has to be prior to the self.

LS: Not prior. There are some selves, not many, which are selves by virtue of self-legislation, creation, but there is nothing higher yet in the nineteenth century. The highest phenomena of the nineteenth century are a few individuals who can do that, that's all. The common barbarism is due to the fact that you have only some highly cultivated individuals, and a barbarous state and a barbarous society. What he hopes for is a society of true selves, where they are not merely outsiders, marginal people, but where they give society its character. Nietzsche's whole doctrine wouldn't allow the distinction between potentiality and actuality because of the teleological implications. What we can say up to this point is that that which limits the freedom of the self does not make intelligible the act of freedom; therefore the meaning of these conditional things depends on what it makes out of it. These conditions are illuminated by the act of creation, they do not illuminate the act of creation itself.

Student: . . .

LS: There is some connection between the simple phenomenon of actors and acting as it goes back to the Greeks. What he has primarily in mind is a modern phenomenon, starting quite from the surface sociologically, but really empirically. It is undeniable that actors and actresses play today a role which they have never played in human history. Until a short while ago they were treated rather as outcasts. Today actors and actresses play an absolutely preponderant role. You could say that is because they earn so much money, but that is already a consequence of a popular demand, a public united by an appreciation of actors and actresses rather than, for example, of great statesmen. The question arises: Does that not have something to do with other aspects of human life? Is the spirit of the actor not (again, I speak sociologically) in the modern intellectuals to a degree which was never the case in the past? Mere vanity existed at all times, but this must be something deeper. Relativism, skepticism, are very powerful in modern life. Doesn't the need to counteract it, while it is still very powerful in oneself, does this not lead to a fundamental insincerity? For example, Nietzsche suspected Thomas Carlyle to be a man of this kind, a man who did not honestly face the problem and tried to shout so that neither he nor anyone else would hear that silent problem, that he had broken with Christianity and did not want to admit it in his own country.[31] Now Carlyle was a very great man compared to much of today, but it is really improper and unbecoming to give contemporary examples. Books like *The Lonely Crowd* and *The Organization Man* deal with this problem.[32]

Nietzsche says here that the actor is the most characteristic phenomenon of modern society. He regarded Richard Wagner to some extent like that—not following the art regardless but squinting at something else, say, the German empire. For example, if you think of the dishonesty which is necessarily implied in many collective research problems, where a coordination is demanded which cannot possibly allow the individual to follow his own way fully. Or the publishers, people who are wholly incompetent to judge what a book should be like: he knows what would sell and you are supposed to adjust your style accordingly. Of course this means selling out. What Nietzsche has in mind is this phenomenon of selling oneself, which can have the very innocent meaning: I put my best foot forward to get that job. I do not say that there are not many books and many doctoral dissertations which are improved by a competent editor, but I am speaking of the more important, more interesting phenomenon which Nietzsche is driving at. Nietzsche has in mind that in modern society the actor, literally and metaphorically understood, has acquired a preponderance which he never had in the past. The state is a brutish fellow. It is subject to another deficiency: lifelessness. In society you have enormous life, goings-on, humming, and yet in a deeper sense it can also be equally lifeless because it is deprived of the true sources of life: the individual concerned with his improvement. Nietzsche raises a much higher claim, the individual as creative. But today, when stimulation of creativity becomes one of the functions of the elementary school, something has obviously gone wrong.

Student: . . .

LS: In one sense the end is as individual as it always was. It is only of such a kind that it permits of being accepted by individuals everywhere . . .[33]

Man must now exercise rule over the whole planet. Man, that is to say, not this or that nation, must become owner of the earth. In this stage, man has become aware of the fact that all values are his creation; hence from now on there can only be conscious creation of values. But what is creative in man is not the consciousness, the ego, but the self, the productive subconscious center of the whole man. So we have to say, more precisely: creation of new values which is accompanied by consciousness. The values have no support other than the individual's creativity.

Man is a creator, but not being omnipotent he is the endangered creator of all values. Here we can see the peculiar mixture of pride on the one hand and delicacy on the other which permeates Nietzsche's writings. One could illustrate Nietzsche's position, by the way, by indicating the difference between him and Freud. The id in Freud is the completely meaningless out of which, in a complicated way, the ego and the superego emerge. For Freud the id is the productive, creative center which creates the superego.

5 Postulated Nature
and Final Truth

Zarathustra, Part i, 16–22

Editor's note: Most of the tape of this session was inaudible. The transcript provides Werner Dannhauser's notes on that lecture.

Leo Strauss: We will review by considering some common points between
Nietzsche and modern social science, to see how Nietzsche concerns us.
Social science distinguishes between facts and values. There is objective knowledge only of facts. It is a fact that there are values, but there
is no objective knowledge of the validity of values. Scientific knowledge
is infinitely progressive; discoveries are unpredictable. This is somehow
connected with the view that all thought is historical. One escapes the
difficulties which arise by [positing an] absolute beginning [composed]
of definitions which are sterilized: science is an artificial island in the flux
of things. There are still difficulties because these questions arise: What is
science? Is science good? This last question cannot be answered scientifi-
cally because that would take value judgments. The choice of science must
be considered arbitrary; there is no responsible way of choosing. Science
must look to the coming of the last man. Man is merely a symbol-using
brute. One can see the problem from another angle: science is infinitely
progressive, so there will always be mystery. Science says: Take a faith to
live side by side with science, but at the same time science must preach
the sovereignty of reason, though reason can't choose. Reason can show
certain values to be based on untruth, like race supremacy, but it cannot
say why the choosing of truth-based values is preferable.
    Nietzsche starts but does not end with these problems. He also thinks
of man as a brute, and also says that no value system has objective support.
But Nietzsche knows that this situation is a radical change, *the* change.
Human life cannot go on as before. He adds another premise, which is
nonrelativistic: we have an awareness of human greatness. On the basis
of this awareness our situation looks like the supreme crisis: either the

superman or the last man. Values must be seen as a human creation. All previous values were meant to appear as given, and as such are useless now. Our objective knowledge of the lack of objective knowledge teaches us that values are creations of men, not of egos but of selves. The alternative to the last man is a society of creative individuals. But the question arises: Is awareness of greatness part of the *nature* of man?

The problem of the superman: in *Zarathustra* it is presented as a doctrine. It is called a doctrine. It is not demonstrated, but a free project. By "free project" Nietzsche does not mean arbitrary project; it is meant to be based on evident premises. We must ask about the truth of the premises. The major premise is that God is dead. With his death there comes the danger of the collapse of the human into the all-too-human. The alternative is the superman. God's death brings crisis, either the greatest degradation or the great overcoming. Atheism is man's degradation or elevation, but it cannot be humanistic. Nietzsche appeals to those who are concerned with human greatness, but Nietzsche does not prove one should be so concerned. A proof is impossible because there is no human nature. Values are creations, creations have raised man. Nietzsche appeals to men who have been raised by Western values. Now that God is dead we need the superman. How does Nietzsche know? Human greatness demands that man dedicate himself to the higher. The primary form of this dedication is the *Volk*, which is the primary moral phenomenon as distinguished from the natural, universal, rational law.

The *Volk* is pre-Christian. It has its own God. Then comes Christianity. See *Beyond Good and Evil*, aphorism 60.[1] The biblical notion of human greatness surpasses any previous notion. With the created value of love of mankind, the *Volk* stops being the primary moral phenomenon. One God replaces many gods. But biblical religion leads to the degradation of otherworldliness. Its decay leads to the individual, the man who lives by his own values, the superman. There will be a this-worldly universalism, loyalty to earth, a transfiguration of passions (connection of high and low). Uniqueness is more important. The task is to be entirely at home in this world, to be loyal to the earth. Regarding the political situation to which this was addressed, Nietzsche saw very clearly the impossibility of continued nationalism. Man must now exercise rule over the whole planet: man, not a given nation, must rule all. From now on there can only be conscious creation. Rather we have to say that from now on the creation of values will be accompanied by consciousness: only the self creates, not the ego. Man is the creator of values but he is not omnipotent.

He is always in danger. That is why in Nietzsche there is always a mixture of pride and delicacy. In Freud's terms: the *id* is the meaningless stratum from which *ego* and *superego* emerge; the *id* creates the *superego*, then the *ego* intervenes.

Man must become superman, master of the world as his world. Man never had this possibility or challenge before. The citizen of the world who contemplates is impossible; to say God is dead means to say that truth is dead. Nor can one say that the physical world is not dead, so let us have pure science. Nietzsche treats this in *Twilight of the Idols*, in "How the 'True World' Finally Turned into a Fiction: The History of an Error." With the true world we have abolished the apparent world. By this Nietzsche means that the apparent world is now the true world.

To explain this, it is necessary to deal with the history of modern science and philosophy. First came the distinction between the primary and the secondary qualities: only primary qualities are considered objective. Then comes the discovery that primary qualities are subjective, too. The primary is the logical construct. We organize sense data; reality is completely inaccessible. The *Ding an sich* is unknowable. We live entirely in a subjective world, unless we understand knowledge not as perceptive of the given but as construction. As construction we have the world, the true world, man's world. But if this is so, why then the creation of the whole man, the completed man, superman? If there is to be truth, there must be a superman who can say, "It's my world," a man entirely at home in the world as his world. Such a man is awake, aware, a philosopher. But this is a new sense of philosophy.

The truth is a free project. Is this truth about truth a free project? Is it, too, a human creation? Or, if man is a rope over an abyss, is this not the essence of man? Is not then the superman the natural end of man? Nietzsche doesn't mean this. He refers to evolution in the Prologue. The movement toward the last man is as natural as the movement toward the overman. Nietzsche's project is negatively based on Christianity, but there is no intelligible necessity for Christianity. The whole historical process is not teleological but a series of creations. Will there not then be a variety of projects, an infinity? No, because all previous projects were not known to be free. Now we know the truth about projects, so that points to a final project. In a sense this will be the end, but there is no necessity to have reached the end.

Let us go back to the speeches. The most important one is the last one in part I. We have seen the demand for a universal goal in the speech

"On the Thousand and One Goals." Nietzsche realizes that there are already such universal goals (most obviously Christianity). He now turns to neighborly love. The previous speech had already implied the rejection of this by showing that greatness comes from antagonism. However, there is this problem: Doesn't universality demand universal love? Nietzsche says yes, but not as such love is commonly understood, for this would lead to the last man. The next one doesn't deserve love. Love may be a mere means of getting approval, an escape, collective selfishness, a mere relation between shadows. These are persuasive empirical arguments. A human relationship based on ignorance of one another is for Nietzsche a false relationship. True neighborly love requires first that one love one's own highest possibility. Transfiguration is made possible by the free project. Good self-love is the basis of our love of others. Nietzsche has in mind people like those who always rush to visit the sick. We think they are saints, but often they never rush to share joys because they want to see only misery. Nietzsche draws our emphatic attention to such swindles. In this sort of insight, he is a very great psychologist.

Speech 17, "On the Way of the Creator." Not all have the right or the power to be a self. Only the true creator has the right to be free. Freedom from versus freedom for: this speech is the origin of the famous distinction. Nietzsche here is the critic of liberalism, which had taken its chances with freedom from. In a sense, Nietzsche returns to the classical view of Plato and Aristotle: there must be freedom for virtue, but how can there be freedom for vice? The best argument for liberalism, the right to bad free speech, is in Milton's *Areopagitica*. Nietzsche says that not all have the right to freedom. What is the basis of the distinction? Did the creator make himself a creator, or did he find something in himself? Nietzsche seems to have recourse to nature here. Nietzsche's problem is the restoration of creativity and freedom. There is a kind of conscience with a view to self-legislation: one gives one's self a law. Kant and Rousseau had thought of self-legislation, but the law was universal. Nietzsche drops the universality. Consciousness and reason are inferior. To have one's own law is the greatest responsibility; there is infinite responsibility accompanied by the possibility of infinite self-contempt.

Speech 18, "On Little Old and Young Women," is a report in dialogue form on a dialogue. Neither the inner nor the outer dialogue is prompted at the initiative of Zarathustra. Like some of Plato's dialogues, this is twice-compelled.[2] This ends with the now very famous shocker: Don't forget the whip. More important is that there is a tacit understanding that the creative individual is necessarily the male. Previously he had hinted at the progress of women, maybe from love to friendship; here he shows the limits of women. He had yet another recourse to nature.

Speech 19, "On the Adder's Bite," relates an experience of Zarathustra's after speech 18 makes clear he has little experience of women. He returns to the general theme of neighborly love; now he treats of the love of enemies. For Nietzsche the biblical judgment and injunction are not delicate enough. Biblical morality is transcended in the direction of greater delicacy, but nobility is not possible at all.

Speech 20, "On Child and Marriage." There seems to be a deliberate mixing of the themes of love and sex, which is Nietzsche's way of showing the kinship. Here a new wholeness of man is stressed. Procreation is regarded as creation by Nietzsche. To really get away with this would require by him a long biological proof and a new eugenic science. Otherwise he is wrong.

Student: How is Nietzsche's morality more delicate?[3] He says: Don't act like a saint especially if you are one. The things formerly included under the concept of urbanity are here presented very extremely.

LS: Nietzsche's points are certainly serious considerations, though on the whole it is easier to err on the side of brutality. An omniscient God humiliates men by knowing all we feel; in part 4 the ugliest man kills God so that he need no longer bear the scrutiny of his ugliness.[4] Pride and shame are inextricably bound together. It seems that Nietzsche reverts to an inverted Rousseauism. Rousseau stressed pity while Nietzsche mentions pride first, but ultimately Nietzsche's pride seems a bit sentimental.

To get back to the speech "On Child and Marriage," a prosaic expression would be a eugenic project, which could work only if Lysenko were right.[5]

Speech 21 deals with free death. Love of life means willingness to die when life is declining. There must be choice even of death. At the proper time, death is to be chosen, not out of dissatisfaction with the earth but to the glory of the highest. The teachers of slow death are those who think that suicide is forbidden. In this speech Jesus comes in. The only proper name in the book is Jesus. There are no Greek names. Jesus did not live long enough. He did not love life enough and he was not in the desert long enough. The ultimate affirmation of life is the free choice of death by suicide when the creative powers begin to fade.

Speech 22, "On the Gift-Giving Virtue," is the last speech of part 1. Zarathustra came to the city to find living companions. He found disciples, now he wants solitude again. This speech is definitely a parody of the New Testament. The free death in the last speech was the alternative to crucifixion. This is the only subdivided speech in part 1. The three changes of voice that Zarathustra has are probably parallel to the three metamorphoses of the mind.

The speech in section 1 identifies the gift-giving virtue as the highest and identifies this virtue with self-love. The speech is directed, however, against a crude hedonism and egoism. Man is neither a beast of prey nor a tame beast; he is not a beast at all. The gift-giving virtue takes the place of charity. It is not a biblical virtue but is meant as part of a loyalty to earthly strength. But anti-Christianity is not the theme of this division. There will be a movement from species to superspecies. But the superspecies will not consist of egoists. Nietzsche does not explain how the superman is related to the supersociety. Virtues belong to the self, which is identified with the body; ultimately, changes of morality are changes of body. The infrastructure is body while the superstructure is spirit. In contrast to this, the Marxist doctrine seems more rational. Nietzsche's apparent "absurdity" is connected with his critique of rationality. Knowledge of good and evil is impossible because they stem from the body. Intimations based on inspired awareness are possible. Body is not always elevated, but only at moments. There is an elevation and resurrection of the body. Creation is the consequence of bodily changes, changes in the subconscious. The scope and limit of moral knowledge are hints, suggestions, and symbols. The gift-giving virtue is a new virtue, not something belonging to the eternal and unchangeable nature of man. In the first division of speech 22, the emphasis is on a critique of hedonism and egoism; the critique of Christianity is in the background.

The second division of the speech emphasizes the novelty of the doctrine. Before now all virtue was ascetic. Now there is a radical change: man will no longer be an experiment. The change is so radical that now all error, chance, and meaninglessness will vanish. Here there is a close kinship to Marx and other leftist radicals: the future is open to an entirely new ideal. The highest individuals will become a chosen people, a self-chosen people. This people will not be of supermen yet, but it will be the precondition for the superman. Division 2 is almost silent about the gift-giving virtue. It is characterized by futurism. The connection with the first division is that the gift-giving virtue belongs to the future, and that it is the gift of Zarathustra. Now the question arises: Is not Zarathustra's creation the final creation? Also note the crucial importance of knowl-

edge: Zarathustra is a teacher. How is a teacher compatible with the creativity of the disciples?

The third division gives a provisional answer to these questions. Zarathustra makes clear what he means by teaching. It is merely an appeal to
creativity, not to belief. Much of this is definitely a parody of the New
Testament. For example, see Matthew 10:33 and Mark 8:38.[6] There is only
an appeal, but can there be so indefinite an appeal? Can there be a simply
open future? If one speaks of history, must one not have an eschatology,
a doctrine of the end of history? The statement that God is dead is now
enlarged to the statement that all gods are dead. When all have found the
self, there will be a great noon. It will not be the arrival of the superman
but the moment when the community can will the superman. It is a great
noon of knowledge.

This must be compared to Hegel. According to Hegel, the historical
process is completed. There is an absolute moment, and the highpoint
of knowledge coincides with the highpoint of society. Hegel coincides
with Napoleon. In this way Hegel avoids the pitfalls of relativism. Let us
now consider Nietzsche's great antagonists, Marx and Hegel. Nietzsche
says that in Hegel the philosopher comes after all has been done and
merely interprets, and that for Hegel there has been a history but now
there won't be. Against this, Marx asserts an open future, but the essential
character of the future is known: complete freedom and the abolition of
exploitation. For Marx there are two absolute moments: Marx stands at
one of them, when the decisive knowledge becomes available; the second
absolute moment is the moment of realization and the establishment of
freedom.

Nietzsche also has two absolute moments: the first is the high noon of
the peak of knowledge; the second is the coming of the superman, Nietzsche's equivalent to Marx's perfect society. But there is this difference:
there is no necessity for the superman; the last man is equally possible.
The second difference is that from noon there is a movement to evening
and a new morning. The world of the superman is followed by a night
followed by another morning. What does Nietzsche have in mind here?
Look at Marxism: you get freedom. It lasts forever, but not quite—the
world will end. We must believe this according to natural science. Marx-
ists don't bother with this because it is millions of years away, but the
length of our stay is philosophically uninteresting. Nietzsche faces this
problem philosophically: there is an infinity of historical processes. His
term for this is eternal return. For Marx and Hegel, there is only one

unique historical process. On the biblical basis there is nothing to say against this, but when you deny the Bible, with what right does one insist on the uniqueness of this historical process? Why should there be just one process? The eternal return is the peak of Nietzsche's teaching, but his motives for it are very hard to discern. A low-level explanation is that there can be no need for uniqueness. It is, however, no objection to say that there is no empirical evidence for the eternal return, for by its very terms there could not be. But if the realm of Marxist freedom or Nietzschean superman comes to an end, is there not a new victory of chance and nonsense over man's meaning-giving will? Can this victory of chance and nonsense following the superman be understood as a victory of the human will? Nietzsche tried to answer affirmatively.

At the end of part I, Nietzsche bears witness to the need for finality. One must take a stand somewhere, *the* stand. Progressivism does not work. In the case of historicism, there is the assertion that all thought is historical, but this is meant as a final insight. Marxism presents itself as the final teaching. In Nietzsche the self/ego distinction is meant to be final. We have become used to distrusting any kind of finality; this is because of the status and progress of science. Newton was once final; today we think there is no final word. We think that what is true of natural science must be true of all knowledge. The difficulty of this appears, however, even in natural science. The method and its amending process is the finality. Finality could only be avoided if the finality is in the questions. In some way Plato saw this.

Student: What is the eternal return?

LS: It was a common doctrine in antiquity. It is one way of seeing the world as permanent; within this permanence there is impermanence, in which history resides. This was the view of Plato and Aristotle. They spoke of cataclysms on earth which destroy civilization. There is fundamentally the same development: from tribe to city to cataclysm. An alternative view is that the visible universe came into being and will perish again. They had no notion of the biblical God. They thought the process would recur. They spoke of the great era; they had a relatively short time in mind, like 36,000 years. Of those who thought the process would recur, some thought it will recur identically. Nietzsche adopted this version.

The eternal return appears to Nietzsche as a moral postulate, not a cosmological doctrine. When man had God, all was thought of as infinitely important. When God dies, levity must follow. If man is to remain capable of high effort, there must be a substitute for God, and that substitute is the eternal return. All will happen again; what I do now will recur infinitely. It is a moral postulate: Live so that you can will your entire life to recur infinitely. But Nietzsche was no mere moralist. He was a philosopher, so this became a philosophical problem. He asks: How can we assume the uniqueness of the historical process? As a philosophical problem this is absolutely crucial, and it is to Nietzsche's credit that he faced what Marx simply seemed to overlook. The relation of the eternal return as a moral postulate to the eternal return as a cosmological doctrine is very dark in Nietzsche. The eternal return also faces another problem. Modernity speaks of the conquest of nature. Man will become the master of all. Perfect mastery means that all can be molded, even man himself. Human nature: What does it mean now? Where do we draw the line? How long will human life be prolonged? Nobody can say. On what philosophical grounds can one reject the possibility of man's immortality? What about the difference between the sexes? Nobody knows how far we can go. Lasswell's very lack of sobriety is instructive in this respect. He speaks of fantastic things. For him the problem of the future is a society of geniuses and its relation to robots. Since the robots will walk and talk, must we give them human rights? The differences between men and machines disappear.[7] Ridicule of Lasswell is theoretically not good enough. If nature is moldable, there are no assignable limits. Now one can say to this: Fine, all our troubles will vanish. The trouble is that the direction of the advance cannot be predicted, for a denial of the nature of man means a denial of the legitimately objective goals. Lasswell's successors may be beasts. Nietzsche would not say: Fine. He realized that one must have recourse to nature. He wanted inequality and the two sexes to remain, and therefore a recourse to nature is indispensable, but how is this possible given the infinite power of the human will? He also asserts the infinity of will. His fantastic way out seems to be to postulate nature, which then gives man limits—but if it is postulated, it is not nature.

The eternal return is not a noble lie. Nietzsche says if you have a dangerous truth in your hand, then open your hand. Nietzsche had no notion of the noble lie. His way of writing is not because of social responsibility. One can't consider Nietzsche insane because of the fantastic nature of his teaching. It may well be that parts of *Zarathustra* are the extreme in idiosyncrasy, but he was the first to see what relativism really means.

The section "On Little Old and Young Women" should be compared to the *Symposium*.

Nietzsche's difficulty with objective truth: If there is objective truth, then dualism becomes necessary. Nietzsche's formula for this is: Pure mind grasps the pure truth. There is something in this formulation, but if the pure mind grasps the pure truth, then one gets to asceticism. Then poetry, which is subintellectual, goes to a lower rank. Nietzsche's concern is with a notion of truth which does not split man into high and low.

Nietzsche's influence today is enormous. He is the father of all those who think of art as the supplement to science. He once formulated his attempt as looking at science from the viewpoint of art and at art from the viewpoint of life. Art is conceived of today as the highest; even social scientists say this. But art is necessarily individual: a novel by Tolstoy is not a novel by Stendhal. In other words, the truth is radically subjective.

Ortega y Gasset, Spengler—all those who speak of the modern crisis are the pupils of Nietzsche. Nietzsche is great enough as a thinker so that his very difficulties are illuminating.

For Nietzsche the knowledge of the truth is the knowledge of something very elusive. In any matter of consequence there can't be clear and distinct knowledge. The truth is so elusive that even the biblical God is not sufficient to express it.

6   Truth, Interpretation, and Intelligibility

Zarathustra, Part 2, 1–12

Leo Strauss: As you know, social science is based on psychology, and ultimately on biology. These sciences present themselves as objective sciences. They are, in part, as such atheistic sciences. Man is understood by them as the unintended product of evolution: man is the unintended product of a process and controlled by a variety of factors. Nietzsche seems frequently to merely adopt these views, but his emphasis is on the atheism, that is to say, an awareness of the infinite significance and consequence of this fact. The modern liberal social scientist would not take this fact too seriously, he would say that he is only an agnostic. The consequence of atheism as Nietzsche understands it is the decay of biblical religion, and that is bound to lead to the decay of biblical morality. Now we speak of a certain decency in Western society, and quite rightly—this decency would reveal itself as a mellowed Christianity. Now this decency has lost its basis by abandoning the faith on which it was originally based, and therefore it is in the process of corrosion. Think of such an external phenomenon as the beatniks. For some generations, the belief in God had found a substitute in the belief in progress, a heaven on earth. This belief in progress had lost its convincing power through two world wars and the spread of communism, which is constitutionally unable to act on the humanitarian principles on which it is based. The social scientist meets these phenomena in the more remote content. He makes objective studies of juvenile delinquency, and he does it on the assumption that juvenile delinquency is something undesirable. He cannot do this job imposed on him by the society to which he belongs without going into an analysis of the conditions of juvenile delinquency, which means ultimately the overall character of our present society and its trend and proclivities. If he wants to do his duty, he must consider Nietzsche's analysis, since that analysis is based on the same principles as his own science, namely, atheism. And he must look out for a remedy; otherwise he merely fiddles while Rome burns.

Nietzsche seems to have seen through the moral substance which is still left, and thus he seeks for a new idea based on the new fundamental premise that God is dead. He believes that there is not only a danger to man of previously unknown dimensions, but at the same time an opportunity never known before: man may become superhuman, the superman. But what Nietzsche says about this superman or about the gods is not, according to him, knowledge, that is to say, demonstrative or communicable knowledge. As such, his method seems to be inferior to what social science, psychology, and biology think. Science views with contempt Nietzsche's unscientific thesis. Nietzsche here turns the table: Is this science what it claims to be? Is it objective knowledge, or is this science not itself motivated by a moral idea, by specific moral taste? As we might say today, is it a mere accident that most social scientists today are liberal? Is this liberalism not built in somehow, without the scientist being aware of it somehow? These sciences, however, present themselves as the outcome of a rational study of man. What they teach can be shown to be true to every human being regardless of his origin, the only requirement being that he has acquired the necessary scientific training. But, Nietzsche contends, how do we know that the rational study of man (granted for a moment that this is the rational study of man) is not essentially blind to the best in man?

Here Nietzsche takes up an issue which existed in the beginning of modern science and was classically formulated by Pascal, by making the distinction between the spirit of geometry and the *esprit de finesse*, the spirit of subtlety. In other words, is the spirit of the mathematical sciences not constitutionally unable to understand the human as human? Do we therefore not need another spirit? Even in ordinary social science we hear sometimes of a given social scientist that he is "perceptive." This trait is not accounted for by any notions of the exactness of the social sciences. Nietzsche goes beyond this. He says there is no objective knowledge: all knowledge rests on hypothetical suppositions. If all knowledge rests on hypothetical presuppositions, all knowledge is ultimately hypothetical. Then the question arises: What is the value of these hypotheses as opposed to other hypotheses? According to the popular view, the value of these hypotheses has to be judged in terms of their enabling men to predict with a view of achieving control of things and of men. Nietzsche raises the question: Why is this *the* criterion? This is a merely dogmatic assumption. Why must the basic hypotheses not rather be judged in terms of what the hypotheses do to the highest in man, not to man's controlling man? As Nietzsche put it, he looks at science from the perspective of art, and at art from the perspective of life. This is a value judgment, to use the common phrase. But is the view of science as predictive not also a value judgment, to say nothing at all about the proposition that man needs science for his survival, which in the age of the nuclear bomb has lost all credibility? Man can survive much better without science.

We see then that social science is not in a position to oppose Nietzsche, because he is infinitely superior to social science in his awareness of what the problems are. This does not mean of course that Nietzsche's teaching is the true teaching. He may be perfectly right by saying that social science does not supply us with objective knowledge. But are we not in need of genuine knowledge? Is not his denial of the possibility of objective knowledge bound up with his denial of the essential difference between men and brutes? Because to say that there is an essential difference between men and brutes is in fact to say that man is a rational animal, and therefore a being which finds its perfection in knowledge, in objective knowledge. Did not Nietzsche himself make too many concessions to Darwin? At any rate, after he has defeated his contemporaries, he must tackle earlier sources, especially Plato and Aristotle. In the *Zarathustra* he does this in the second part. But we have already found a clear reference to the issue in the speech "On the Chairs of Virtue," in part 1, where he caricatures traditional moral doctrine by the assertion that according to that doctrine the end of virtue is sleep. What Nietzsche has in mind is an understanding of virtue as something like peace of mind or moderation, quiet contemplation. Nietzsche opposed this in the name of creativity, which presupposes the very opposite of peace of mind, namely, chaos.

Now we turn to the second part of the *Zarathustra*. The first speech is called "The Child with the Mirror." You remember the symbol of the child from the first speech in the first part—the camel, the lion, and the child. Even now, Zarathustra is not yet a child, he is distinguished from a child. Zarathustra descends again to men, but no longer to the people (as in the initial speech when he addressed the people), nor to all, but to those whom he loves; yet according to his notion of friendship, they may well prove his enemies. The child tells Zarathustra to look in the mirror. Zarathustra himself does not look into the mirror, but looking in the mirror at the request of the child . . . he sees the devil's grimace, the image of what his enemies have made of his doctrine. His descent is due entirely to love, not to need. Like a god, he possesses only wealth and no poverty.

The six following speeches are polemic; they deal again with the contemporary forms of badness. The second speech, "Upon the Blessed Isles," where his friends lived, this speech restates Zarathustra's thesis. It is afternoon, autumn, harvest time. You remember the reference to the noon, the peak of knowledge, at the end of the first part. Zarathustra does not say now that God is dead, as he said before. He says God is a supposition, a conjecture: he can never be more than a conjecture, a mere possibility, an empty possibility; he can never be known, fully known by man; he can never become thinkable in the full sense. What is to be true must be the work of the whole man; otherwise it remains a ghost which saps man's creativity, for it implies that there is a fixed limit to his creativity.

> Reader: God is a conjecture; but I desire that your conjectures should be limited by what is thinkable. Could you *think* a god? But this is what the will to truth should mean to you: that everything be changed into what is thinkable for man, visible for man, feelable by man. You should think through your own senses to their consequences.
>
> And what you have called world, that shall be created only by you: your reason, your image, your will, your love shall thus be realized. And verily, for your own bliss, you lovers of knowledge.
>
> And how would you bear life without this hope, you lovers of knowledge? You could not have been born either into the incomprehensible or into the irrational.
>
> But let me reveal my heart to you entirely, my friends: *if* there were gods, how could I endure not to be a god! *Hence* there are no gods. Though I drew this conclusion, now it draws me.[1]

LS: This seems to be a particularly blasphemous and absurd statement. Nietzsche disdains to give any justification for this statement. Let me explain the background. In the Platonic dialogue *Euthyphro*, the problem of piety is discussed. Piety in the popular opinion appears to be doing what the gods tell men to do. Yet there is also another notion of piety according to which piety consists in loving God, following God, walking in his way, imitating him, becoming like God, and the last conclusion would be becoming a God. We can very well raise the question: Is this not absurd? Isn't man mortal, perishable, changeable, and God unmoved and imperishable? Let us read the sequel.

> Reader: God is a conjecture; but who could drain all the agony of this conjecture without dying? Shall his faith be taken away from the creator, and from the eagle, his soaring to eagle heights?

God is a thought that makes crooked all that is straight, and makes turn whatever stands. How? Should time be gone, and all that is impermanent a mere lie? To think this is a dizzy whirl for human bones, and a vomit for the stomach; verily, I call it the turning sickness to conjecture thus. Evil I call it, and misanthropic—all this teaching of the One and the Plenum and the Unmoved and the Sated and the Permanent. All the permanent—that is only a parable. And the poets lie too much.

It is of time and becoming that the best parables should speak: let them be a praise and a justification of all impermanence.[2]

LS: Nietzsche rejects the very notion of the unmoved and imperishable as an utterly incredible conjecture in the name of time and becoming, change, perishing, suffering. These are the conditions of creativity. The alternative, that there are determinate natures, that there is a good life according to nature and not as a free project, is rejected in accordance with the general modern tenets. Think of the well-known fact that it is now impossible to speak of the fine arts as imitative arts; it is a matter of course that they are understood as noetic. All these things are implied. Nietzsche only draws the last conclusion: there cannot be anything beyond time and beyond becoming. That is the ultimate reason why there cannot be a God. There is a further reference in the sequel on page 199, paragraph 4.

Reader: Whatever in me has feeling, suffers and is in prison; but my will always comes to me as my liberator and joy-bringer. Willing liberates: that is the true teaching of will and liberty—thus Zarathustra teaches it.[3]

LS: The way in which man is affected. . . what is imposed, that is sheer suffering. Only will liberates. What does this imply? Ultimately, something like the . . . nature, what is imposed on us, what is given us, and this must be opposed to the will. The will alone can free man. You remember the passage at the end of the first part: the contrast of charms and senselessness; meaning and sense come into being only by virtue of man's giving meaning to that which is in itself merely accidental and senseless. There is a given; otherwise there would be nothing on which to imprint sense, but which meaning it has depends entirely on the will.

Reader: Willing no more and esteeming no more and creating no more—oh, that this great weariness might always remain far from me! In knowledge too I feel only my will's joy in begetting and becoming; and if there is innocence in my knowledge, it is because the will to beget is in it. Away from God and gods this will has lured me; what could one create if gods existed?[4]

LS: In other words, if there were superhuman beings, it would be the end of creativity. What is given is the object of knowledge, but all is either a mere fact as merely given, or else it is seen in the light of the will. But is not the former—the merely given, the mere fact—not true knowledge, pure knowledge? Nietzsche says no. The given cannot be understood as the object of pure knowledge, but only as connected with the tired will. There is no ethically neutral knowledge. The knowledge of the given must be interpreted, and to abandon interpretation is also an interpretation. We shall see that this cannot be simply maintained, but is nevertheless important.

The next speech: "On the Pitying." This is connected with the preceding speech by the proposition of the traditional belief in God as infinite love, the all-seeing God. Given the imperfection of man, this infinite love must turn into infinite pity and therewith, according to Nietzsche, into the destruction of God as the most perfect being because of the destructive character of pitying. In this speech, Zarathustra turns into the knower in his relation to other men who are not knowers, and he says he is related to other men as men are to brutes. This is an old story. But Nietzsche understands this relation of the knower to the not-knower in a radically different way.

Reader: My friends, a gibe was related to your friend: "Look at Zarathustra! Does he not walk among us as if we were animals?"

But it were better said: "He who has knowledge walks among men *as* among animals."

To him who has knowledge, man himself is "the animal with red cheeks." How did this come about? Is it not because man has had to be ashamed too often? O my friends! Thus speaks he who has knowledge: shame, shame, shame—that is the history of man.[5]

LS: Man has become man by shame. This was already discussed in the beginning in the Prologue. Man has become man from the ape, or worm, or whatever it may be, and he is ashamed of this origin, by suffering from this origin. There is then an inseparable connection between suffering and elevation, and this leads to the further consequence throughout the work that the idea of the abolition of suffering is identical with the idea of the abolition of any possible human greatness.

Let us contrast Nietzsche's view with the common view that there is such an idea as moral progress. Man raises himself above the brutes: he asserts eventually that there is an essential difference between men and brutes and that his origin is different from that of brutes. This assertion is due to human pride. There is a view that modern science is an attack on human pride. First, with Copernicus, the earth becomes an insignificant planet—it is no longer the center; then, Darwin. Therefore, there is a rather common view that man's humanity is merely disguised brutality. One cannot speak of man's being higher than the brutes. The practical consequence is, as was indicated in the beginning, the last man. Nietzsche in a way accepts this notion of the history of man, but he interprets it radically differently: he says that humanity is modified brutality. It is not disguised but transfigured brutality. Man can be proud and should be proud, but he knows his lowly origin. His pride is therefore only the reverse side of his shame.

Nietzsche agrees with Darwin (i.e., the modern notion of the origin of man), but he disagrees with him as to the cause of evolution. Nietzsche sees this cause in creativity. His expression for that is, as we shall see later, the will to power. From this point of view we have simply two different theories of evolution, namely, the Darwinian or mechanical, and the creative evolution, as it was called by one of Nietzsche's many pupils, Bergson.[6] But this would be misleading. Nietzsche's doctrine is not theoretical, as Bergson's tends to be. Nietzsche implies: Is creativity theoretically knowable? If not, and that is Nietzsche's contention, an ethically neutral knowledge of the fact of evolution is essentially incomplete and must be interpreted. The interpretation depends on the human experience, the self-experience of the interpreter. In other words, the Darwinian interpretation is only a reflection of Darwin's understanding of man as a competing animal. In other words, you can establish that there is a history of the species in general, but this is hopelessly incomplete and can never be made complete by any progress of science. It must be interpreted, but this interpretation is necessarily ethically differentiated, not ethically neutral. Nietzsche makes here a very important distinction between the knower and the noble man: the noble man is not identical with the knower. Knowledge is here presented as ethically neutral. It is a fact that man has become man by overcoming, or repression, or concealment. From this point of view, knowledge is debunking. Nietzsche says: No, knowledge is not essentially debunking; debunking is a certain interpretation, it is a certain view of knowledge for destruction or degrading. This use is no longer essential to knowledge. Debunking has its root in the debasement of the shame, as a concealment of defect, of the shameful part of our being—*la partie honteuse*—and this shame is suffering or based on suffering. One can respect that suffering as a condition of the mind. One can have shame out of respect for the highest, the aspiration which drives to overcome it.

Shame, and this is the immediate subject of the speech, must take the place of pity. Pity is here understood as attentiveness to other men's suffering, weakness, and degradation. This concern with the suffering of others is really degrading. This theme is developed throughout this speech. Shame is respect for the pride of others; its root is therefore one's own pride. Pity has nothing to do with pride. Now let us turn to page 201, paragraph 2.

> Reader: Great indebtedness does not make men grateful, but vengeful; and if a little charity is not forgotten, it turns into a gnawing worm.
>
> "Be reserved in accepting! Distinguish by accepting!" Thus I advise those who have nothing to give.
>
> But I am a giver of gifts: I like to give, as a friend to friends. Strangers, however, and the poor may themselves pluck the fruit from my tree: that will cause them less shame.
>
> But beggars should be abolished entirely! Verily, it is annoying to give to them and it is annoying not to give to them.[7]

LS: These remarks of Nietzsche remind somehow of those who are called the French moralists, La Rochefoucauld and others. The noble soul can be grateful, grateful and not vengeful, of its low origin. One could of course raise the question which we discussed last time: Why can there not be a much greater robustness regarding the unreasonable sensitivity of oneself toward others? There are beggars who are proud men. In other words, why not an urbane irony rather than delicate respect for all kinds of beings?

On all these points Nietzsche is a kind of inverted Rousseau, and one can perhaps state this more precisely by reverting to certain well-known doctrines of Rousseau on the one hand, and Nietzsche on the other. When comparing Nietzsche and Rousseau, it seems at first that Nietzsche is more virile than Rousseau, but this is not necessarily so.

Consider the ideal of the citizen of Geneva. Now what is Rousseau's scheme? Rousseau says there are two fundamental desires. One is for self-preservation, which he calls *amour de soi*, love of oneself. This is good and natural. However, it can degenerate and does degenerate into what he calls *amour-propre*, vanity. And vanity is the root of all evil, our concern with what others think of us; therefore all opposition to innate qualities has to do with vanity. The natural view is somehow the acceptance of natural equality at this point. Rousseau asserts that pity belongs to the natural man. The man not corrupted by society is selfish; he is concerned with self-preservation but only with his self-preservation, not what others think about him. His relation to others is that of pity. This scheme is accepted by Nietzsche in form but changed in substance. Nietzsche puts on the positive side pride and shame, in other words, that which Rousseau had called *amour-propre*. Nietzsche replaces the whole concept of self-love, the concern with self-preservation, with the will to power, the will to overcome it, the will to superiority. Nietzsche's primary distinction is not between self-love and vanity, but between the healthy will to power and the sick or poor will to power. Let us read on page 201, paragraph 7.

Reader: Worst of all, however, are petty thoughts. Verily, even evil deeds are better than petty thoughts.

To be sure, you say: "The pleasure in a lot of petty nastiness saves us from many a big evil deed." But here one should not wish to save.

An evil deed is like a boil: it itches and irritates and breaks open—it speaks honestly. "Behold, I am disease"—thus speaks the evil deed; that is its honesty.

But a petty thought is like a fungus: it creeps and stoops and does not want to be anywhere—until the whole body is rotten and withered with little fungi.[8]

LS: Nietzsche speaks of the fungus growth. We all know that many people are made sick by petty thoughts and ought to speak up, and perhaps even act up. But is this universal? One can't forget that for some the acting out leads to murder. Nietzsche's emphasis on sincerity has contributed to the modern sincerity fetish.

The next speech is "On Priests." You see the connection: atheism, pity, aid in the present day of Christian morality are embodied in the priest. We will read the first two paragraphs on page 205.

Reader: But blood is the worst witness of truth; blood poisons even the purest doctrine and turns it into delusion and hatred of the heart. And if a man goes through fire for his doctrine—what does that prove? Verily, it is more if your own doctrine comes out of your own fire.

A sultry heart and a cold head: where these two meet there arises the roaring wind, the "Redeemer."[9]

LS: Nietzsche here brings up a broader problem. There is an aphorism in *Beyond Good and Evil*, number 87, which expresses what Nietzsche says there perhaps more clearly:

Heart in bond, spirit free. When one places one's heart in firm bonds and keeps it locked up, one can afford to give one's spirit many liberties. I already said this once. But people do not believe me—unless they know it already—[10]

This formulation is, I think, clear. You cannot have both a free heart and a free mind, contrary to the liberal view. If you have a free heart, the heart is in control of the mind. You can also have a free mind, but then you must keep your heart under control. This is Nietzsche's solution, which reminds, I think, of the classical view. What Nietzsche means by a cold head is this: no intellectual passion, no passionate concern with knowledge, with one's own problems (otherwise it would not be passionate, since they are not your problems), with one's own problems as problems.

I refer to the next speech, "On the Virtuous." Let us read on page 208, paragraphs 6 through 7. The main thing is that the notion of the rewards of virtue must be completely dismissed. Even the statement that virtue is its own reward is still too low because it brings in the very notion of reward.

Reader: Oh, my friends, that your self be in your deed as the mother is in her child—let that be *your* word concerning virtue!

Verily, I may have taken a hundred words from you and the dearest toys of your virtue, and now you are angry with me, as children are angry. They played by the sea, and a wave came and carried off their toy to the depths: now they are crying. But the same wave shall bring them new toys and shower new colorful shells before them. Thus they will be comforted; and like them, you too, my friends, shall have your comfortings—and new colorful shells.

Thus spoke Zarathustra.[11]

LS: Nietzsche has debunked the traditional notions of virtue. All virtues are toys, which means the greatest seriousness which is indicated by the word virtue. We must not forget that the virtuous man is called by the Greeks the serious man, and I think this is still true today. What Nietzsche says is that this greatest seriousness of man is inseparable from the lightness; hence no notion of reward. This is true of all virtues at all times, if they were virtues. But the new virtues are not artifacts, but they stem from the ocean and preserve the sounds of the ocean. They are natural, they are natural in a way in which the traditional virtues are not natural.

I go on to the next speech, "On the Rabble." The opposite of the traditional virtues or the traditionally virtuous men—the good and the best—are the vicious. The opposite of the virtuous in Nietzsche's sense are the rabble. You see here the political, antidemocratic implication, which is surely there. By the way, the term rabble was also used by such good democrats as Thomas Jefferson, as you may remember.

Now what is the rabble? People without a sense of honor and without cleanliness. Here Nietzsche expresses again the infinite suffering, but this must be rightly understood. It is not a mere idiosyncrasy of Nietzsche. Infinite suffering is only the other side of the infinite pride, the infinite delicacy. This is connected with the fact that Nietzsche seems to visualize man's infinite possibilities.

> Reader: *Letter.* A letter is an unannounced visit; the mailman, the mediator of impolite incursions. One ought to have one hour in every eight days for receiving letters, and then take a bath.[12]

LS: How exaggerated. How superior is the older view that we must be good citizens in the city of God, and that city requires that all kinds of people are members: poisonous snakes, skunks. Of course it is wise to avoid the poisonous snakes and the skunks.

We now come a bit closer to the whole political problem in the next speech, "On the Tarantulas." The tarantulas are the preachers of equality. Their motivation is resentment, revenge. Their speeches of justice only conceal their revenge. From Nietzsche's point of view, there exists an essential connection between the egalitarianism of modern times and the biblical belief in God. Nietzsche was of course not the first to say this: you remember Tocqueville in *Democracy in America* makes this contention.[13] Nietzsche turns it around. Now let us turn to page 212, paragraph 4.

Reader: They are like enthusiasts, yet it is not the heart that fires them—but revenge. And when they become elegant and cold, it is not the spirit but envy that makes them elegant and cold. Their jealousy leads them even on the paths of thinkers; and this is the sign of their jealousy: they always go too far, till their weariness must in the end lie down to sleep in the snow.[14]

LS: This is a very sensible statement, but the question is whether this extremism is not also characteristic of the counter-tarantula Nietzsche. Let us turn to page 213.

Reader: I do not wish to be mixed up and confused with these preachers of equality. For, to *me* justice speaks thus: "Men are not equal." Nor shall they become equal! What would my love of the overman be if I spoke otherwise?

On a thousand bridges and paths they shall throng to the future, and ever more war and inequality shall divide them: thus does my great love make me speak. In their hostilities they shall become inventors of images and ghosts, and with their images and ghosts they shall yet fight the highest fight against one another. Good and evil, and rich and poor, and high and low, and all the names of values—arms shall they be and clattering signs that life must overcome itself again and again.

Life wants to build itself up into the heights with pillars and steps; it wants to look into vast distances and out toward stirring beauties: therefore it requires height. And because it requires height, it requires steps and contradiction among the steps and the climbers. Life wants to climb and to overcome itself climbing.[15]

LS: Here the argument against equality is sketched. The love of the superman implies a radical anti-egalitarianism. There are two different reasons which we must distinguish. If we want the highest development of the individual, we demand inequality in the sense of dissimilarity, known in the general discussions of today as pluralism. For Nietzsche, inequality is the condition for any high achievement. One can argue as follows: originally, the demand for equality meant the equality of the citizen as citizen, which means that certain conditions must be fulfilled so that the citizens can be equal citizens. This had radically been changed already in Nietzsche's time, and even more so today. Today, egalitarianism implies the equality of cultures. The old European egalitarian doctrines implied somehow a fundamental superiority of Europe, not that this could not also be acquired by non-Europeans, but it so happens that Europe was the place where the egalitarian view, the democratic idea, was developed. Today the equality of all cultures is demanded, but one cannot leave it at that. To be logical, one would have to say equality not only in space but also in time: the equality of all generations. Here you see immediately the contradiction between equality and progress. If you want progress, you cannot simply be egalitarian. But this is only one point; the other point can be stated as follows: if there is need for height, there is need for low. One could say there is enough around us which is lower than man and therefore there is no need for low human beings. I read you aphorism 257 in *Beyond Good and Evil*:

Every heightening of the type "man" hitherto has been the work of an aristocratic society—and thus it will always be; a society which believes in a long ladder of rank order and value differences in men, which needs slavery in some sense. Without the *pathos of distance* as it grows out of the deep-seated differences of caste, out of the constant view, the downward view, that the ruling caste gets of its subordinates and tools, out of its equally constant exercise in obeying and commanding, in keeping apart and keeping a distance—without this pathos of distance there could not grow that other more mysterious pathos, that longing for ever greater distances within the soul itself, the evolving of ever higher, rarer, more spacious, more widely arched, more comprehensive states—in short: the heightening of the type "man," the continued "self-mastery of man," to take a moral formula in a supra-moral sense. To be sure, we must not yield to humanitarian self-deception about the history of the origins of an aristo-cratic society (in other words, the presuppositions for the heightening of the type "man"): the truth is hard.[16]

The ultimate reason is indicated toward the end by the formula that life is will to power—i.e., will to superiority. This theme will be taken up later, but in a way this is the crucial problem for Nietzsche. If you re-member what we discussed last time, a society of men, free and equal, made possible by the conquest of nature—there is no longer any need for any human being to do the low chores, and others leading a life of leisure; it is now possible for all men to do this. One can say that this is really a demand for justice if there is plenty: Why should not everything be made accessible to everyone, provided he has the desire and the ability? However, Nietzsche's vision is the opposite of Marx's vision.

In the next speech he turns to the philosopher. He proceeds in the following way. First he speaks of the famous pagans, then there follow three songs—"The Night Song," "The Dancing Song," and "The Tomb Song"—and thereafter "Of Self-Overcoming." Now let us first see what Nietzsche's criticism of traditional philosophy is.

> Reader: You have served the people and the superstition of the people, all you famous wise men—and *not* truth. And that is precisely why you were accorded respect. And that is also why your lack of faith was tolerated: it was a joke and a circuitous route to the people. Thus the master lets his slaves have their way and is even amused by their pranks.
>
> But the free spirit, the enemy of fetters, the non-adorer who dwells in the woods, is as hateful to the people as a wolf to dogs. To hound him out of his lair—that is what the people have ever called "a sense of decency"; and against him the people still set their fiercest dogs.
>
> "Truth is there: after all, the people are there! Let those who seek beware!"—these words have echoed through the ages. You wanted to prove your people right in their reverence: that is what you called "will to truth," you famous wise men.[17]

LS: I believe you are all familiar with this opinion. It is now the content of every ordinary textbook in the history of political or social thought, only not so forcefully expressed. What do you hear? That all those famous doctrines are merely the selection or articulation of the opinions prevailing at the time. The traditional philosopher was part of his time and part of his people. The traditional philosopher finds reasons for what the society accepts. You may note here a literary reference which is revealing. He distinguishes the famous sages from the free minds and he compares them to wolves as distinguished from dogs . . .[18]

> Reader: And verily, you famous wise men, you servants of the people, you yourselves have grown with the spirit and virtue of the people—and the people through you. In your honor I say this.

LS: In other words, he means that when he says that values are mere ideologies, they fulfill a salutary function.

> Reader: But even in your virtues you remain for me part of the people, the dumb-eyed people—the people, who do not know what spirit is.

Spirit is the life that itself cuts into life: with its own agony it increases its own knowledge. Did you know that?

And the happiness of the spirit is this: to be anointed and through tears to be consecrated as a sacrificial animal. Did you know that?

And the blindness of the blind and their seeking and groping shall yet bear witness to the power of the sun, into which they have looked. Did you know that?

And the lover of knowledge shall learn to *build* with mountains. It means little that the spirit moves mountains. Did you know that?[19]

LS: Now the people is characterized by ignorance of the spirit: spirit here means also mind; one could say the people are ignorant of intellectuality. Now spirit or mind is like turning against life. The famous sages were life which did not turn against life. Now what does that mean, life turning against life, especially when you think of the praise of those wolves, the sophists? Life turning against life means primarily a passionate critique of life in the name of a higher form of life. Spirit or mind is not rationality, according to Nietzsche, but inspiration: something in man, out of man, coming over man. There is an aphorism in *Beyond Good and Evil* to which I want to refer, number 211, which is a commentary on Nietzsche's criticism of traditional philosophy:

I insist that we finally stop mistaking the workers in philosophy, and the scientific people generally, for philosophers, that this is the very point at which we must sternly give "to each his own," which means not too much to the former and not far too little to the latter.

It may be necessary to the education of a genuine philosopher that he should have stood once on all the steps on which his servants, the scientific workers in philosophy, have now stopped—*must* have stopped; he himself must perhaps have been a critic and a skeptic and a dogmatist and a historian, not to mention poet, collector, traveller, riddle-reader, moralist, seer, "free thinker," and almost everything else, in order to run the entire circumference of human values and value-feelings, in order to be *able* to gaze with many eyes and many consciences from the heights to any distance, from the depths to any height, from the corners to any open spaces. But all these are only prerequisites for his task. The task itself is something else: it demands that he *create values*.

Those philosophical workers in the noble tradition of Kant and Hegel have to determine and formalize some large reservoir of value-judgments, that is *former value-creations*, which have come to the fore and for a certain length of time are called "truth." They may lie in the realm of logic or of politics (morality) or of esthetics. The role of the researchers is to make everything that has heretofore happened and been evaluated into a visible, thinkable, comprehensible and handy pattern; to abbreviate everything that is long, to abbreviate time itself; to *overpower* the entire past. It is an enormous and wonderful task in whose service any subtle pride and any tough will may surely take satisfaction. *But the real philosophers are commanders and legislators.* They say, "It *shall* be thus!" They determine the "whither" and the "to what end" of mankind—having the preliminary work of all the workers in philosophy, the overpowerers of the past, at their disposal. But they grope with creative hands toward the future— everything that is and was becomes their means, their instrument, their hammer. Their "knowing" is *creating.* Their creating is legislative. Their will to truth is—*will to power.* Are there such philosophers today? Were there ever such philosophers? *Must* there not be such philosophers? . . .[20]

The answers are obvious. There are a few more passages on page 216.

Reader: You know only the spark of the spirit, but you do not see the anvil it is, nor the cruelty of its hammer.

Verily, you do not know the pride of the spirit! But even less would you endure the modesty of the spirit, if ever it would speak.[21]

LS: In other words, the same spirit which is so proud and places such a high demand on itself is also much more modest than the spirit of traditional wisdom. Can you understand that? Well, all these famous sages said: "I teach the truth." Surely this is not modest, and Nietzsche says they did not know that they taught only the "closed truth." In the sequel, he develops the theme that the traditional philosophers are lukewarm, neither hot nor cold, a theme to which I believe Dante refers in the beginning of the *Divine Comedy* when he describes limbo.[22] He speaks of the lukewarm on the one hand, and the philosophers on the other: they were surely not extremists. Then Nietzsche turns to the three songs which are of course impossible to interpret. The function of the three songs is to indicate what distinguishes philosophy in Nietzsche's sense from all traditional thought, and that can be done only by presenting his human experience and, as it were, asking us if the traditional philosophers, even the greatest, had such experience. The answer, I think, can very well be negative.

"The Night Song": there is night, but Zarathustra is light; hot and cold; only giving, not taking; in complete solitude. He wishes he could be one who could take from others: "a craving for love is within me," not love. A craving for being loved or for loving? This is not quite clear.

Now if the creative self is the source of all meaning, it exists in a world of meaninglessness. I think this is the necessary consequence: it exists in a world of complete darkness.

In "The Dancing Song," the central song, Zarathustra is night if seen in the perspective of ordinary men, but his companion is Cupid, who sleeps during the day. Zarathustra sings a song in praise of life unfathomable. Life itself denies that she is unfathomable: "But I am merely changeable and wild and a woman in every way, and not virtuous." But Zarathustra does not believe her. He loves only life and life alone. He loves wisdom only because it reminds him of life; wisdom is similar to life. Is wisdom not perhaps identical with life? In an earlier writing, "The Advantage and Disadvantage of History," he had spoken of an opposition between life and wisdom, and he understood by wisdom objectivity or objective science. It was the opposition between creativity/life and objectivity/wisdom. Zarathustra's wisdom, as distinguished from that of the scientist, is not the opposite of life. I also refer you to the passage in the preface of *Beyond Good and Evil* where truth is referred to as a woman.[23] Truth is not God.

"The Tomb Song" takes up again the theme of "The Night Song." Zarathustra was not always solitary. There was a time when he loved human beings and was loved by them.

Reader: And once I wanted to dance as I had never danced before: over all the heavens I wanted to dance. Then you persuaded my dearest singer. And he struck up a horrible dismal tune; alas, he tooted in my ears like a gloomy horn. Murderous singer, tool of malice, most innocent yourself! I stood ready for the best dance, when you murdered my ecstasy with your sounds.

LS: There is a reference to Wagner. This is also part of this presentation which distinguishes Zarathustra-Nietzsche from all previous philosophers.

Reader: Only in the dance do I know how to tell the parable of the highest things: and now my highest parable remained unspoken in my limbs.[24]

LS: In a way, this remains so: the truth cannot be open, it is elusive. Life is not identical with wisdom, though they are somehow akin but in such a way that the full meaning of life can never be given. One cannot call the truth given, because from Nietzsche's point of view this would be merely the text without interpretation and in itself meaningless. The interpretation depends on the creative act of the interpreter. But the interpretation that is given exists as much as the mere text, and therefore one cannot say the interpretation is not true, only the text is true. Positivism says only the text is true, everything else is arbitrary or subjective. From Nietzsche's point of view, to know means not merely to be cognizant of a thing but to interpret, to create, to be a poet. Let us read an interpretation of this on page 682.

Reader: And as for our future, one will hardly find us again on the paths of those Egyptian youths who endanger temples by night, embrace statues, and want by all means to unveil, uncover, and put into a bright light whatever is kept concealed for good reasons. No, this bad taste, this will to truth, to "truth at any price," this youthful madness in the love of truth, have lost their charm for us: for that we are too experienced, too serious, too gay, too burned, too *deep*. We no longer believe that truth remains truth when the veils are withdrawn—we have lived enough not to believe this. Today we consider it a matter of decency not to wish to see everything naked, or to be present at everything, or to understand and "know" everything. *Tout comprendre—c'est tout mépriser.*

"Is it true that God is present *everywhere?*" a little girl asked her mother; "I think that's indecent"—a hint for philosophers! One should have more respect for the bashfulness with which nature has hidden behind riddles and iridescent uncertainties. Perhaps truth is a woman who has reasons for not letting us see her reasons? Perhaps her name is—to speak Greek—*Baubo?*

Oh, those Greeks! They knew how to live. What is required for that is to stop courageously at the surface, the fold, the skin, to adore appearance, to believe in forms, tones, words, in the whole Olympus of appearance. Those Greeks were superficial—*out of profundity*. And is not this precisely what we are again coming back to, we daredevils of the spirit who have climbed the highest and most dangerous peak of present thought and looked around from up there—we who have looked *down* from there? Are we not, precisely in this respect, Greeks? Adorers of forms, of tones, of words? And therefore *artists?*[25]

LS: Also the passage we read last time, "How the True World Finally Became a Fable"—the whole problem of subjectivity and objectivity. Traditional notions of understanding, which lead to present-day science, make a distinction between the subjective and the objective, according to which only the objective is truly true. In the approach of modern science, which Nietzsche here follows, they lead to a meaningless truth. As he put it: to understand everything is to decide to debunk it. What is the way out? Nietzsche says in the first place that we must realize that this so-called objective truth is not objective; it rests on basic hypotheses which are as subjective as any creation of a poet may be. Therefore, the question is not objectivity versus subjectivity, but narrow and poor subjectivity against broad and rich subjectivity. From that point of view, the deepest poem is infinitely truer than any science can be. This does not solve the problem, but it is a very important step toward a solution. Today it is a very popular view that novels are more revealing of man than scientific studies. Art is more perceptive. There cannot be, even ideally, that kind of objectivity, of universal agreement, as is possible within science.

The next speech[26] is of particular importance, from our point of view perhaps the most important. Let us read the beginning.

Reader: "Will to truth," you who are wisest call that which impels you and fills you with lust?

LS: He is again speaking of the wise men, but not quite of the same people as in the first speech. He no longer speaks of the famous wise men. Nietzsche is here not concerned with historical references, and it may well be that in many cases the same thinkers were both.

Reader: A will to the thinkability of all beings: this *I* call your will. You want to *make* all being thinkable, for you doubt with well-founded suspicion that it is already thinkable.[27]

LS: The will to truth is said to have animated all philosophers. Nietzsche says that this is a misunderstanding. They did not will the truth, they willed thinkability. What fact accessible to our inspection is meant here? One can say philosophy is an attempt to understand and know everything. This is a very provisional statement, but not misleading because it reminds us of the comprehensiveness which is essential to philosophy. The will to know everything implies that everything is in principle knowable. How do we know that everything is knowable? Maybe this is only a dogmatic assumption made by the Greeks and inherited by us. This is what Nietzsche is driving at. The alternative position is that being is as such elusive. This is Nietzsche's objection to traditional philosophy, and this is lined up with the problem of creativity, the superman, and all those other things which he has in mind. So the will to know the truth is the will to thinkability, in other words, the will to make all things thinkable. The philosophers of the past have tried unconsciously to imprint their will, their character, on reality and then claim that this is the truth. This is developed in prose in the first chapter of *Beyond Good and Evil*. The intelligibility of the whole is the basic premise of philosophy and is an unsupported dogmatic premise. But there was of course also another tradition in a way opposed to the Greek tradition, the biblical tradition, in which the highest being, the source of all being, is not intelligible or thinkable but radically mysterious. From Nietzsche's point of view, the Bible does not solve the problem at all because the biblical God is perfectly intelligible to himself and therefore not in himself nonintelligible. Here we have to remind ourselves of that extreme statement which we read: "if there were a God, how could I help wishing not to be God."[28] In other words, if the highest principle is intelligible to himself, men cannot help trying to imitate God, to become like God. Nietzsche asserts that being as being is elusive: "We do not possess the truth"—"we," that is, Nietzsche and later philosophers as distinguished from the whole tradition of philosophy. The older thinkers said that we possess the truth in principle, because they regarded the truth as knowable. This contention of Nietzsche that being is elusive, in opposition to the classical view that being is distinguishable, is today much more credible. In this as well as in many other respects, Nietzsche spells out what modern men, insofar as they are modern men, think. This view that being is elusive is today so evident because it is implied in the progressive character of modern science. Everything is subject to revision. Science is as such infinitely progressive; in the nature of the case there can never be an end to science. But if the progress is infinite, the mystery is equally infinite because there is something which is not yet known; therefore, to say that being is elusive is only to spell out what modern science has not spelled out but what it necessarily implies.

But Nietzsche means something else, too: all meaning, all articulation, all values originate in men, in the self, the self being the elusive depth of man. There could not be creativity if there were not such an elusive depth. Creativity implies elusiveness. If you can predict what a man will create, you cannot really speak of creation. Take the extreme case: if you can predict what a man is going to say, while it may be very charming, it is surely the opposite of creativity. So creativity means elusiveness, but since the self is the origin of all meaning, it implies that the ground of everything is elusive.

If philosophy in the traditional sense was to make being thinkable, what is the motive for that? What is the reasonable explanation for that? Let us say a desire for certainty. Nietzsche's answer as he develops it here is that it is in the nature of life to do that, but not as life is commonly understood (so that it would mean the means for survival, for self-preservation or comfortable self-preservation), but life as the will to power. And this is the theme of Nietzsche's will to power.

Student: What about the difference between the knower and the noble?

LS: Man appears to the knower as the beast which has red cheeks. The red cheeks refer to the country squires as distinguished from those pale companions of Socrates. "Thus speaks he who has knowledge: shame, shame, shame." Looking around in social science today, is this not true? Isn't this what Comte, Marx, and all those other schools which enter into the big stream called social science say? All those things which appear so grand and impressive have a low origin, if you analyze them. Nietzsche says that there is a certain stratum which is common to Nietzsche and to those evolutionary societies. But the noble man is not simply identical with the knower. What Nietzsche says is that he will never find the mere knower. There is always something within man, and the meaning and form it takes depends on whether the knower is noble or base. If he is base, he uses these things for the humiliation of men, for the degradation of men; if he is noble, he will use it for the elevation of men. This means, as it were, that you don't look so much at the low things that went into it but at the acts of overcoming, by virtue of which men change from quasi-brutes into men. Commonsensically speaking, Nietzsche can of course not deny that there is a certain sphere where all human beings, if they are in their senses, will agree. Science, you might say, is the normal effort of man to enlarge this dimension where all men as men, provided they have the necessary conditions, will agree. But the whole body of knowledge of science, especially of social science, is of course only to a very small part merely given. After all, we constantly use concepts, and these various concepts demand one another and belong together in a certain overall interpretation of man. This overall interpretation of man is expressed in the conceptual framework. It is practically impossible (though not theoretically) to make a distinction, because every scientific finding, even in the social sciences, is already expressed in that framework. So there exists something which truly unbiased men, whatever their will may be, would agree to. That, I think, Nietzsche cannot consistently deny, but what he does insist on is that this is very trivial. It becomes meaningful only by virtue of the interpretation, and what is presented to us as objective science is a specific interpretation of the given which is as little morally neutral as interpretations given by Nietzsche. I believe that an analysis of the more ambitious social scientists would show this. Of course, when a man says at the beginning of his book: "These are my value judgments and everything that follows from now on is straight science," this is nonsense. The so-called value judgments affect his very findings since they are inherent in the very concepts which he arrives at. I think what is important is an awareness of the fact, or at least of the possibility, that this may be true of our social science and therefore it might not have the dignity and the compelling character of the truth.

Let us assume that Nietzsche has a point in saying that the vision of the last man is in fact guiding what is called now social science. I think one could give some proof of that. If one were to analyze the work of Lasswell, one would see that the problem which is in the foreground is democracy—to defend, support, and elaborate democracy—but on the other hand, the crucial importance of the scientist, including the social scientist. This immediately confronts you with the problem of technocracy versus democracy. If science takes on a crucial social significance, who is the decision maker in the end? Not the sovereign people but the scientist. But this by no means goes to the root of the thing, because they think they have discovered that, contrary to an older notion, the solution to the social problem—security, wealth, etc.—is not sufficient for making people happy. There is the problem of the individual which remains. Some people who are very well off still commit suicide. These personal problems affect also political men: statesmen, Supreme Court judges (there is a tremendous literature on this subject). Therefore we need another science apart from economics to make men balanced, normal. This science is understood by Lasswell to be psychoanalysis. So in a way the crowning science is not economics, surely not in Lasswell, but psychiatry.[29]

But what does that mean, if you read the passage here on the last man?

Everyone is a cog in the machine; there are no disturbing aspirations any-more. One of my former students, who is now a professor, had this expe-rience: he had a student who was greatly disturbed by the fact that he was no longer able to do what he wanted to do as a political scientist. Then he underwent psychoanalytic treatment. As a consequence, he became perfectly composed, all these disturbances stopped, and he was no longer worried about his essential defects. This professor asked me: "Is he really better off now?" Well, he is no longer worried, but he has also forgotten the aspiration which gave him a value which he now completely lacks. I also remember a statement by a pharmaceutical company. There was a picture of Cesare Borgia in all his devilish splendor. Now, they say: If Ce-sare Borgia had taken this pill, he would no longer be Cesare Borgia and would be all right. But Machiavelli says that some things were taken care of by Cesare Borgia because he did not take these pills. In other words, there is something to these last men. If Lasswell were strictly logical, he would have to demand strict psychoanalytocracy. The men who make the ultimate decisions are psychoanalysts. After all, what does Congress know about psychology? Someone who studies Lasswell more carefully than I am able to do might offer this suggestion: every citizen becomes a psychoanalyst. This may sound like a joke, but I think Lasswell is admi-rable here, in spite of all the things he does, because he does not consider reputation as other people do and he lets many cats out of the bag which others keep in the bag.

Of course one can find visions or ideas which are basically all right in all social science. As I have said many times in classes, there are of course old-fashioned political scientists—and this cannot be criticized from any point of view—people who assume a public role and are perfectly sensi-ble, but this is not especially characteristic of present-day social science. After all, political science is the oldest discipline. Furthermore, there are people who do very limited, sensible jobs which are necessary and use-ful, but they have their center outside themselves. Citizens impose on them for the common good. No one would object to that. What I had in mind is the overall notion of social scientists which is chiefly presented by people who once were the Young Turks thirty years ago, who are now already dignitaries, and their notion about the meaning of social science, which is the only question with which I am concerned.

Student: . . .

LS: Your question implies in a way the answer. Nietzsche is not an idealist, because the self for him is the body. That is clearly "anti-idealistic."

For Nietzsche, reinterpretation is in terms of good and bad, of values, and this is mere talk if it is not followed by action. Nietzsche surely wanted to change the world. This word of Marx is directed against Hegel with perfect justice, because Hegel did not want to change the world in any sense. He wanted to change it less than Aristotle. Aristotle realized that most societies were imperfect and, if possible, they should be improved, whereas Hegel says, in principle at least, that no more meaningful change is possible. Marx's change is based on a previous interpretation known by the name of dialectical materialism. That Marx's interpretation permitted the formation of a political party, whereas Nietzsche's interpretation made impossible the formation of a political party and made impossible any political activity on the part of Nietzsche is surely true. One could perhaps say this. The victory of communism and the defeat of fascism reflect this difference: Marx showed a way to political action; Nietzsche could not show it. Nietzsche had made impossible, especially in Germany, the acceptance of liberal democracy and socialism.

You must not forget that the continental conservatives, i.e., Bismarck, took the view that liberal democracy is only the first step, and if it is permitted to work itself out, it will lead to socialism and communism. Of course Bismarck says it won't work, it will lead to chaos. This Bismarckian notion however was also Nietzsche's notion. Bismarck saw a kind of alliance between throne and altar, but he was not always consistent. You may remember his famous fight, *Kulturkampf*, with Germany's Catholic clergy. What characterized Nietzsche was that he was sure that conservatism will not do. There may be resistance for some time, but by this very fact we increase the power of the assailants. What would be possible would be a third thing: neither conservatism nor progressivism but, to speak in political language, a radicalism of the right. Nietzsche of course used language which could later on be used by the radicalism of the right, but this is neither the depth nor the importance of Nietzsche. Nietzsche's appeal was to the individual, and his concern was with the creativity of the individual, and this is absolutely incompatible with political action. However, the fact that it had political meaning is inescapable.

Therefore, one can say that by making people dissatisfied with the left in any sense of the word and with the existing right in any sense of the word, which conclusion could the young confused people possibly draw? To that extent, Nietzsche's responsibility is undeniable, contrary to the absolutely untrue remarks of Kaufmann. But it is a subtle question. The fact that Nietzsche would have been the first to run away does not solve the issue. In my opinion, the relation of Nietzsche to National Socialism is like that of Rousseau to the Jacobins. Rousseau was not a Jacobin and would have loathed it, of course, but Rousseau made possible the Jacobins' perversion of his doctrine. Nietzsche made possible that perversion of his doctrine which is National Socialism. You cannot speak of the blond beast in terms of praise, you cannot say the extermination of millions of men is necessary, but it would be extremely foolish to say that since this is so, Nietzsche is a fascist. By the same token, one would have to reject Rousseau for the terror of the French Revolution.[30]

Later on I will refer to a writing in Nietzsche in which he presents this notion which would be wholly nonpolitical: the last man will come. That's inevitable. On the other hand, there will be isolated individuals, and these can be supermen in a sense—in other words, no political solution at all. But this is not sufficient. I think he was thinking in terms of a political rejuvenation of the West also. Nothing is more meaningless than these apologetics which Kaufmann here uses and which are unworthy especially of Nietzsche. If I respect the man, I respect him for what he was and not as a figment of my imagination.

Student: . . .[31]

LS: We speak of a man in terms of the human and the superhuman. One can also speak in the same sense of the finite and the infinite. Now if man is to become superman, he is in this sense to become infinite: to the extent to which he takes on the attributes of the superhuman. This infinity of a being, which is surely not omnipotent, creates a radical change according to which pride becomes infinite pride. Since this being is a suffering being from Nietzsche's point of view, this goes together with infinite suffering. For instance, the suffering from the imperfection of man must take on this infinity, if viewed in the light of what men could be, which is so much higher than the common idea of man understanding human perfection. This has something to do with the old story of infinite malleability, which means, in other words, there is no nature of man sufficiently defined to give men an indication of a specifically human perfection. But this Nietzsche shares with all these specifically modern thinkers. What is characteristic in Nietzsche is that he draws the conclusion that man must become superhuman, and therefore the extremism, the infinity, and the intensity of these demands which you observe in every page of the *Zarathustra*.

Nietzsche may not have sufficiently seen the tremendous developments of technology which make possible the extinction of the human race. But still there is the increase in leisure without people being trained to make use of it. There must be, in the formula of the Romans, bread and circuses, in other words, no aspiration. I believe if one would analyze the situation, especially in this country—all this juvenile delinquency—one would see a certain disappointment, an absence of aspiration as at least one factor. Nietzsche's last man is perfectly nice, he is not a murderer. But if there were murder, Nietzsche would say this would affect the police problem but not the overall human problem. The best men of that society would be mere philistines, so that one could perhaps turn it around, as Nietzsche sometimes does, and say that criminals in that society may precisely be those who are choked by these acts.

7 Will to Power and Self-Overcoming

Zarathustra, Part 2, 15–20

Leo Strauss: The second part, as distinguished from the first part, almost explicitly deals with philosophy, whereas the first part deals chiefly with the Bible or Christianity except for the speech "On the Chairs of Virtue," which deals with philosophy.

The thesis of the first part, "God is dead," is now enlarged to the notion of the unmoved or imperishable as a conjecture inimical to life, that is to say, to time and becoming, to creativity. Nietzsche then turns to various forms of human life which are inimical to creativity, forms which are not as such philosophical. I refer especially to the speech "On the Tarantulas," i.e., to the speech on equality. Philosophy becomes again the theme of the second part, after it was the theme near the beginning in the speech "On the Blessed Islands" and in the speeches "Of Famous Sages" and "On Self-Overcoming." The famous sages proved to be mere servants of the people and of the people's beliefs: to put it in the language of our time, rationalizers or ideologists. But this is not sufficient; therefore the subject of philosophy is taken up again in the speech "On Self-Overcoming." Between those two speeches, "Of Famous Sages" and "On Self-Overcoming," we find three songs: "The Night Song," "The Dance Song," and "The Tomb Song." These songs express, without formulating it, what has been lacking in previous philosophies: the fullness and depth of life. The philosopher of the future, we may say, will be a synthesis of the philosopher and the poet, especially the lyric poet. Here we may remind ourselves of a saying by Cicero, transmitted by Seneca: "Cicero denies that he would have time to read lyrical poetry even if his lifetime were doubled."[1]

The speech "On Self-Overcoming" is the most explicitly philosophic speech hitherto. Nietzsche contends that the will to truth is a form of the will to power, and that the will to power is the fundamental character of all living beings, nay, of all beings. Here the difficulty arises: Is the doctrine of the will to power itself an expression of the self-consciousness of the will to power? In other words, has the will to power become conscious of itself in Nietzsche, or is the doctrine a direct expression of Nietzsche's own will to power? Is the doctrine of the will to power meant to be objectively true or is it a creation? At any rate, this much is clear: Nietzsche's philosophy differs from all earlier philosophies not only in its content or substance, but in its mode as well. It is not simply a doctrine which is meant to be objectively true.

Now before he continues his explication of the will to power, Nietzsche turns to various parts or fragments of the philosopher in the traditional sense, especially the contemporary forms of this phenomenon. The first subject was the sublime ones, the penitents of the spirit, those who have ceased to regard the truth as beautiful or edifying but who seek the truth for the sake of the truth without any other concern, and therefore in particular they seek the ugly truth: men who are true to themselves. In the speech "On the Country of Education," he deals with the involuntary destroyers of all culture and all faith because they are the detached onlookers of all cultures and faiths. Mr. Benjamin made a very good suggestion:"education," of course, is a proper translation of the German word *Bildung*, if you understand education in the sense in which it is used in the title of Henry Adams's education, where it does not mean of course only the education he received at the universities but the whole forming and formation of a man.[2] In the following speeches, this discussion is continued of the fragments or parts of the philosopher in the primary sense, in the pre-Nietzschean sense, of the term.

We turn then to the speech "On Immaculate Knowledge."[3] Nietzsche criticizes here the idea of contemplative knowledge. He opposes that to creative knowledge, and he expresses this relation by using the figure of the moon and the sun. The moon, which does not give fertility and light to anything, contemplative knowledge; the sun, the origin of light and life, creative knowledge. Let us turn to page 234, paragraph 5.

Reader: "This would be the highest to my mind"—thus says your lying spirit to itself—"to look at life without desire and not, like a dog, with my tongue hanging out. To be happy in looking, with a will that has died and without the grasping and greed of selfishness, the whole body cold and ashen, but with drunken moon eyes. This I should like best"—thus the seduced seduces himself—"to love the earth as the moon loves her, and to touch her beauty only with my eyes. And this is what the immaculate perception of all things shall mean to me: that I want nothing from them, except to be allowed to lie prostrate before them like a mirror with a hundred eyes."[4]

LS: This is not meant to apply to the originators of the contemplative ideal, to the Greek philosophers, and this appears from the following consideration: these contemplators are contemplators of life, of change in various manifestations. The original contemplators were contemplators of what is always and unchanging. But we know now that there is nothing unchanging or eternal; the seeming sempiternal or eternal is only the decayed temporal. You are all familiar with this view; for example, Sabine is a popular exposition of this view.[5] If you take the doctrine of natural law, you will find that this is a Stoic doctrine, which emerged at a certain time after the breakdown of the Greek *polis*. So this doctrine, which presents itself as the doctrine of the eternal or sempiternal, is in fact only a reflection of the temporal. This is the point of view which emerged and became notorious in the second half of the nineteenth century. The sempiternal or eternal is only the decayed temporal; hence the object of contemplation can only be life, creative life, but only as an object. Here you have the inferiority: the noncreators look uncreatively at creative life. Now let us turn to page 235.

Reader: Verily, it is not as creators, procreators, and those who have joy in becoming that you love the earth. Where is innocence? Where there is a will to procreate. And he who wants to create beyond himself has the purest will.

Where is beauty? Where I must will with all my will; where I want to love and perish that an image may not remain a mere image. Loving and perishing: that has rhymed for eternities. The will to love, that is to be willing also to die. Thus I speak to you cowards!

But now your emasculated leers wish to be called "contemplation." And that which permits itself to be touched by cowardly glances you would baptize "beautiful." How you soil noble names! . . .

Look there: how she approaches impatiently over the sea. Do you not feel the thirst and the hot breath of her love? She would suck at the sea and drink its depth into her heights; and the sea's desire rises toward her with a thousand breasts. It wants to be kissed and sucked by the thirst of the sun; it wants to become air and height and a footpath of light, and itself light.

Verily, like the sun I love life and all deep seas. And this is what perceptive knowledge means to me: all that is deep shall rise up to my heights.[6]

LS: Nietzsche contrasts here his notion of knowledge with the older notion. In other words, to understand this passage we must remember the distinction between the knower and the noble which Nietzsche made before. There, the knower as knower seemed to be neutral as contrasted to the noble or the base. Knowledge is as such incomplete and must be interpreted; this interpretation is fundamentally twofold: the noble and the base interpretation. The base interpretation would be a materialistic interpretation.

Now this distinction is dropped. This sunlight love of life and this concern with the deep or the low is an integral part of knowledge. The distinction between knowledge and noble or base is meaningful superficially, it is meaningful regarding the derivative. But the fundamental phenomenon of life is the self, the creative self. For example, I can observe a society and gather certain data which everyone can see, but this has obviously nothing to do with the core of the thought or the work of this man. The core is the creative self. The creative self, however, cannot be experienced, hence known, by man insofar as he is a detached observer or a detached self-observer. Knowledge in the highest sense accompanies the creative act or presupposes it in another way, but it cannot be divorced from it.

The creative thinker then is opposed to the contemplative thinker. This has a prehistory of which I mention only one important part. We have always thought of the difference between Nietzsche and Marx; we must think of it here too. Marx said against Hegel that in the Hegelian scheme the philosopher comes *post festum*, after the festival, after everything has been done, after the creative activity of society. Marx also said in the same spirit: Hitherto philosophers have interpreted the world, but what counts is that the world be changed.[7] This has something to do with Nietzsche's problem. The mere interpreters are like Nietzsche's contemplators: the moon, as distinguished from the sun. Marx opposed this especially to Hegel's view. According to this view, self-consciousness is not as such created, it comes at the end. According to Nietzsche, philosophy is itself created, and therefore it cannot be simply self-consciousness. It cannot be self-consciousness strictly speaking for the other reason: that the creative self is elusive and can never be fully comprehended. Still one may say that, compared with earlier thought, Nietzsche's philosophy is meant to be self-consciousness in the decisive respect: all earlier philosophers did not know that the will to power was at the root to their will to truth. Nietzsche knows it.

Now we come to the following speech, which is particularly unpleasant to read for people like myself: "Of Scholars." The scholar is also a fragment of the philosopher. Here it becomes clear that Zarathustra is Nietzsche. Nietzsche was a scholar; he wrote a very impressive chapter on "We Scholars," translated badly in English under the title "We Intellectuals." Everyone knows that intellectuals and scholars are two different things.

Now Zarathustra-Nietzsche was once a scholar but he is no longer a scholar. He rejected scholarship. This speech is followed by the speech "On Poets." Zarathustra is still a poet. Now let us see what he has to say about these poor people.

> Reader: I am too hot and burned by my own thoughts; often it nearly takes my breath away. Then I must go out into the open and away from all dusty rooms. But they sit cool in the cool shade: in everything they want to be mere spectators, and they beware of sitting where the sun burns on the steps. Like those who stand in the street and gape at the people who pass by, they too wait and gape at thoughts that others have thought.
>
> If you seize them with your hands they raise a cloud of dust like flour bags, involuntarily; but who could guess that their dust comes from grain and from the yellow delight of summer fields?[8]

LS: What is scholarship? According to Nietzsche, it is rethinking the thoughts of others. One could easily show that, for example, the political historian, who deals with deeds rather than thoughts, must also be concerned with thought. For example, how could you arrive at a history of the Civil War when the core of it would be the understanding of Lincoln's or Jefferson Davis's thought? So every scholar rethinks the thoughts of others. These others may be societies or individuals. The thoughts of scholars are derivative from the thoughts of the original thinkers. On the way from the original thinkers to the scholars, the thought loses its seminal power, its fertility. From fresh grain it becomes flour. It would be unfair of such a superior mind like Nietzsche's to speak about such poor men like ourselves, who could become mere scholars. But why this harshness? He has to counteract the claim of the scholars. The scholars tend to be very boastful. They know and they can prove what they assert. If they assert that Kant wrote this particular piece in the year 1776, they can prove it, whereas Kant himself could not prove his whole philosophy. They know that X taught the doctrine Y, but X himself need not possess objective knowledge of Y. The trouble is only that the knowledge which they possess is inferior in significance to the questionable knowledge of the one who thinks.

Nietzsche goes on to develop how certain weaknesses in the character of scholars have something to do with that defect.

> Reader: They watch each other closely and mistrustfully. Inventive in petty cleverness, they wait for those whose knowledge walks on lame feet: like spiders they wait. I have always seen them carefully preparing poison; and they always put on gloves of glass to do it. They also know how to play with loaded dice; and I have seen them play so eagerly that they sweated.[9]

LS: I would like to tell you a story about a professor at an entirely different university, who is a first-rate scholar. They had a guest from another country speaking on a Greek subject. This man, who was a Greek scholar . . . But of course there are other specimens, too. The essential connection is this: this pettiness is the reverse side of this pretense. The knowledge involved is of lower rank; it is a pretense that fortifies the whole scheme.

> Reader: We are alien to each other, and their virtues are even more distressful to me than their falseness and their loaded dice. And when I lived with them, I lived above them. That is why they developed a grudge against me. They did not want to hear how someone was living over their heads; and so they put wood and earth and filth between me and their heads. Thus they muffled the sound of my steps: and so far I have been heard least well by the most scholarly. Between themselves and me they laid all human faults and weaknesses: "false ceilings" they call them in their houses. And yet I live *over* their heads with my thoughts; and even if I wanted to walk upon my own mistakes, I would still be over their heads.
>
> For men are *not* equal: thus speaks justice. And what I want, they would have no right to want![10]

LS: You see the obvious autobiographical elements in this speech. The conclusion is of a probable nature and will come back again. The inequality of men—we are tempted to say the natural inequality of men; whether we can succumb to this temptation without falsifying Nietzsche's thought remains to be seen.

Now we turn to the last speech of this section, "On Poets." You see that this is a dialogue. We have read a dialogue before, in "The Old and Young Females." The old and young females recur here in this speech. They seem to be the favorite topic of the poets, so that there is a connection between these two dialogues. But the first dialogue was compulsory in a twofold way: Zarathustra was compelled to a dialogue by an old woman. The reason for this was Zarathustra's lack of experience with women. Here Zarathustra is fully experienced; whereas he has ceased to be a scholar, he is still a poet, as he explicitly says. Yet even the present dialogue is compulsory to some extent. The poet is brought up not by Zarathustra but by the disciple. Let us read the beginning.

Reader: "Since I have come to know the body better," Zarathustra said to one of his disciples, "the spirit is to me only quasi-spirit; and all that is 'permanent' is also a mere parable."

LS: These words stem from the end of Goethe's *Faust*.[11] Nietzsche has Goethe in mind, perhaps more than anyone else. This will sound to those of you who admire Goethe sometimes very outrageous.

Reader: "I have heard you say that once before," the disciple replied; "and at that time you added, 'But the poets lie too much.' Why did you say that the poets lie too much?"

"Why?" said Zarathustra. "You ask, why? I am not one of those whom one may ask about their why. Is my experience but of yesterday? It was long ago that I experienced the reasons for my opinions. Would I not have to be a barrel of memory if I wanted to carry my reasons around with me? It is already too much for me to remember my own opinions; and many a bird flies away. And now and then I also find a stray in my dovecot that is strange to me and trembles when I place my hand on it."[12]

LS: For an interpretation, I would steer you to a passage from the *Twilight of the Idols*, page 475, dealing with Socrates.[13] You see, Nietzsche seems to deal in a very snobbish way, and therefore in a very offensive way, with reason.

Reader: With Socrates, Greek taste changes in favor of dialectics. What really happened there? Above all, a *noble* taste is thus vanquished; with dialectics the plebs come to the top. Before Socrates, dialectic manners were repudiated in good society: they were considered bad manners, they were compromising. The young were warned against them. Furthermore, all such presentations of one's reasons were distrusted. Honest things, like honest men, do not carry their reasons in their hands like that. It is indecent to show all five fingers. What must first be proved is worth little. Wherever authority still forms part of good bearing, where one does not give reasons but commands, the dialectician is a kind of buffoon: one laughs at him, one does not take him seriously. Socrates was the buffoon *who got himself taken seriously*: what really happened there?[14]

LS: This illustrates, though it does not explain, our passage. Nietzsche rejects here the demand for sufficient reason, and he says that this demand is based on the fact that ultimately there is no sufficient reason. Provisionally I can give sufficient reason, but if we went on and on we would get to a point which can no longer be justified. Here this is called authority. Ultimately, we come back to something which is called, in the formula of the modern poet: Thus I will, thus I command. Will should stand in the place of reason. But Nietzsche is not a worshiper of authority in the simple sense of the term. How then can he accept this authoritarianism? I read to you a passage from *Beyond Good and Evil*, aphorism 231: "Learning transforms us." This sentence is also relevant for the present speech for the following reason: Nietzsche blames the poets for not learning sufficiently.

It does what all nutrition does, namely, much more than merely "maintain," as the physiologists know. But fundamentally, "way down below" in us, there is something unteachable, a bedrock of intellectual destiny, of predestined decision, of answers to predestined, selected questions. In the presence of every cardinal problem there speaks an unchangeable "This is myself." On the problem man-woman, for example, a thinker cannot relearn anything but only learn to the end—only discover fully what is "in him." At certain times we find certain solutions to problems which create a strong faith in *us* in particular; one will perhaps call them one's convictions. Later, one sees in them only the footprints leading to self-understanding, the signposts pointing to the problem which *we are*, more correctly, to the great stupidity which we are, to our intellectual destiny, to the *unteachable* "way down below."[15]

In other words, what Nietzsche means is that authority in the old sense has lost all its power for Nietzsche. But what takes its place? Ultimately,

ZARATHUSTRA, PART 2, 15–20   111

his own creativity, the creativity of the self, but this is something within him which he can no longer justify and defend. In this respect, it is closer to authority in the old sense than to authority.[16]

This raises of course a great distinction between a man who is merely obstinate and one who is, as Nietzsche means it, opinionated. Or more radically: What then is truth? What is truth if the ultimate we can find in any great thinker is this self which he can develop but not as such modify? Does not truth become poetry? Therefore, Nietzsche must make clear the difference between Zarathustra and the poets. Let us turn to page 239.

Reader: "Faith does not make me blessed," he said, "especially not faith in me. But suppose somebody said in all seriousness, the poets lie too much: he would be right; *we* do lie too much. We also know too little and we are bad learners; so we simply have to lie. And who among us poets has not adulterated his wine? Many a poisonous hodgepodge has been contrived in our cellars; much that is indescribable was accomplished there."

LS: This is also a quotation at the end of *Faust*,[17] but it is a parody on it.

Reader: "And because we know so little, the poor in spirit please us heartily, particularly when they are young females. And we are covetous even of those things which the old females tell each other in the evening. That is what we ourselves call the Eternal-Feminine in us. And, as if there were a special secret access to knowledge, *buried* for those who learn something, we believe in the people and their 'wisdom.'

"This, however, all poets believe: that whoever pricks up his ears as he lies in the grass or on lonely slopes will find out something about those things that are between heaven and earth. And when they feel tender sentiments stirring, the poets always fancy that nature herself is in love with them; and that she is creeping to their ears to tell them secrets and amorous flatteries; and of this they brag and boast before all mortals.

"Alas, there are so many things between heaven and earth of which only the poets have dreamed.

"And especially *above* the heavens: for all gods are poets' parables, poets' prevarications. Verily, it always lifts us higher—specifically, to the realm of the clouds: upon these we place our motley bastards and call them gods and overmen. For they are just light enough for these chairs—all these gods and overmen. Ah, how weary I am of all the imperfection which must at all costs become event! Ah, how weary I am of poets!"[18]

LS: I do not claim to be able to give an interpretation of this, but some points become clear to me. The poets are characterized by lack of intellectual honesty. Knowledge, as we said, is interpretation of a text, of a meaningless given to which meaning is given by an interpretation. But one must not falsify the given: one must take it as it is, one must grasp it as it is. One must not ascribe givenness to what is interpretation or creation. The poets do not make that distinction. Furthermore, the poetic creativity is distinguished from Zarathustra's creativity. The poetic creativity depends on the popular mind, and it produces "other words," images which transcend the word. Poetry is not loyal to the earth; it idealizes. In some places, the speech on the poets seems to be particularly unclear, not to say absurd. For example, page 240, paragraph 6: "Some lust and some boredom: that has so far been their best reflection." Well, it is hard to recognize what he means by that. Let us turn to page 241.

Reader: "Verily, their spirit itself is the peacock of peacocks and a sea of vanity! The spirit of the poet craves spectators—even if only buffaloes.

"But I have grown weary of this spirit; and I foresee that it will grow weary of itself. I have already seen the poets changed, with their glances turned back on themselves. I saw ascetics of the spirit approach; they grew out of the poets."[19]

LS: These ascetics or penitents of the spirit were those hunters of the ugly truth of which he spoke at the beginning of this section in the speech "On the Tarantulas." A radically new kind of philosopher must come, characterized by intellectual probity: those who accept the ugly truth, by which Nietzsche surely does not mean naturalistic notes. It is possible that the understanding of certain post-Nietzschean poetry, perhaps Rilke, would help in understanding this speech. Perhaps in the light of that new kind of poetry, all earlier poetry appears to be superficial because it idealized or posited an ideal world instead of penetrating the earthy and revealing the depth of the earth.

At this point a new section begins. Nietzsche will return to the philosopher in that new section, but from a different point of view. This new section is the last section of the second part of Zarathustra. The most important speech is the one on redemption, but it is preceded by the speeches "On Great Events" and "The Soothsayer."

"Great events" is a term carefully chosen and must be distinguished from the term "greatest event." In aphorism 285 of Beyond Good and Evil

ZARATHUSTRA, PART 2, 15–20   113

we find this remark: "The greatest events and thoughts—and the greatest thoughts are the greatest events—are comprehended most slowly."[20] An example of such a greatest event, and the most important example, is the death of God. Now let us read from the beginning.

> Reader: There is an island in the sea—not far from Zarathustra's blessed isles—on which a fire-spewing mountain smokes continually; and the people say of it, and especially the old women among the people say, that it has been placed like a huge rock before the gate to the underworld, and that the narrow path that leads to this gate to the underworld goes through the fire-spewing mountain. . . .
>
> At the time these seamen landed at the isle of fire there was a rumor abroad that Zarathustra had disappeared; and when his friends were asked, they said that he had embarked by night without saying where he intended to go. Thus uneasiness arose; and after three days the story of the seamen was added to this uneasiness; and now all the people said that the devil had taken Zarathustra. His disciples laughed at such talk to be sure, and one of them even said, "Sooner would I believe that Zarathustra has taken the devil." But deep in their souls they were all of them full of worry and longing; thus their joy was great when on the fifth day Zarathustra appeared among them.[21]

LS: Zarathustra descends not to hell, as the common people believe, but to the underworld. The underworld is located on the island of the rabbits. It is hard to understand this. I happen to know that an island of rabbits occurs in a story by Heine, whom Nietzsche knew very well. The story is "Die Götter im Exil," "The Gods in Exile." In that story, an island of the rabbits is described, on which Jupiter lives, dethroned and poor. This is not altogether irrelevant because there is an important relation between Nietzsche and Heine, which has to do with two things: in the first place, a desire for the restoration of paganism versus biblical spiritualism and asceticism; and secondly, Heine was one of the leaders in the revolt against Goethe, a revolt which was adopted by Nietzsche, as you could see from the third essay in *Untimely Meditations*.[22]

But what does this mean? We cannot possibly read the whole story; I mention the most important point, which appears in the sequel. Now what is the fire hound? The fire hound appears to be the spirit of revolution, of egalitarian subversion. Its location (and this is a suggestion of mine) is France. What about the crew and the captain who shoot rabbits?

Everyone knows Zarathustra except the captain. My suggestion is that this is the war of 1870, and the captain is Bismarck. Nietzsche wants to bring out the utter insignificance of the war of 1870, which was regarded in Germany as the crowning event establishing the unity of Germany. As compared with the revolutionary movement of Europe, the Franco-Prussian war is like shooting rabbits, a minor incident in that great and vast political movement. One thing is clear: the fire hound is the spirit of egalitarian revolution.

Now let us go on page 243.

Reader: "'Believe me, friend Hellishnoise: the greatest events—they are not our loudest but our stillest hours. Not around the inventors of new noise, but around the inventors of new values does the world revolve; it revolves *inaudibly*.

"'Admit it! Whenever your noise and smoke were gone, very little had happened. What does it matter if a town became a mummy and a statue lies in the mud? And this word I shall add for those who overthrow statues: nothing is more foolish than casting salt into the sea and statues into the mud. The statue lay in the mud of your contempt; but precisely this is its law, that out of contempt life and living beauty come back to it.'"[23]

LS: It appears from the sequel that Zarathustra is opposed to the two opponents who control the contemporary scene: the revolution on the one hand, and state and church on the other. What he does want becomes clear from the appearance of another fire hound in the sequel, page 244.

Reader: "At last, he grew calmer and his gasping eased; and as soon as he was calm I said, laughing, 'You are angry, fire hound; so I am right about you! And that I may continue to be right, let me tell you about another fire hound. He really speaks out of the heart of the earth. He exhales gold and golden rain; thus his heart wants it. What are ashes and smoke and hot slime to him? Laughter flutters out of him like colorful clouds; nor is he well disposed toward your gurgling and spewing and intestinal rumblings. This gold, however, and this laughter he takes from the heart of the earth; for—know this—*the heart of the earth is of gold!*'"[24]

LS: This other fire hound is equally revolutionary; therefore he is also called a fire hound. We have seen before, when we discussed the speech "On the Tarantulas," that Nietzsche appeared as a counter-tarantula.

Similarly, he appears here as another fire hound. But the revolution which Nietzsche has in mind is opposed to the egalitarian revolution, and it is not only the egalitarianism to which he is opposed but also its radically rebellious character. Nietzsche's revolution, paradoxical as it may sound, is not a rebellious revolution. At the end of the speech, it is stressed that at the heart of the earth is gold: there is no hell, there is nothing to fight against. It is the heart of the earth, not the heart of heaven; therefore, loyalty to the earth. Where people had located hell, there is in truth pure gold.

A word about the end of this speech.

Reader: "What shall I think of that?" said Zarathustra; "am I a ghost then? But it must have been my shadow. I suppose you have heard of the wanderer and his shadow? This, however, is clear: I must watch it more closely—else it may yet spoil my reputation."

And once more Zarathustra shook his head and wondered. "What shall I think of that?" he said once more. "Why did the ghost cry, 'It is time! It is high time!' High time for *what?*"[25]

LS: Does this ring a bell? Think of the ambiguity of the word "high time." In one sense this refers to the urgency, but in the more literal sense of the word, to the highest time. At the end of the first part he speaks of the high noon, the moment men become aware of the possibility and necessity of the superman.

The next speech, "The Soothsayer," is not entitled, like the previous speeches, i.e., "on such and such," but simply "The Soothsayer." Let us read the beginning of this speech.

Reader: "—And I saw a great sadness descend upon mankind. The best grew weary of their works. A doctrine appeared, accompanied by a faith: 'All is empty, all is the same, all has been!'"[26]

LS: "The same" is in German *gleich*, which also means equal. Nietzsche discusses here the opponent of the egalitarian revolution, the opponent not on the political level but on the spiritual and intellectual level. That is pessimism, as is indicated especially in the work of Schopenhauer. As is indicated by the word "all is the same, all is equal," it is in fact also egalitarian. For a fuller understanding of this whole section, one would have to read Nietzsche's *Untimely Meditations*, where he presents three figures who determine modern man: Rousseau, Goethe, and Schopenhauer. Rousseau is of course the tarantula, the preacher of equality and as such rejected from the very beginning. Goethe is rejected as too contemplative, too much concerned with preserving. Schopenhauer is presented there as a true educator, but this Schopenhauer, as Nietzsche knew already at the time, was already Nietzsche in the guise of Schopenhauer. The true Schopenhauer, the true pessimist, was rejected at the beginning.[27]

Now why is he called the soothsayer? He doesn't speak at all of the future, or does he? He speaks about the future by denying a future. There is no future. After Nietzsche, and with the use of Nietzschean means, Spengler's *Decline of the West* made this claim familiar.

In the sequel is the description of a terrifying dream which Zarathustra had, page 246.

Reader: "I had turned my back on all life, thus I dreamed. I had become a night watchman and a guardian of tombs upon the lonely mountain castle of death. Up there I guarded his coffins: the musty vaults were full of such marks of triumph. Life had been overcome, looked at me out of glass coffins. I breathed the odor of dusty eternities: sultry and dusty lay my soul. And who could have aired his soul there?

"The brightness of midnight was always about me; loneliness crouched next to it; and as a third, death-rattle silence, the worst of my friends. I had keys, the rustiest of all keys; and I knew how to use them to open the most creaking of all gates. Like a wickedly angry croaking, the sound ran through the long corridors when the gate's wings moved: fiendishly cried this bird, ferocious at being awakened. Yet still more terrible and heart-constricting was the moment when silence returned and it grew quiet about me, and I sat alone in this treacherous silence.

"Thus time passed and crawled, if time still existed—how should I know? But eventually that happened which awakened me. Thrice, strokes struck at the gate like thunder; the vaults echoed and howled thrice; then I went to the gate. 'Alpa,' I cried, 'who is carrying his ashes up the mountain? Alpa! Alpa! Who is carrying his ashes up the mountain?' And I pressed the key and tried to lift the gate and exerted myself; but still it did not give an inch. Then a roaring wind tore its wings apart; whistling, shrilling, and piecing, it cast up a black coffin before me.

"And amid the roaring and whistling and shrilling the coffin burst and spewed out a thousandfold laughter. And from a thousand grimaces of children, angels, owls, fools, and butterflies as big as children, it laughed and mocked and roared at me. Then I was terribly frightened; it threw me to the ground. And I cried in horror as I have never cried. And my own cry awakened me—and I came to my senses."[28]

LS: Zarathustra himself had been a pessimist. Nietzsche himself had been a pupil of Schopenhauer. But then he had a dream, a dream of re-generation, of a new life. But as it appears, it is only a caricature of a new life. In the sequel, the disciple interprets the dream; he sees only that Zarathustra is the soothsayer of the overcoming of death. This soothsayer is ambiguous: he is a pessimist and Zarathustra in the extreme. But this interpretation is wrong, or at least insufficient, as is indicated at the end of the speech. Is then Zarathustra not the redeemer from death? . . .

This speech, as well as the next and then the last of this part of *Zarathustra*, will not end with "Thus spoke Zarathustra." These three speeches correspond to the three songs: "The Night Song," "Dancing Song," "Tomb Song." The last speech which did not end with "Thus spoke Zarathustra" was "The Tomb Song," and here again the dream.

Now we come to the speech "On Redemption," which is the most important speech of this section of the second part. But before I turn to that, I would like to know whether you have any questions.

Student: . . .

LS: There is something which is missing and which is identified in a very provisional way in the next speech. But the great pessimism is already clear: the heart of the earth is gold. If this is so, then the world cannot be the worst of all possible worlds. At the end of the first part, he spoke of the new morning following the evening, but at that time we didn't know yet why this is necessary. That is the first speech in which the subject of the eternal return comes up, to such an extent that we can see that Nietzsche's reason for it is in the next speech.

Student: . . .[29]

LS: The will to power appears to be, on the one hand, a recent doctrine, starting from phenomena and leading us up to the will to power as the ground. He partly did that in the speech "On Self-Overcoming." Or is the will to power a mere postulate? But even if it is a postulate, must there not be some reasons why the postulate is required? If someone makes an assertion which has no plausibility at all, that wouldn't do under any circumstances, but if the man proves by his way of thinking and in all other possible ways that he is a genius, that would not make any impression on anyone, I hope. Some reasoning surely must come in. The question is only whether the reasoning has this character: that he leads us up to a certain point, say, to an insoluble problem, and then he suggests something which is no longer demonstrable. Only in retrospect can he suggest that this is a solution to the problem, he can ascend no further. This would be one way in which it could be done. In other words, there must be some reason. The point is only to what extent can it be sufficient reasoning.

Student: . . .

LS: This self-accusation, "Are you a wooer of truth or are you a madman, a poet?," that problem remains unclear until the end. Yet the kinship between the philosopher and the poet is much closer in Nietzsche than it was in the world of philosophy. That is one of the great difficulties.

Let us now begin the next speech.[30] This speech continues the argument of the speech "On Self-Overcoming." The self-overcoming is not only the self-overcoming of the lower by the higher will, but of the will as such. It must be redemption from the will, in a sense, and we can say this is the turning point of the whole work. I believe this speech is almost literally the center of the book. Remember also the first speech in the first part, where he distinguished between the spirit of the camel, "thou shalt," the spirit of the lion, "I will," and the spirit as child, for which he did not give a name. "I will" is somehow not the highest, and yet it must be will somehow. Now let us begin at the beginning.

Reader: When Zarathustra crossed over the great bridge one day the cripples and beggars surrounded him, and a hunchback spoke to him thus: "Behold, Zarathustra. The people too learn from you and come to believe in your doctrine; but before they will believe you entirely one thing is still needed: you must first persuade us cripples."[31]

LS: The hunchback suggests to Zarathustra that he too become a healer.

Reader: But Zarathustra replied thus to the man who had spoken: "When one takes away the hump from the hunchback one takes away his spirit— thus teach the people. And when one restores his eyes to the blind man he sees too many wicked things on earth, and he will curse whoever healed him. But whoever makes the lame walk does him the greatest harm: for when he can walk his vices run away with him—thus teach the people about cripples. And why should Zarathustra not learn from the people when the people learn from Zarathustra?"

LS: In other words, Zarathustra declines the suggestion of the hunch-back and justifies his declining on the basis of popular wisdom. Even the people know that the defective is necessary, and in this sense good.

Reader: "But this is what matters least to me since I have been among men: to see that this one lacks an eye and that one an ear and a third a leg, while there are others who have lost their tongues or their noses or their heads. I see, and have seen, what is worse, and many things so vile that I do not want to speak of everything; and concerning some things I do not even like to be silent: for there are human beings who lack everything, except one thing of which they have too much—human beings who are nothing but a big eye or a big mouth or a big belly or anything at all that is big. Inverse cripples I call them."[32]

LS: And he develops this: the bodily defects are the least important ones. The greatest defects are not seen by the people at all; the greatest defects are the defects of those men whom the people revere as great men. Here this question arises. Popular wisdom has made the assertion that the defective is necessary and in this sense good. Can one say of these greatest defects too that they are necessary? Let us turn to an earlier pas-sage, on page 209.

Reader: And some who turned away from life only turned away from the rabble: they did not want to share well and flame and fruit with the rabble.

And some who went into the wilderness and suffered thirst with the beasts of prey merely did not want to sit around the cistern with filthy camel drivers.

And some who came along like annihilators and like a hailstorm to all orchards merely wanted to put a foot into the gaping jaws of the rabble to plug up its throat.

The bite on which I gagged the most is not the knowledge that life itself requires hostility and death and torture-crosses—but once I asked, and I was almost choked by my questions: What? does life require even the rabble? Are poisoned wells required, and stinking fires and soiled dreams and maggots in the bread of life?[33]

LS: Here you see again: the bodily defects are a minor question. Let us turn back to page 250.

Reader: When Zarathustra had spoken thus to the hunchback and to those whose mouthpiece and advocate the hunchback was, he turned to his disciples in profound dismay and said: "Verily, my friends, I walk among men as among the fragments and limbs of men. This is what is terrible for my eyes, that I find man in ruins and scattered as over a battlefield or a butcher-field. And when my eyes flee from the now to the past, they always find the same: fragments and limbs and dreadful accidents—but no human beings.

"The now and the past on earth—alas, my friends, that is what *I* find most unendurable; and I should not know how to live if I were not also a seer of that which must come. A seer, a willer, a creator, a future himself and a bridge to the future—and alas, also, as it were, a cripple at this bridge: all this is Zarathustra.

"And you too have often asked yourselves, 'Who is Zarathustra to us? What shall we[34] call him? And, like myself, you replied to yourselves with questions. Is he a promiser? or a fulfiller? A conqueror? or an inheritor? An autumn? or a plowshare? A physician? or one who has recovered? Is he a poet? or truthful? A liberator? or a tamer? good? or evil?

"I walk among men as among the fragments of the future—that future which I envisage. And this is all my creating and striving, that I create and carry together into One what is fragment and riddle and dreadful accident."[35]

LS: What he says here is this. Hitherto all men, including Zarathustra, were fragments, scattered parts. No one was complete. Some centuries prior to Nietzsche, people had talked of a complete man in terms of a universal man. From this point of view, we may say the superman would seem to be the universal man. Differently stated, hitherto chance ruled, and this leads to the following notion of the future: the conquest of chance, conquest of fragmentariness. We have seen this conquest of chance and fragmentariness before.

Let us turn to page 189.

Reader: Not only the reason of millennia, but their madness too, breaks out in us. It is dangerous to be an heir. Still we fight step by step with the giant, accident; and over the whole of humanity there has ruled so far only nonsense—no sense.[36]

LS: In other passages of the *Zarathustra*, for example on page 183,[37] paragraph 5, you will find that the superfluous ones should never have been born. In later writings, Nietzsche expresses this in a much more extreme way. For example, in the *Ecce Homo*, in the chapter on *The Birth of Tragedy*, he says: "Every[38] new party of life, which takes into its hands the greatest of all tasks, the higher breeding of the human race, including the merciless extinction of everything decadent and parasitical, will make possible again that Too-much[39]of life on earth, out of which early Greek culture[40] has stemmed."[41] What does this mean? Men have been incomplete up until now, some even decadent and parasitical. Doesn't the conquest of chance, practically speaking, consist in a eugenics which includes, from the point of view of *Beyond Good and Evil*, the extinction of the low, the sick, and the degenerate?[42] That this element exists in Nietzsche would be dishonest to deny, but it is indeed not the highest level in Nietzsche, the level of Zarathustra. In this speech he speaks of redeeming chance, which is not the same as conquering chance. He had also spoken earlier, in "Self-Overcoming," of knowledge as redeeming being, as distinguished from conquering being.

Now what does this redemption of chance mean? That he explains in the sequel.

Reader: "And how could I bear to be a man if man were not also a creator and guesser of riddles and redeemer of accidents?

"To redeem those who lived in the past and to recreate all 'it was' into a 'thus I willed it'—that alone should I call redemption."[43]

LS: Redemption of chance, of accident, of the fragments—and they are what they are by virtue of the human past, in this sense redemption of the past. But redemption is not conquest but affirmation of chance, of the past, of the fragments. This is a very radical and surprising change we must try to understand. First of all, one could say that this is a wholly unnecessary suggestion because redemption is implied in the conquest of chance: think of Marxism and other doctrines. Is the redemption of the past not implied in the fact that the past is the basis of the future? All suffering and idiocy of the past was required to bring about the consummation. Is this not *the* vindication of suffering and idiocy? This was seen already by Kant in his sketch on the philosophy of history, and taken up by Hegel and Marx. We can say now only this much: this is not what Nietzsche means.

Reader: "Will—that is the name of the liberator and joy-bringer; thus I taught you, my friends. But now learn this too: the will itself is still a prisoner. Willing liberates; but what is it that puts even the liberator himself in fetters?"

LS: The previous teaching regarding the will was fundamentally incomplete, because it did not consider the essential limitation of the will. That is what concerns him now.

Reader: "'It was'—that is the name of the will's gnashing of teeth and most secret melancholy. Powerless against what has been done, he is an angry spectator of all that is past. The will cannot will backwards; and that he cannot break time and time's covetousness, that is the will's loneliest melancholy."[44]

LS: This expression "it was" occurs in a very emphatic way already in the beginning of "Advantage and Disadvantage of History." There he says that man is an animal which cannot forget. The brutes forget immediately.[45] Man lives therefore as much in the past as in the present. Remembering the past makes it impossible for us to be as completely sincere as the brutes, prevents us from being entirely what we are, namely, what we are now. We are also always what we no longer are. Our existence is an *imperfectum* which can never be perfected. Man cannot forget; hence he sees everywhere becoming, as distinguished from being. This applies especially to the way in which he sees himself, in which the individual sees himself. To the extent to which a man cannot forget, there is no being, no character. Only to the extent to which men can forget, to the extent to which man can be unhistorical, can he be creative, for creation is in the moment, in the present moment. But this forgetting of the past does not liberate us from the past, from the fragmentariness, from the ape in us.

Here in *Zarathustra* the argument runs as follows. The will desires to be sovereign, to be simply creative, but it depends on the given, that is to say, on the past. The will is impotent regarding the past as past. The past is irrevocable, the past cannot be willed. But past is not only one of the three dimensions of time—past, present, future—it is the character of time as such: time passes. In rebelling against the past, the will rebels against time, against the desire of time, that is to say, the desire to pass away. But we may ask again: Was the past not willed when the future was willed? The past, we said, is a condition of the future. Yet this overlooks the fact that the past *was* without being willed, the willing comes in only afterwards. Will then is frustrated by the past, by time.

Now what does the will do in order to counteract its defeat by time? This question is answered in the sequel.

Reader: "Willing liberates; what means does the will devise for himself to get rid of his melancholy and to mock his dungeon? Alas, every prisoner becomes a fool; and the imprisoned will redeems himself foolishly. That time does not run backwards, that is his wrath; 'that which was' is the name of the stone he cannot move. And so he moves stones out of wrath and displeasure, and he wreaks revenge on whatever does not feel wrath and displeasure as he does. Thus the will, the liberator, took to hurting; and on all who can suffer he wreaks revenge for his inability to go backwards. This, indeed this alone, is what *revenge* is: the will's ill will against time and its 'it was.'

"Verily, a great folly dwells in our will; and it has become a curse for everything human that this folly has acquired spirit.

"*The spirit of revenge*, my friends, has so far been the subject of man's best reflection; and where there was suffering, one always wanted punishment too."[46]

LS: What then does the will do in order to counteract its defeat by the passing of time? Nietzsche's answer: it turns into revenge. As he said, man's best thought was his spirit of revenge. All previous thought, including the best, is characterized by the spirit of revenge. What does this mean? The will negates what it cannot will: it negates the past, time, passing away, the perishable. The will conjectures something imperishable, unchanging, eternal. It engages in a flight from the perishable into the afterworld, into calumny of the earthly. The will postulates eternity in order to escape from time, from passing away, from death. Differently stated, the eternal is a postulate in order to escape from uncertainty, because the eternal or sempiternal is the only subject of knowledge proper. Here then Nietzsche gives his final analysis of philosophy in the pre-Nietzschean sense of the term: it is an escape from time.

In the sequel, Nietzsche shows how this is connected with the moralistic interpretation which pervaded the past and to some extent Nietzsche's own time, therefore what he calls in his more popular later writings "the spirit of resentment" which characterizes the biblical tradition and modern morality. Nietzsche has spoken of the spirit of revenge before: he traced the egalitarian revolution to the spirit of revenge. In a vulgar sense, this has of course been said: the poor are envious of the rich. The spirit of revenge is effective in the egalitarian revolution and it is effective in all earlier thought, biblical or philosophic. What is that connection? The eternal or sempiternal is only a derivative from the temporal, but this derivation is due to man's desire to escape from the temporal, to escape from the perishable. Therefore, man postulates something which is in no way exposed to a tradition.

But after all, you have only to read Marx and Engels to see that there is nothing eternal about the egalitarian revolution. Or is this a deception? Well, what about the realm of freedom? If something eternal is postulated and accepted, when this is regarded as higher in dignity than the perishable, a degradation of human life is the consequence of the admission of the eternal. Now, ideas are regarded as eternal. The ideas as such render questionable the actual or the real, because even if something actual should be in agreement with the ideas, it owes its dignity to the idea, it does not have dignity in itself. The idea as idea remains the standard; every idea is in principle therefore conducive to revolutionary purposes. Any universal or abstract principle has necessarily a revolutionary and disturbing effect, and this is the origin of the revolutionary movements of modern times which, after all, started from the eternal or natural rights of man. This was pushed aside in the nineteenth century, but it still lingered on. But there is no transcendent standard, no ideals. But what about the superman? Does the project of the superman not include a condemnation of previous men? Has Nietzsche not been moralizing throughout the work, condemning previous men and especially the last man? The superman must somehow include acceptance of the previous men and of the last man.

Student: . . .

LS: The past is irrevocable and is no longer in any way subject to the will. It can nevertheless be willed. That's the paradox toward which he is driving. Paradox, however, does not mean here absurdity, it means simply deviating from accepted opinion.

Take the superman: Given this tremendous power and desire, technical knowledge, etc., why not a society of supermen? In a certain sense, the realm of freedom is of course the society of supermen. All are creative: redeemed from necessity, all become creative. What is Nietzsche's objection to this? Why is this impossible from his point of view? Or undesirable? Why shouldn't the man who says "extinction of all degenerates" not also engage in speculation about the most extreme achievements? Is there not a certain tension between the criticism of all previous men, and yet demanding the survival in this time and age of all these intellectuals? If inequality presupposes a higher dignity of human beings, one cannot wish for the abolition of inequality. Nietzsche's doctrine somehow presupposes that there is an order of nature. What is the status of nature? Has he not undermined completely the notion of nature by the same reasoning by which objective truth has been called into question? The willing of the past as that act by which nature creates is in a fantastic way debased by the will of Zarathustra, which wills the past.[47]

Student: . . .[48]

LS: For example, the superman as Nietzsche understands him necessarily presupposes Christianity. If the superman is Caesar with the soul of Christ, from Nietzsche's point of view there is no possibility in the Hegelian way of constructing the emergence of Christianity as an essential necessity: it just happened. To this extent, the notion of the superman cannot be understood as part of an intelligible teleological process.

8 Summary and Review

Fusing Plato and the Creative Self

Leo Strauss: We have reached the center of *Zarathustra* and should recon-
sider the whole problem by beginning at the beginning. Before we awake
to awareness of the fundamental questions, we have already made up our
minds, or our minds have been made up for us by others. Before we begin
to think—which means to think for ourselves—we possess already opinions or convictions. In a society like ours, those opinions frequently stem
from philosophies. There are always in societies like ours ruling schools
of thought into which we grow up. Prior to our own investigations we
cannot know which of these present-day schools, if any, possesses the
truth or teaches the truth, so we must be duly respectful in regard to
each of these schools, at least to begin with. But for the same reason, we
must withhold this respect; for all we know to begin with, any of these
schools which was taught in the past may have taught the truth. We are
of course inclined to be more impressed by the contemporary, the contemporary which is the most audible—let us say the most noisy, the
most powerful—and we are inclined to mistake that which rules for the
heights or that which deserves to rule. In lesser things, we see easily that
this respect for the powerful and established merely because it is powerful
and established is foolish or vulgar, but with regard to the power of contemporary thought we are much more easily deceived. One reason is
this: only contemporary schools of thought can possess knowledge of the
contemporary situation, but knowledge of the contemporary situation is
of no use whatever if we do not possess knowledge of the principles in
the light of which the contemporary situation is to be understood, to be
judged, and to be developed. Thinkers who knew absolutely nothing of
the contemporary situation may well have possessed knowledge of those
principles, and vice versa.

Yet, however open-minded and truly liberal we may wish to be, those
inclinations and insights drive each of us toward one or the other avail-

able schools of thought. Very, very few men at any time tried to walk a way never before trodden by any man before. Now prior to investigation, these men who tried to walk a way never before trodden by any man before do not deserve higher respect than the available schools, for these ways may be the ways of madness. But on the other hand, we must also say they have the same right to be heard as anyone else if they fulfill the minimum requirements, the fulfillment of which gives a man the right to be heard. They have a right not to be silenced on the ground they thought something unheard of, or that they teach something entirely new. We cannot reject their teachings because they contradict all previous re-nowned teachings. We cannot demand of these innovators that they must justify themselves before the tribunal, and they deny it rightly. There is no right of the first occupants in the realm of the mind. A simile for it would be "First come, first served"—which is a very healthy principle, but in matters of possession. In the realm of the mind such right cannot be admitted.

Now if we look around us, we see four schools of thought: positivism, existentialism, Marxism, and communism. In the academic life of the West (especially in the Anglo-Saxon countries, as we all know), there is a preponderance of positivism. The claim of positivism is not baseless. Pos-itivism is based on the only authority which in one way or another is still recognized by everyone today, the authority of modern natural science, and it is further based on the reasonable demand for unity of knowledge. From these two premises it follows that the universal extension of the successful methods of natural science (that is to say, fundamentally of the methods of mathematical physics) to every subject matter, above all to man and the human affairs, must be demanded. In other words, these people say the only genuine knowledge is scientific knowledge, and what scientific knowledge is, is defined by the analysis of scientific method as practiced today. But there is this difficulty: Is it possible to extend the scientific study along the methods of natural science to man and human affairs without distorting and impoverishing the phenomena as we know them prior to the scientific treatment? Is man not *sui generis*? Is there not an essential difference between man and nonman? Does the scientific study of man not amount to the understanding of men in terms of the subhuman? Does this not imply a degradation of man? The explicit form which positivism takes in application to man is the distinction between facts and values. Before the tribunal of science—that is to say, before the tribunal of the highest form of knowledge, the only form of genuine knowledge—all values are equal. This leads, in effect, by a simple consideration of statistics, to a preponderance of the lowest values and therewith to the degradation of man. Is a value-free social science possible at all? As you may know, I think it is not, but I cannot now enter onto this well-trodden way.

If the insufficiency of positivism is realized but the positivist conception of science and knowledge is fundamentally accepted, existentialism arises. I know that this needs many qualifications, but allow me for the time being this freedom. Existentialism is *the* contemporary alternative to positivism, for both communism and Marxism have their roots in positivistic thought. Existentialism has two roots, historically: Kierkegaard and Nietzsche. Kierkegaard was a Christian, and his whole teaching served the establishment of the Christian plane. The philosophic root of existentialism is therefore to be sought in Nietzsche and in Nietzsche alone. There are other reasons supporting that. In the first place, Kierkegaard, who lived more than a hundred years ago, became known outside of Denmark only in the early decades of this century, in the wake of Nietzsche's entrance. We could refer further to the testimony of *the* existentialist, the greatest representative of it, namely, Heidegger: to understand existentialism one must start from Nietzsche.[1]

There is a further consideration. Nietzsche is *the* critic of communism on the basis of the same principle which is also the basis of communism, and this principle is formulated by Nietzsche in the sentence "God is dead." But the question is: Must we not question the modern premises as such, the premises common to positivism, Nietzsche, and Marxism? This is done in effect by communism, although the communism of our age is neo-communism and therefore not simply identical with original communism. However this may be, within communism as philosophy, disregarding the theological part and therefore also the philosophical teaching of classical antiquity on which communism rests (Plato, Aristotle, Cicero, etc.), we find the notion of natural law and natural right. This notion, which is rejected by all present-day schools, compels us to go beyond the horizon of the contemporary. We approach Nietzsche therefore from the point of view as to its explicit or implicit relation to natural right.

The notion of natural right or natural law (I do not go now into the question of the difference) is based on the premise that nature gives us guidance in matters of human conduct, that nature is good. The modern rejection of natural right is based on the questioning of this premise. This questioning is expressed in Descartes's universal doubt, in the suspicion that we might owe our being to an evil spirit. It is implied in the notion of the conquest of nature and, for example, in Hobbes's notion of the state of nature as a state to be avoided, to be left. The place of nature is taken in modern thought first by reason, and then by history.

The peculiar position of Nietzsche is this. He starts from history as the guiding concept and tries to restore nature, bypassing reason. He bypasses reason on the basis of his criticism of reason: reason, the ego, is only the servant of the self—and the self, as he puts it in an overstatement, is the god. One could expect for a moment that the movement of Nietzsche's thought goes from history to natural right. That it is not entirely wrong, we shall see later; but in the main, this expectation is disappointed. There is some obstacle to the restoration of natural right in Nietzsche's thought. What is that obstacle? Perhaps this obstacle is *the* modern obstacle, and by trying to understand it we can understand the modern premise more clearly.

Nietzsche's chief work according to his own deliberation is *Thus Spoke Zarathustra*. The starting point, as you remember, is "God is dead." This is the greatest event in the life of man, his supreme crisis. The primary consequence of this event is the prospect of the last man: the man who has ceased to aspire, who knows no longer any heroism, any dedication, any reverence. Needless to say, Nietzsche does not speak of psychoanalysis, because psychoanalysis emerged out of Nietzsche. Nietzsche merely says: "No shepherd and one herd, everyone wills the same, everyone is the same, everyone is equal. He who feels differently goes voluntarily to the lunatic asylum."[2] But this formulation of Nietzsche presupposes of course that there is no cure for feeling differently, whereas psychoanalysis is such a cure. In other words, psychoanalysis really completes Nietzsche's vision of the last man: perfect conformity. Nietzsche's presentation of the last man is a presentation from the anticommunist point of view of what the communist realm of freedom would in fact be. The communist realm of freedom claims to be the stage where human creativity as the creativity of all and each begins, but, as Nietzsche suggests, the realm of freedom is utterly incompatible with any creativity. Yet while the movement in the direction of the last man is very powerful, its victory is not necessary. The death of God, which makes possible the greatest degradation of man, the last man, makes also possible the highest elevation of man. The denial of all superhuman beings makes possible that man himself becomes superhuman. This is the meaning of the expression "the superman." The superman is characterized by creativity, by conscious creativity, by consciousness of the fact that all meaning and value originates in man—not in God, nor in nature. The superman is a knower, therefore, because he has this crucial self-consciousness; therefore, Nietzsche can also call him the philosopher of the future. He is therefore characterized by pride and delicacy: he is a creator, the pride; he is a vulnerable creator, the delicacy.

The delicacy takes the place of pity in particular, the delicacy which respects the pride of others, whereas pity hurts that pride. We must also emphasize the fact that this creator is radically lonely and therefore in the highest degree suffering. The notion of the superman is, to say the least, not politically neutral. Nietzsche rejects both the left and the right, both the egalitarian revolution and the state, but his appeal to creativity, his calling and awakening of the creative individual, is bound to have political effects, while Nietzsche is unable to show a way to political effects. Therefore, Nietzsche's political effect leads necessarily to a perversion of his teaching. This perversion is fascism. Here is the great difference between Nietzsche and Marx. It has been said that both Lenin and Stalin had perverted Marxism, and this may be true to a certain extent, but they surely perverted Marxist teaching much less than people like Hitler and Mussolini perverted Nietzsche's teaching.

The notion of the superman presupposes the death of God, that is to say, the rejection of everything unchangeable, unmoved, imperishable. The place of being is taken by becoming, the place of eternity is taken by time. But what is the essential character of becoming, in Nietzsche's view? Nietzsche says "will to power." This doctrine of the will to power is arrived at by starting from human phenomena, and least of all from political phenomena. What Nietzsche has in mind is akin to what is called by Dewey and others growth.[3] That is a somewhat difficult expression. In the older notion of growth, it was understood that there is a limit to growth. As the German proverb puts it: Care has been taken that the trees do not grow into heaven. Therefore, becoming is necessarily a movement toward the peak, toward what is, where becoming finds its end. I do not deny that there is not a great deal of difference between will to power as Nietzsche understands it and growth as Dewey and others understand it, namely, this: if beings grow, there is no notion of a limit. There will be some which will take away the light from the others—think of trees in the woods. To put it bluntly, someone will get hurt. Either you accept that hurting or you must do something to stop growth. There is no sufficient awareness of this on the part of the people who talk of growth, whereas Nietzsche was fully aware of it when he spoke of the will to power.

Now whatever the primary human phenomena may be for Nietzsche in developing the will to power—and I think the phenomenon of knowledge is probably more important than anything else—Nietzsche feels compelled to universalize the will to power. Will to power is not only the essence of man, will to power is the fundamental characteristic of everything living. The will to power doctrine is meant to account for the upward movement in evolution, in human history, without the assumption of a preexisting end, a pregiven end, which as such elicits the growth, the upward movement. Therefore, the will to power is strictly applied to Plato's view of *erōs*, the love for something toward which you aspire which is in its own right prior to your own desire. The doctrine of the will to power differs from earlier metaphysical suggestions not only in substance, because will to power is obviously not God, but it differs also in its mode. There is nothing which is always; corresponding to that, there is no pure mind which perceives that which is always. Reason, the intellect, the ego, is a mere surface of the self. Hence knowledge must be understood as a function of the whole man; it cannot be understood as an actualization of the mere intellect. Knowledge is a function of the whole man, of the self, and since the self is the body, it is also a function of the organism, as some people say. Knowledge therefore is ultimately a modification of the will to power: it is an activity of the living being, and the living being is essentially the will to power. Knowledge is ultimately not perceptive but creative, imprinting a pattern on the meaningless given, as distinguished from perceiving a pattern. Only knowledge in this sense can be accepted by Nietzsche in the last analysis, and that is what he means by one of the songs in the *Zarathustra*: that there is a kinship between life and wisdom, wisdom understood as something of the fundamental character of life, namely, will to power, i.e., imprinting a pattern, not perceiving a pattern.

But what does truth come to mean under these conditions? Is not Nietzsche's doctrine of the will to power a manifestation of Nietzsche's will to power or of Nietzsche's individuality? With what right can he regard this doctrine as superior to other suggestions? All knowledge, as he puts it, is perspectivity, belonging to a specific perspective and possibly valid only with a view to that perspective. There is not *the* perspective of *the* knower, of the pure mind. There is no objective knowledge, there is no objective knowledge which is not fragmentary and therefore insufficient for giving us guidance. To the extent to which there is something like objective knowledge, it must be completed by interpretation, as Nietzsche calls it. But interpretations have a different cognitive status than the awareness of the text, the merely objective and given which no one can gainsay. Now if all knowledge of any relevance is perspectivity, the superior perspective must be the more comprehensive perspective. Accordingly, Nietzsche's doctrine of the will to power understands itself at a certain stage as the best suggestion hitherto: not the final philosophy, but the philosophy of the future. There is a necessity for doing that which can be stated as follows. If this doctrine of the will to power is meant to be finally true, there would be an end of creativity of the highest order, because from Nietzsche's point of view the philosophic doctrines are human creations. But what we want, apparently, is an infinite progress of ever higher creation, of ever broader perspectives. In this connection, we might read a beautiful statement of the difficulty here in the last aphorism of Nietzsche's *Dawn of the Morning*.[4]

Nietzsche calls philosophy the most spiritual form of the will to power.[5] What does this spirituality mean? It means the will to power turned against itself. The will to power, as we find it in the organic world and in man most of the time, is an attempt to overpower and incorporate other things. But on the highest stage, the will to power turned against itself. The polemic intention against all spiritualism compels him to overstate the importance of the body.

What is the "or"? Maybe discover a land which is completely unknown to anyone, including ourselves? What Nietzsche indicates here is this problem: Must it not necessarily be directed toward an end of the progress? Is progress possible without wishing for a final stage? At one point or another this must become clear to us, if it is not to be a senseless striving.

To repeat, Nietzsche has a metaphysical doctrine which differs from all earlier metaphysical doctrines. But it is equally important, and perhaps more important, that it differs from all earlier metaphysical doctrines also in its mode. This mode is that the doctrine of the will to power is not simply a theoretical doctrine but is somehow connected with Nietzsche's creativity. There is a fundamental difference between Nietzsche's perspective and all earlier perspectives. Every great thinker has a perspective of his own, but the perspectives of all earlier thinkers have something in common which distinguishes all of them from Nietzsche's perspective, for all earlier philosophers absolutized their perspectives. They did not know that their teaching was relative to a specific perspective, whereas Nietzsche knows that all knowledge, including his own, is perceptivity. In other words, it is the problem you all know even today from vulgar relativism. The will to power doctrine may be an interpretation of that insight. Therefore, the interpretation may be Nietzsche's peculiarity, but the insight into the perspectival character of all knowledge is in itself final. I read you a passage from *Ecce Homo*. The *Ecce Homo* contains a summary of an appreciation by Nietzsche of all his writings. In his appreciation of the *Dawn of Morning*, section 2, he says: "My task is to prepare a moment of the highest self-consciousness of mankind, a great noon where mankind looks into the future, where mankind leaves the dominion of chance and where it poses the question of the 'why' and 'for what' for the first time as mankind."[6] Here it is implied that this is *the* creation. Nietzsche claims to be the first who states *the* question, and by stating the question he prepares the great noon, the high noon, the peak of mankind. There is a peak, there is a finality. Here it is implied that the question is higher in rank[7] than any answer. This question then supplies the broadest perspective, not only a broader perspective than any other perspective but the broadest perspective, the absolute perspective. Why? Because the essential character of all knowledge has now become clear, or if we accept the hypothesis of the will to power, the will to power has become conscious of itself in Nietzsche, and this is the absolute moment. In all previous stages the will to power was active in thinkers, but not aware of it. Now it is aware of it, and that is the radical and absolute difference.

Every worldview or system of values is a creation. This is not only an assertion of Nietzsche, but it is also taught to every freshman in college. But this assertion that every worldview or system of values is a creation is *not* a creation but an insight, and the most fundamental of all insights. Or stated differently: objective truth, the truth that is discoverable by science, for example, is incomplete. Men can live only by subjective truth. This whole thought and the reasoning supporting it is not itself a subjective truth. Human life is a horizon-forming project, and therefore we can only live by such projects—only by creativity, by the creations of ourselves or others. But this understanding of human life as a horizon-forming project is not itself a horizon-forming project; therefore we arrive ultimately at a theoretical insight which claims to be final, and which is the most important insight and therefore the final truth. This is not essentially affected by the fact that these insights presuppose the experience of creativity. While the experience of creativity is a presupposition of the theoretical thesis, the thesis itself is a theoretical assertion. *The* truth is discovered on the basis of the first man who had full self-consciousness of *the* creative act. The creative act is of course not the creation of this painting and that piece of music, but the first conscious creation of a worldview and a value system.

There is not *the* true world, the objective world beyond the appearance of the many subjective worlds relative to people, relative to individuals. And we are concerned with an infinite variety of subjective worlds, and on this basis with the contention that this subjective world is superior which is a creation of the richest individuality. But this creation is according to Nietzsche accompanied or at least conditioned by the self-consciousness of the mind's creativity. In this highest phase, we may say the self-consciousness is objective truth in this sense and coincides with the creative act, the subjective truth. We can perhaps say the superman stands as a kind of imaginary focus for the coincidence of objective and subjective truth. *The* truth is inaccessible to a noncreative man, that is to say, to us who are not creative men. But Nietzsche calls us to creativity.

There is a strict parallel to that in Kierkegaard, namely, the appeal to make the jump. This is fundamentally the same problem. Here we can state the difficulty simply by mere quotations because this notion, historically speaking, was prepared by a German thinker prior to Kierkegaard: Jacobi.[8] Jacobi had a conversation with Lessing in which he demanded from Lessing the *salto mortale*, the mortal jump. Lessing said that he was too old for jumping, to which Jacobi replied: That is not the difficulty, you have only to go on this elastic point and you will be jumped. To which Lessing remarked: This is already the jump, to go to that elastic point.[9] In other words, there is no way to talk away the problem, or to minimize it, or to sweeten it, but still one can say the jump must somehow be prepared. In plain English, we must be led by argument to the point where we can jump from and where the case is made of the necessity of the jump.

But before we continue, we must keep one thing in mind. Nietzsche's notion of knowledge or truth is based on the awareness not indeed that there must be an absolute moment, but on the awareness that there *is* an absolute moment. The absolute moment is the peak, the high noon of mankind. But by admitting a peak, one admits descent. This descent—in Marxist language, what comes after the realm of freedom—ends either in everlasting meaninglessness and even the extinction of human life altogether, or else return, and then in principle eternal return. Nietzsche, in contradistinction to Marx and Hegel, faces this problem of the end of the peak. Knowledge is concerned primarily or exclusively with nature. Knowledge means, as we have seen, either imprinting a character on the

characterless given, or else perceiving the character of the given, which has
in itself a character, articulation. A parallel movement of thought, parallel
to what we observed regarding knowledge, can also be observed regarding
nature. How are Nietzsche's peculiar understandings of nature parallel to
his understandings of knowledge?
I take three aphorisms of *Beyond Good and Evil.* The first is aphorism 9:

"In moderation, according to nature" you wish to live? Oh noble Stoics!
How your words deceive! Think of a being like Nature, immoderately
wasteful, immoderately indifferent, devoid of intentions and considerate-
nesses, devoid of compassion and a sense of justice, fruitful and desolate
and uncertain at the same time: think of Indifference on the throne—how
could you live in moderation according to this indifference? Living—isn't
it precisely a wishing-to-be-different from this Nature? Doesn't living
mean evaluating, preferring, being unjust, being limited, wanting to be
different? But supposing your imperative "to live in moderation, according
to nature" only means "to live in moderation, according to life"—how then
could you live *otherwise?* Why make a principle of something that you are
and have to be? The truth is quite another matter: while rapturously pre-
tending to read the canon of your law out of nature, you actually want the
opposite—you strange play-actors and self-deceivers! Your pride wants
to dictate your morality, your ideal, to nature (even to nature!). It wants to
incorporate itself in nature; you demand that nature be nature "in moderation, according to the Stoa"; you want to remake all existence to mirror
your own existence; you want an enormous everlasting glorification of stoicism! With all your love for truth, you force yourselves to see nature *falsely,*
i.e. stoically—so long, so insistently, so hypnotically petrified, until you can
no longer see it any other way. And in the end some abysmal arrogance
gives you the insane hope that, *because* you know how to tyrannize over
yourselves (stoicism is self-tyranny), you can also tyrannize over nature—
for isn't the Stoic a *part* of nature? . . . But all this is an old, everlasting story.
What happened to the Stoics still happens today, as soon as a philosophy
begins to have faith in itself. It always creates the world in its own image;
it cannot do otherwise, for philosophy *is* this tyrannical desire; it is the
most spiritual will to power, to "creation of the world," to the *causa prima.*[10]

This is the clearest and most precise formulation of what Nietzsche
means also by philosophy: a will which imprints itself on the meaningless

given. Nietzsche's view of science is exactly the same: this is not philosophy in the strict and narrow sense. Now what does he say here? Nature is indifferent. How can it possibly be a guide for man? It becomes a guide for man only by falsification. Men infer these ideas in nature, and then of course they find it bad. You all know this thought, for this is what Sabine and others say (though not as beautifully) all the time. But Nietzsche suggests a change: maybe they do not mean by nature, nature proper; maybe they mean by nature life. And then Nietzsche says also that life as life does not supply a standard because we naturally live according to life, which is of course based on the premise that life does not have a direction. We may very well deviate from the ways of life. Man—a specific man, say, Hegel, Nietzsche, Hobbes—imposes his will to power on the meaningless. His idea has no other basis than his will to power.

Now let us turn to a much later aphorism, aphorism 230, which also is very interesting but unfortunately much too long, so let us read the end:

> They are beautiful, glittering, jingling, festive words: candor, love for truth, love for wisdom, self-sacrifice for insight, heroism of the truthful! Something about them swells one's pride. But we anchorites and marmots, we have convinced ourselves long ago, in all the secrecy of our anchorite's conscience, that this worthy word-pomp too belongs to the old lying bangles, to all the deceptive junk and gold dust of unconscious human vanity; that even beneath such flattering colors and cosmetics the frightful basic text *homo natura* must be recognized for what it is. For to retranslate man back into nature, to master the many vain enthusiastic glosses which have been scribbled and painted over the everlasting text *homo natura*, so that man might henceforth stand before man as he stands today before that *other* nature, hardened under the discipline of science, with unafraid Oedipus eyes and stopped up Ulysses ears, deaf to the lures of the old metaphysical bird catchers who have been fluting in at him all too long that "you are more! You are superior! You are of another origin!"—this may be a strange, mad task, but who could deny that it is a *task!* Why did we choose it, this mad task? Or, to ask it with different words, "Why insight, anyway?" Everyone will ask us this. And we, pressed for an answer, having asked the same question of ourselves hundreds of times, we have found and shall find no better answer—[11]

He had given the answer before, when he said will to power turning against itself or the most spiritual form of cruelty, as he said in the earlier part of this aphorism. Knowledge is the will to power turning against itself—the overcoming becomes self-overcoming—in opposition to knowledge as creativity, which means imprinting one's will to power on the given. What he speaks of here, the intellectual honesty, he has spoken of before in *Zarathustra* in the speech "On the Sublime Ones"; the men who are the ugly hungerers for the ugly truth, the full dedication to the truth without any expectation of guidance from it. Here we find, to re-translate man into the eternal fundamental text, that man is nature, *homo natura*. What does he mean by that? How is nature here understood? Nature is here somehow understood in contradistinction to creativity. It is not clear that the nature meant here is much more than that desolate nature, indifference itself as power, of which he had spoken in aphorism 9.

Now let us turn to aphorism 188. I want to point out one crucial feature. Throughout this aphorism the word nature is used in quotation marks. Only in the last few lines does he drop the quotation marks.

Every morality, in contrast to *laisser aller*, is a work of tyranny against "nature" and also against "reason." But this is not an objection to it, not unless one wished to decree (proceeding from some sort of morality) that all types of tyranny and irrationality are to be forbidden. What is essential and of inestimable value in each morality is that it is a long-lasting re-straint. To understand Stoicism or Port-Royal or Puritanism, it is well to remember the restraints under which any language hitherto has reached its peak of power and subtlety—the restraint of metrics, the tyranny of rhyme and rhythm. How much trouble have the poets and orators of each nation always taken (not excepting several of today's prose writers) with an inexorable conscience in their ear, "for the sake of a folly" say the Util-itarian fools who think they are clever, "in deference to arbitrary laws" say the anarchists who imagine they are "free," in fact freethinkers. The strange fact, however, is that everything of freedom, subtlety, boldness, dance, and craftsmanlike certainty that one can find on earth, whether it applies to thinking, or ruling, or speaking, or persuading—in the arts as well as in codes of conduct—would never have developed save through the "tyranny of such arbitrary laws." Indeed, the probability is strong that *this* is "nature" and "natural"—and *not*—*laisser aller!* Every artist knows how far his most "natural" condition is from the feeling of letting oneself go, how rigorously and subtly he obeys a thousandfold law in the moments of "inspiration," in his free ordering, locating, disposing, and formgiving, how his laws mock at all formulation into concepts, precisely because they are so rigorous and well-defined (even the firmest concept, compared to them, has something teeming, manifold, and ambiguous about it). The essential thing "in heaven and on earth," it seems, is—to say it once more—that there be obedience, long continued obedience in some one direction. When this happens, something worthwhile always comes of it in the end, something which makes living worthwhile; virtue, for example, or art or music or dance or reason or spirituality—something that transfigures us, something subtly refined, or mad, or divine. The long bondage of the spirit, the long repression in the communicability of thoughts, the discipline assumed by the thinker to think within an ecclesiastical or court-imposed system or within the framework of Aristotelian assumptions, the enduring, intellectual will to interpret all that happens according to the Christian scheme, to discover and justify the Christian God in every accident—all this violence, arbitrariness, rigor, gruesomeness, and anti-rationality turned out to be the means for disciplining the European spirit into strength, ruthless inquisitiveness, and subtle flexibility. We must admit, of course, that much which is irreplaceable in energy and spirit was suppressed, choked out, and ruined in the same process (for here, as everywhere, "nature" shows up as that which it is, in all its wasteful and *indifferent* magnificence which outrages us but which is a mark of its distinction). That European thinkers for millenniums thought only in order to prove something (today the case is reversed and we distrust any thinker who is out to prove something), that they always knew very definitely what was *supposed* to be the result of their most rigorous thinking (think of the example of Asiatic astrology or today's harmless Christian-moral interpretation of personal events as happening "to the greater glory of God" or "for the good of the soul"!)—all this tyranny, this arbitrariness, this rigorous and grandiose stupidity has *disciplined* and *educated* the spirit. It seems that slavery, in both its coarser and its finer application, is the indispensable means for even spiritual discipline and cultivation. Look at any morality—you will see that it is its "nature" to teach hatred of *laisser aller*, of too much freedom, and to implant the need for limited horizons, for the nearest task. It teaches the *narrowing of perspectives*, in other words stupidity in a certain sense, as a necessary condition for life and growth. "Thou shalt obey, someone or other, and for a long time; *if not*, you perish and lose your last self-respect"—this seems to me to be the moral imperative of nature. It is neither categorical, to be sure, as old Kant demanded (observe the "if not"!), nor is it directed to any individual. What does nature care about an individual! But it is directed to peoples, races, times, classes, and—above all—to the whole animal known as "man," to *mankind*.[12]

You see here this interesting transition from nature in quotation marks to nature without it.

Nature is, to begin with, a traditional and hence merely questionable concept, but in the course of his reflection nature becomes nontraditional. We learn only one thing about nature here: nature dictates obedience. But after we have read the speech in *Zarathustra* on self-overcoming, we know already that it is the root to *the* thought of Nietzsche, because obedience is correlative to command, and this interplay of obedience and command is the most fundamental characteristic of the will to power. The conclusion from this is that nature is the will to power and no longer the mere desolateness distinguished from life or living of which he spoke in aphorism 9. Nature is the will to power, and there is a variety of levels of the will to power. That means there is a natural order, a hierarchy.

And now we come to a very extraordinary thing. In the *Antichrist*, in aphorism 57, Nietzsche contrasts the biblical and Christian morality with the Hindu morality, the code of Manu. There Nietzsche discerned the Platonic notion of the natural hierarchy. So Nietzsche's last word on nature is that it implies a natural order. Nature as the natural order is not by being willed, but in itself. In this strange way, Nietzsche, perhaps only for some moments, restores the Platonic position. His whole doctrine depends on this doctrine of hierarchy, which he very rarely calls a natural hierarchy. Nature has become a problem for Nietzsche, but on the other hand he is in need of it, and this underlies the doctrine of the eternal return, which we have begun to discuss last time.

Student: . . .

LS: The eradication of the will to power would be mere nothingness, because even suicide wouldn't do. Nietzsche would say of man that it is still easier to will nothingness than not to will. In a certain modification, the will to power would still be there. The only thing which can be called an overcoming of the will to power is the will to power turning against itself, and this is, in the highest form, the attempt to know: not to imprint one's fact on what is, but to let it be what it is and to see what it is. This is the attitude of men of intellectual fortitude, the sublime ones. Nietzsche regarded this as the highest form of spirituality which is still possible prior to this radical change.

In order not to misunderstand Nietzsche, you must only think of the alternative which he opposed. According to Nietzsche, nature is will to power. One could say that according to Plato, nature is *erōs*. Both say becoming and perishing as distinguished from anything eternal. But what is the essence of this becoming? For Plato it is aspiration toward something. If you think of Aristotle, what is nature is form in act. Nietzsche rejects this. Nietzsche would say there cannot be an entelechy, there cannot be a form which in its operation is *the* perfection of the being. For him, on the highest level this nature means overcoming: there cannot be a peak. The difficulty in Nietzsche is of course that he must reserve a peak at the end, the high noon. Aristotle starts from the notion that there must be an order of beings. What I contend is that Nietzsche is driven back to that: Nietzsche believes only that his notion of the will to power can make intelligible the genesis of form insofar as there is always a transcending of a given stage. He has to find a formula for nature which accounts for "evolution."

The other question is whether it is possible to assert the superiority of one stage of human history to an earlier stage without having a standard outside of the progressive process. The historicist thinkers try to maintain the notion of progress while rejecting a transcendence of aim. In the case of Hegel and Marx, this is supplied by the contradictions: if you have a given stage of history, you start by contradiction. Now either there is simply a decay, or if it remains alive (this nation, or class, or whatever), there will be a higher stage in which the contradiction is solved. It is higher because it has solved a problem which was insoluble in the lower stage. In physics, for example, present-day physics is regarded as higher than Newtonian physics, not because they possess *the* truth nor because they possess a clearer notion of the ideal goal of physics, but simply because they know all of Newton, they can solve his problems, and can in addition solve problems which he could not solve. Nietzsche rejects this idea of contradiction because this in itself would lead to the possibility of a final stage in which all contradictions are resolved. Nietzsche's primary intention is to find a formula which permits the infinity of progress, and that means that at every stage of man there is something in man by virtue of which he transcends it for the mere fact that it is given. In a later stage of the argument, he says that there must be a peak, otherwise there cannot be truth. How does this help in understanding the genesis of man, and how far would this enable one even to say that man is higher than the brutes? Could not one say that, taking the will to power on a subhuman level: Is not man from that point of view more powerful than all the brutes? In other words, he beats them at their own game and therefore, taking the standards of lions and tigers, man, by virtue of his intellect, has more power than the subintellect . . .

The interesting thing in Nietzsche is, I think, that he raises the modern notion of human suffering to the highest pitch . . . I believe that in the problem of the past, of time, is concealed the whole problem of nature. The difficulty Nietzsche has when he identifies nature with the will to power is to explain nature as a not-willed order, as an order which is not intelligible, which is due to acts of the will to power: let us say of the character of the will to power itself.

I have tried to show how Nietzsche somehow succeeds, without obvious internal contradiction, to solve the question of knowledge and the question of nature. This does not mean that it is true; it means simply that the immediate and massive objections are not immediately justified. We must turn to the difficulty which Nietzsche himself saw and which is discussed in the speech "On Redemption." This difficulty leads him to the doctrine of the eternal return. Nietzsche thinks that the only difficulty to which his doctrine is exposed is solved by the doctrine of the eternal return. We must see whether this is justified, and secondly, if not, what is the obstacle.

9 Greek Philosophy and the Bible; Nature and History

Zarathustra, Part 2, 20–22

Leo Strauss: I would like to repeat a part of my argument of last time because it is of some difficulty. Nietzsche's doctrine of the will to power, I said, differs from earlier philosophies not only in substance but in its mode as well, for the earlier philosophers conceived of themselves as contemplative, as grasping what is; and in particular, what is—this substance—was thought to be the mind. They conceived of themselves as expressions of full self-consciousness of the mind. But for Nietzsche, contemplative knowledge is inferior to creative knowledge. I remind you of his similes: the moon, contemplative knowledge, in contradistinction to the sun. The highest form of knowledge is light-giving and life-giving knowledge. This is the creation of superior men, of their free project rooted in their fundamental will, in their selves. If this is so, if all previous philosophies were mistaken in thinking that they had grasped the truth independent of this, but that these philosophers were actually projecting their selves, there is of necessity a variety of such creations.

Now Nietzsche's first suggestion is this. All knowledge, as he puts it, is perspectivity. There is not *the* perspective: all knowledge is relative to a specific perspective, but there are narrower and broader perspectives. Nietzsche's own doctrine of the will to power is meant to correspond to the best or broadest perspective which has emerged hitherto, but he is compelled to advance to the assertion that his perspective is not only the broadest perspective hitherto but *the* broadest perspective, the final perspective, the absolute perspective. This absoluteness can be established only by the fact that the essence of life or being has now for the first time been grasped, that essence being the will to power. The absoluteness of the perspective is established by the fact that life has now for the first time become conscious of itself, that it knows now what it truly is. There is then in Nietzsche's doctrine a coincidence of the creative act by virtue of which he posits the will to power and of self-consciousness of the creative act, and therewith of self-consciousness of the essence of life. Nietzsche knows that he is the creator of this doctrine, but creation is not only a peculiarity of Nietzsche or any other thinker, creativity is the essence of life itself. Life itself can be understood only through its peak. At the peak of life, the most spiritual will to power is philosophy.

Nietzsche's doctrine, I said, is a coincidence of imprinting his stamp on what is and at the same time recognizing this stamp. His poetry, his self-expression, and his wooing the truth are ultimately the same, although the tension between his poetry and his wooing the truth remain on every level of his thought and being except the highest. This coincidence is very difficult to understand, but on the other hand, it is important to see that this is not merely a crazy notion of a man who finally went insane but that there is a necessity for this view, and we must wonder whether we have a better solution. I will explain that. The negative premise of Nietzsche's understanding of his knowledge and ultimately of all knowledge is this: there is no pure mind. This old Platonic-Aristotelian assumption is rejected by him. But if there is no pure mind, cognition must be understood as a function of life, a function of something which is not mind or reason or ego, but deeper. Thus it follows that the understanding of the whole is on the highest level a projection of the self.

Let me state what Nietzsche is driving at somewhat differently, and later on contrast it with the view which is most popular today. Philosophy is knowledge of what is. It must be, in the last resort, understanding of all beings in the light of the highest being. That was the traditional view of philosophy. It must be understanding of all beings in the light of the highest being, because otherwise the highest would be reduced to the lowest, which is the characteristic thesis of materialism. But the highest being according to Nietzsche is not God but man. Now man changes by virtue of his creative acts; therefore if we want to understand what is, we cannot possibly leave it at looking at the essence of man. There is no essence of man, but we must look at man in his changes. Differently stated, the various philosophies which have existed correspond to the variety of cultures. That means, however, that there are many truths, as many truths as there are cultures. The variety of philosophies corresponding to the variety of selves is only a modification of this view; it is not fundamentally different. Now once one becomes aware of the relativity of philosophies to life, be it the cultures or the self, one must be aware of the fact that cognition in the highest sense is creation. But this historical insight is final and one; hence the corresponding creative act following the historical insight, the creative act proportional to the historical insight, can be only one such act as *the* final creation.

These things may surely seem to be fantastic to positivists, and positivism is the most powerful force in academic life today. The question which one must address to positivism is this. Positivism claims to be an understanding of knowledge, especially of the highest form of knowledge— i.e., of science—and philosophy is being reduced to an understanding of science as the highest form of knowledge. Positivism surely doesn't admit a pure mind so that science would be the actuality of the pure mind; it must conceive of science as a function of a certain organism, the human organism. It must also conceive of science as a historical phenomenon. If this is taken seriously, it follows that the scientific view of the whole is one view among a variety of such views. With what right can the scientific view claim to be superior to the other views? Because it is truer. But does not positivism define truth on the basis of scientific method? Is then the truth of the scientific worldview not circular? Positivism cannot say that the scientific view is superior because it is better, for no scientific value judgments are possible. Science, positivistically understood, cannot answer the question: Why science? What is the meaning of science? For example, there was an article in the *American Political Science Review* in which McClosky says that conservatives are backward people, implying that liberals are progressive and healthy people.[1] There is a connection between conservatism and obscurantism, and liberalism and science. This is an implicit attempt to prove the goodness of science. I don't want to go into the empirical correctness of McClosky's thesis, but you see the difficulty: science is identical with or at least essential to mental health. Once he says this, he admits objective value judgments and contradicts the basic principle of his position—or science is merely the preference of some fellows and "superstition" or nonscience is the preference of others. The question of the goodness of science cannot be answered. If this is so, the choice of science is from the point of view of science a groundless choice. To understand the choice, we cannot possibly have recourse to scientific psychology, for scientific psychology explains the choice of science on the basis of the choice of science. The ultimate phenomenon at which we would arrive by starting from the positivistic notion is an abyss of freedom, which as an abyss cannot be understood but only pointed to, and that is reduced to a simple formula: existentialism.

Now as for Nietzsche, the speech about the abyss must be mindful of the fact that man, however radically distinguished from the brutes, is an animal. There must be then a formula, a necessarily enigmatic formula, which comprises all living beings, all beings, and this formula is the will to power. Nietzsche's problem, which is underlying all these immense difficulties, arises from what one may call historicism, from the enmeshed and real insight into the essentially historical character of all thought. In trying to meet these difficulties, Nietzsche became entangled in certain fundamental difficulties which led later thinkers not to a return to prehistoricism but to suggestions entirely different from Nietzsche's, although akin to them ultimately. I shall speak of this later because this is exactly what existentialism amounts to: an attempt to free Nietzsche's critique of all earlier thought from certain apparent relapses into a universal doctrine. But first let me come back to the difficulty of the position as it was felt by Nietzsche.

Student: . . .

LS: There is indeed a stratum of objective knowledge which is in principle unaffected by historical change. Nietzsche's argument in many places allows for the alternative of objective knowledge which is essentially incomplete and not life-giving. But what he is driving at is an ultimate unity of the truth. Science rests on certain principles which it can never establish, which it presupposes. To mention only the most massive one: the principle of causality. A deeper inspection of the history of science shows that there is a great variety of such hypotheses and even a sequence of such hypotheses, a history of the fundamental premises of human thought, a history of "systems of categories." If you say science works, the other systems also work. Science works according to its criteria of working: steady progress and steady refining of its methods. But why is this a necessary criterion? Positivists cannot answer these questions. There was a time where people said this magic science didn't have any effect. If one enlarges this simple commonsensical consideration, one arrives at the view that science is a human effort by which men can reliably predict, and this concern with prediction must be understood as required for the needs of men. That was the older view.

When Nietzsche opposes the will to power to the will to life, the will to life would never make intelligible the concern with overcoming, transcending, which is most visible on the highest level of human life— which according to Nietzsche is ultimately the only way you can account for evolution. If a man develops a new theory, even in science, there is some value. The present theories are not quite sufficient; he must invent something. What about the status of these so-called creative acts? Surely they will be submitted to certain tests. Nietzsche would also admit this; therefore he can call the will to power a hypothesis, but there is this difference. Since it is a doctrine regarding man, the proper test is not in a laboratory: since Nietzsche calls men to a greater effort, tests can only be given by life. Nietzsche talks of experiment, in German, *Versuch*. But *Versuch*, experiment, is in German almost *Versuchung*, temptation.[2] The true experiment of the doctrine would be whether it can be lived upon. Nietzsche would grant that any laboratory test of present-day man would not concern the possibility of the superman, because that possibility has not been tested. The fact of the matter is that we cannot do away with the simple old-fashioned notion of knowledge, of truth, which in certain severe modifications lives on in modern science.

How do we get higher notions of life? Man was originally not much better than an ape. How come we have a much richer understanding of time? Not because there is a tendency in man as man toward perfection which is determined by his nature. Nietzsche's answer would be that he is the heir of a very great tradition, the Greek and the biblical tradition. Man has become much more than an ape could possibly be by creative acts. He begins by remembering the great tradition, but the molders of morality eventually outlived that morality. This cannot be anticipated at the beginning, because you cannot know the outcome, and then certain individuals, i.e., Napoleon and Goethe, show a new possibility of man which never existed before. Nietzsche tries to get a coherent picture of this new possibility. In other words, the historical consciousness enters into the recognition of good. Nietzsche says that everything good is inherited, which means that everything good is acquired. Man does not have a natural gift in the sense that he has those imposed on him by nature, nor are there any goals dictated to him by his own reason. All such goals originate in creative acts, in acts which could not possibly be anticipated before they were made. There is no teleology, and therefore Nietzsche starts from this accumulated evidence which in its present form is in a state of decay. The peaks of former creations are now seen by him as insufficient for man, who has been thoroughly molded. Up to now, all societies have been partial societies, however large they may have been, but now man is confronted with the task of becoming the ruler of the earth in a more strict sense, namely, that the human race has a unity and will have to rule. This radical change in the situation of man is greater than the transition from the so-called city-states to the national state, because in all these other cases there was always an enemy outside, and this is insignificant compared to the emergence of a single society. For this, all previous knowledge is insufficient. The fundamental disproportion between rationality used through insight and the complete absence of reason regarding the foundation is surely a fundamental defect. The view that the historical consciousness can never reach the horizon of man as man—the alleged awareness that we cannot transcend a specific historical horizon—is today very common. The official positivistic view is that science is somehow exempt from historicism, whereas values are not. The question is whether science can escape that flux of history.

For Nietzsche there was a peak from which man has fallen ever since, and that was early Greece, Greece prior to Socrates. But that is only part of the story. He polemically overstated his own "completeness." As you have seen in the *Zarathustra*, however, there is something wholly alien to the Greeks—loving man for the sake of God—and this is the highest flight of man hitherto, as he says. What does this mean? The love of man for the sake of something superior to man. There is no valid reason, no pattern, and yet at a certain moment a problem presents itself. Now, for the first time, man understands that ideas are creations. Therefore, from this moment on the final value system is possible. Looking back, this is the peak. One can try to reconstruct in a given way how this meeting of Greek thought and Christianity emerged in Nietzsche's solution . . .

The difference between Hegel and Nietzsche in this respect is this: For Hegel the final understanding follows the completion of history. The perfect society is followed by Hegel's understanding of this society and history, i.e., by the understanding of the completion of the creative acts. For Nietzsche the height of self-consciousness precedes the point of view. Therefore there is an open future in Nietzsche and Marx; there is no open future in Hegel.

Student: . . .

LS: Let us reread the last three paragraphs of the first part of *Zara-thustra*.

Reader: And that is the great noon when man stands in the middle of his way between beast and overman and celebrates his way to the evening as his highest hope: for it is the way to a new morning.

Then will he who goes under bless himself for being one who goes over and beyond; and the sun of his knowledge will stand at high noon for him.

"*Dead are all gods: now we want the overman to live*"—on that great noon, let this be our last will.

Thus spoke Zarathustra.[3]

LS: From the last part it follows that at the high noon the superman is willed, not yet there. Taking these temporal designations, we would have to say man's way to the evening is his highest hope. But man's highest hope is the superman; therefore the superman has to be located in the evening. The evening is followed by a night, surely, and the night is followed by a new morning. What does he mean by that? If there is a peak and then a descent—the complete end of all possible history, the destruction of the human race—[then the new morning is the] eternal return. Nietzsche has this great difficulty: all futurists, meaning most modern men living in the expectation of a future of the human race, do not face the question that this future, however glorious it may be, will be followed by the destruction of the human race, according to what the science on which the future is based says. Nietzsche tries to solve the problem by eternal return. That means a will to the future in one direction, which is at once a will to an ever-further future which is no longer that of the superman but that of the return of the past. The eternal return is Nietzsche's solution to that difficulty, of which he was aware.

First let me describe this difficulty in a very provisional way, on the basis of what I said last time about the kinship of Nietzsche's concept of the will to power to the concept of growth. Both concepts have one thing in common. They are distinguished from ordinary progressivism by the following fact. Progressivism may mean a concern with the progress of the mind and progress of institutions, impersonal progress, but Nietzsche is concerned with the individual. Let us think of the growth first. He who says growth also says (whether he admits it or not) decay, perishing, death. If he wants to be serious about his belief in growth, he cannot evade that and regard it as a kind of accident—a traffic accident, one might say, and traffic marches on. But what is needed, precisely on this basis, is a meditation on death, not merely meditation on life. At the beginning of modern times, Spinoza opposed the traditional meditation on death and tried to replace it with a meditation on life.[4] But now, when we speak of growth, we must again have a meditation on death. One can say provisionally that Nietzsche's meditation on death is his doctrine of eternal return. But if this doctrine is inadequate as a meditation on death—and I believe one can say it is because it teaches the eternity of life—then one must find a more consistent and worked-out meditation on death on a Nietzschean basis, and that is existentialism. The first clear reference to eternal return occurs in the speech "On Redemption" in the second part, but we know there was an indication of it at the end of the first part, in the passage we just read. Now this speech, "On Redemption," starts with a presentation of human defects. But more radically stated: All men have been and are hitherto fragments. This fragmentariness is to be overcome and would be overcome by the superman, who from this point of view would be the universal man. In other words, as Nietzsche also puts it there: Hitherto chance ruled; now the conquest of chance will be possible. But after Nietzsche has made these suggestions, there is apparently a sudden change: not the conquest of fragmentariness and chance, but the redemption of fragmentariness and chance. This redemption does not consist in the conquest of chance in that you would say the conquest of chance has been made possible by chance, but redemption consists in the willing of the fragmentariness, the affirmation of fragmentariness, the affirmation of chance.

Why is this so? Nietzsche speaks here in the sequel about the essential limitation of the will, of the will to power: the will cannot will the past as past. The will can of course will things which were in the past, but past is the fundamental character of time: time passes. The will is impotent regarding time, it rebels against time. This rebellion is identical with the spirit of revenge. Nietzsche says here that all previous thought of the highest order was characterized by the spirit of revenge: the revenge on time, on pastness, perishability. Because all previous thought culminated in the conjecture of something timeless, imperishable, unchangeable, eternal, in order to escape from the temporal, all previous thought culminated in conjectural afterworlds. Now, the spirit of revenge had been mentioned before in the section on the tarantula, the egalitarian revolutionary. What is the connection between, say, Plato, a very unegalitarian man, and the egalitarian revolutionary? In the first place, the egalitarian revolution had been guided, in its earlier stages anyway, by rights of man—universal, unchanging, abstract principles whose realization was supposed to lead to a millennium, which millennium in its turn was meant to last forever. As regards the Bible and Plato, the peaks of previous thought, it is characterized by a rebellion against nature as coming into being and perishing as such. Nature, as the realm of coming into being and perishing, is denied because it is transcended with a view to a being which does not come into being, which is in this sense transnatural, supernatural, and therefore degrades the natural. The egalitarian revolution is, in its forms contemporary with Nietzsche, the rebellion against the practically most important characteristic of nature, namely, the order of rank or inequality.

Now let us read the end of that section. "On Redemption," page 253.

Reader: "I led you away from these fables when I taught you, 'The will is a creator.' All 'it was' is a fragment, a riddle, a dreadful accident—until the creative will says to it, 'But thus I willed it.' Until the creative will says to it, 'But thus I will it; thus shall I will it.'

"But has the will yet spoken thus? And when will that happen? Has the will been unharnessed yet from his own folly? Has the will yet become his own redeemer and joy-bringer? Has he unlearned the spirit of revenge and all gnashing of teeth? And who taught him reconciliation with time and something higher than any reconciliation? For that will which is the will to power must will something higher than any reconciliation; but how shall this be brought about? Who could teach him also to will backwards?"[5]

LS: The superman becomes possible through the liberation from the spirit of revenge, from every need for the eternal which is beyond the perishable. This consists in willing the flux: to will the time, to will the past, and that means to will the return of the past. The will ceases to be frustrated when it wills the return of the past. Willing eternal return is the victory of the will, and this highest victory can be the peak of the will. Through liberation from the spirit of revenge, the will becomes properly willed because it is the liberation from that which frustrates will. What we must understand is this: Nietzsche does not abandon the will to the future, he wills the future while willing the past in one act. He says one cannot will the future without willing the past, namely, return to the past. Hegel and Marx also said one cannot will the future without willing the past insofar as the future is not possible if the past had not been as it was, but here Nietzsche means willing the return to the past. We will the future and the past, but that is possible only if there is a circuit. The development of this follows in the third part of the Zarathustra.

Let us read the end of this speech.

Reader: At this point in his speech it happened that Zarathustra suddenly stopped and looked altogether like one who has received a severe shock. Appalled, he looked at his disciples; his eyes pierced their thoughts and the thoughts behind their thoughts as with arrows. But after a little while he laughed again and, pacified, he said: "It is difficult to live with people because silence is so difficult. Especially for one who is garrulous."

Thus spoke Zarathustra.

The hunchback, however, had listened to this discourse and covered his face the while; but when he heard Zarathustra laugh he looked up curiously and said slowly: "But why does Zarathustra speak otherwise to us than to his disciples?"

Zarathustra answered: "What is surprising in that? With hunchbacks one may well speak in a hunchbacked way."

"All right," said the hunchback; "and one may well tell pupils tales out of school. But why does Zarathustra speak otherwise to his pupils than to himself?"[6]

LS: Zarathustra had not spoken of eternal return to his pupils, but to a hunchback one can speak in a hunchback way. And also, what is more important, what the doctrine of eternal return amounts to is affirmation, acceptance of the hunchbacks, and that means of course of the fragments, of man as fragments.

The end of the speech is the natural transition to the next speech, which is called "On Human Prudence." It seems that Zarathustra speaks not only differently to different men, but also to himself. As you see from the title, he calls it not merely prudence but human prudence, which is not a perfect translation of "Von der Menschenklugheit." Prudence, how- ever, occurs also in a nonhuman being in the *Zarathustra*: the serpent, which is the most prudent of the beasts. But the question would be: In what sense is Zarathustra prudent? It is difficult to see but very impor- tant, because what Nietzsche does in writing, or what Zarathustra does in speaking, requires some prudence, as seems to be indicated by the fact that Zarathustra speaks to himself differently than he speaks to his dis- ciples. This is an old question in the history of philosophy. The most obvi- ous difference is indicated in the first section. Zarathustra's prudence has nothing to do with caution. Why this is so we must try to understand. We might find in this connection some answer about the peculiar character of Nietzsche's writing.

10 Eternal Recurrence

Zarathustra, Part 2, 21; Part 3, 1–13

Leo Strauss: I have been asked what the social significance of the teaching of the superman is, and what the meaning of the appeal to creativity is for men who are to live together. In order to answer this question, I suggest that we read a passage in this book on page 314.

Reader: This is my pity for all that is past: I see how all of it is abandoned— abandoned to the pleasure, the spirit, the madness of every generation, which comes along and reinterprets all that has been as a bridge to itself.

A great despot might come along, a shrewd monster who, according to his pleasure and displeasure, might constrain and strain all that is past till it becomes a bridge to him, a harbinger and herald and cockcrow.

This, however, is the other danger and what prompts my further pity: whoever is of the rabble, thinks back as far as the grandfather; with the grandfather, however, time ends.

Thus all that is past and abandoned: for one day the rabble might become master and drown all time in shallow waters.

Therefore, my brothers, a *new nobility* is needed to be the adversary of all rabble and of all that is despotic and to write anew upon new tablets the word "noble."

For many who are noble are needed, and noble men of many kinds, that there may be a nobility. Or as I once said in a parable: "Precisely this is godlike that there are gods, but no God."[1]

LS: I shall not now go into a deeper analysis of this passage, but will limit myself to the most obvious message: the dangers are tyranny, on the one hand; and mass rule, on the other. For Nietzsche, the difference between democracy and mass rule is not important; therefore there is need for a new nobility.

To understand this, let us look for one moment at the discussion of the problem of democracy in the nineteenth century. The most famous statement there is Tocqueville's *Democracy in America*. Tocqueville was a French nobleman who became in a way a traitor to his class: he became convinced of the necessity for accepting democracy. After spending a year in this country, he became satisfied that democracy as a decent thing was possible. The French Revolution had not demonstrated that fact; therefore the American experience was so crucial. But in accepting democracy, Tocqueville contrasted democracy with *the* alternative, the *ancien régime*, the old regime of France, the aristocracy. He compared these two regimes in a detached way. The decision was made not on the grounds of an intrinsic superiority of democracy but on the ground that history, providence, has decided in favor of democracy. Now one of the crucial points in Tocqueville's analysis is what has now become popularized in the name of "other-directedness."[2] People who are guided by what others say, think, and believe, as distinguished from characters who stand on their own feet, is the characteristic of democracy and the danger of democracy, whereas aristocracy, he believed, was much more favorable to the development of rugged individualism. One must keep this in mind to understand Nietzsche.

If you want a simple answer (which, however, is too simple to be true), one could say Nietzsche wrote in the expectation of a new nobility—he was sure that the old nobility was completely finished—which then could rule. Let us assume for one moment that this is what Nietzsche was driving at. All the elitism around the 1900s somehow stems from Nietzsche's thought. The question becomes how to get this new nobility. Nietzsche was not concerned with this question, because he was sure that the only way to get it would be by the awakening of individuals willing to be individuals in this strict sense. Those, however, who were closer to political action had to think of practical means, and out of that came fascism and National Socialism. There were of course also other considerations, for example, economic problems about which Nietzsche didn't say anything to speak of.

There is another question, which I would like to state as follows. Nietzsche is not primarily concerned with the political problem, and this has both its merits and its demerits. I will now speak of the merits. Nietzsche thought it impossible to find a purely political solution to the problem. This would mean, for example, an institutional solution. The political problem is for him a moral problem, and one can perhaps say—with a misuse of the term which is today fashionable, although not altogether misleading—with a religious solution, in spite of his atheism. In Nietz-sche's opinion, a society is not possible without a culture of its own. A culture requires ultimately some commitment, which we may loosely call a religion. This is Nietzsche's chief concern: a regeneration of man. What this would mean in terms of institutions, etc., is of no concern to him.

I would like to illustrate this. Let us take such a trivial everyday prob-lem as juvenile delinquency. People think about it and try to do something about it, but it could very well be that all their thinking and all their devices are absolutely useless. It could be that juvenile delinquency is con-nected with the deep crisis of our society as a whole. It could be true that this phenomenon is due to a loss of hope in the younger generation, or to the absence of great public tasks which arouse public spirit. Now if this is so, it is obvious that juvenile delinquency cannot be treated in isolation, and a regeneration of the society as a whole would be necessary. Whether the palliatives are gentle or tough is a very secondary question compared to the question of society as a whole. What to do in such a situation—not the immediate social action, which might very well be useless—but regeneration of society? Now enlarge this problem, which has no parallel in any earlier crisis; then you understand why Nietzsche was so vague and indefinite regarding the practical problems.

In our reading of the *Zarathustra*, we have now reached the center of Nietzsche's teaching, and that is the teaching of eternal return. According to Nietzsche himself, this is the center. Everything depends on it. Why? Let us remind ourselves of the context within which the doctrine of the eternal return is suggested. Again, I return to the beginning: the death of God and the possibility of the superman; secondly, the death of God and the new understanding of both man and the whole to which man belongs. This new understanding is expressed in the thesis that nature or life is will to power in opposition to *erōs* in the Platonic sense, as striving toward given ends, unchanging ends, transcendent ends. The will to power gen-erates the ends—the will to power in contradistinction to the modern alternative, the will to mere life, because the will to life does not account for the upward thrust, for the overcoming of the lower, for the creativity in evolution. Now the superman is the highest form of the will to power, and therefore the two notions belong together.

I must now turn to the subject of philosophy. Philosophy is according to Nietzsche the most spiritual will to power. I refer again to *Beyond Good and Evil*, aphorism 9, where Nietzsche says what happened to the Stoics still happens today as soon as a philosophy begins to have faith in itself:

"It always creates the world in its own image; it cannot do otherwise, for philosophy *is* this tyrannical desire; it is the most spiritual will to power, to 'creation of the world,' to the *causa prima.*"³ Why is philosophy the will to the *causa prima*, to the first cause? Because the meaning, the articulation, of the merely given is the first cause of any particular meaning, and philosophy as such an attempt is the first cause. Now philosophy is the most spiritual will to power. In its highest form hitherto, the most spiritual form of the will to power has been animated by the spirit of revenge, i.e., by revenge against becoming and perishing, against fragmentariness and defectiveness. Out of this spirit the philosophers conjectured something eternal, unchanging, perfect, and final. This means they try to run away from the temporal, the changing, the fragmentary and never completed. Nietzsche's philosophy of the will to power is the highest form of the most spiritual will to power because it is the first philosophy which is free from the spirit of revenge as he defined it. It does not rebel against becoming and perishing but accepts it and affirms it. It affirms it infinitely. This infinite affirmation of becoming and perishing is the belief in eternal return: no end of becoming, no end of perishing. Nietzsche's philosophy is at the same time the highest act of the will to power and therefore the creation of a worldview, yet at the same time, it is the self-consciousness of the will to power. Therefore, it is at the same time creative and purely cognitive. The will to power is at the same time willed and independent of being willed. In this doctrine, the "I will" is transformed into or overcome by the "I am," the subject to which he had alluded in the first speech, "Of the Three Metamorphoses."

Now I would like to explain this a bit more. This doctrine may be paradoxical and may even seem absurd, but we must see what drove Nietzsche to that. What drove him to that were not particular idiosyncrasies of that individual who later became insane, but premises which he shared with most of his contemporaries and most of the academic community today. In the first place, the premise is: Knowledge is creation and not sense perception. Sense perception must be interpreted. This interpretation of sense perception is not based on a mental perception, say, of forms or ideas, but creation—in present-day language, logical constructs. It is an uglier word than creation, but on the other hand it is proper because there is creativity in these logical constructs. The second premise, you might say, is the old Kantian view: the understanding prescribes nature its laws. The second view, which is also different from Kant, is of course that there are not *the* categories, *the* values, but there is a historical variety of those categories and values. Today this is a very common view regarding the values, obviously, but even regarding the categories.

Now if we start from these premises the following question arises. It is a fact that there are not *the* categories and *the* values but a historical variety of values, so that you cannot say to begin with that one is preferable to the other. Let us call this historicism. Then the question arises: What is the status of the mind which is aware of that historicism? There is always a mind which creates categories and values, but we are now concerned with a mind which is aware of this fundamental relativity. If this mind is shrunk historically, then the difficulty arises that if there is a transhistorical mind, God knows what it may know in addition to the historicity of human thought. So to be consistent, one is compelled to say that the mind which is aware of historicity is itself historical or within history. The historical consciousness, as the Germans called it, is itself a historical phenomenon. The answer to this question is that the historical consciousness belongs indeed to history but to a privileged place, because it is the self-consciousness of history or it is the self-consciousness of the ground of historical change.

Let us take as a simple example Marx's dialectical materialism. Dialectical materialism claims that it reveals the grounds of all change and therefore also the ground of all categories and all values. The ways of production are the grounds of all historical change; then there is a superstructure, and in this superstructure we find the categories and values. Now at all times the categories and values of people reflected their specific situations—say, of the feudal nobility—but each claimed to be the truth, the final absolute truth. But they were all wrong. The proletariat is the first class without an ideology, ideology in Marxist language meaning a false view about the whole. The class consciousness of the proletariat is the true consciousness because it is or implies self-consciousness of the historical process as a whole. Yet there is this difficulty. Consciousness according to Marx depends on being; therefore the consciousness of the proletariat depends on the being of the proletariat. Now the proletariat prior to the revolution is not the victorious proletariat. How then can we figure out in advance how the proletariat molded by the victorious revolution will think and therefore be? Hence if dialectical materialism is to be true, it must be the consciousness of a being which is complete prior to the victory of the proletariat. But this being cannot be the proletariat, this being can only be the thinker, i.e., Marx. The self-consciousness of the ground of historical change must be the end of history in the sense that it must be identical with the discovery of *the* categories and *the* value system. I say discovery because previously we did not have a discovery strictly speaking but a creation of categories and values. In Nietzsche's opinion, the whole Marxist notion leads to the last man, and this is due to the fact that for Marxism, Hegelianism is merely a liberation and also the most terrible danger. And in addition, there is no reflection in Marxism about the end of the realm of freedom of the communist society.

For Nietzsche too the historical insight belongs to a privileged place in the historical process because it is the self-consciousness of history. But this means to begin with simply the end of history, for after one knows that all categories and all values are creations, one can no longer create them. This knowledge paralyzes. One can no longer believe in them if one knows that they are creations. The first consequence then is what Nietzsche calls nihilism or, as he expresses it in the *Zarathustra*, everything is empty, everything is the same, everything was. There is no future because there is no longer creativity. How then can there be a future after this self-consciousness of history has been achieved? Answer: if the self-consciousness of the grounds of historical change is itself a creative act, and in fact the highest creative act. The world as seen by Nietzsche *is* by virtue of being willed by Nietzsche. Only in this way can the paralyzing effect of final knowledge be overcome. This willing, namely, eternal return, changes man radically if it is accepted: it changes man from man to superman.

Let me try to state this problem again. Let us start from Plato. In Plato the difference between opinion and knowledge is crucial. Opinion according to Plato has to do with coming into being, and knowledge or science has to do with what is always and unchangeable. This does not mean that there cannot be opinions about the unchangeable. So opinion takes on a broader meaning and means not merely opinion regarding coming into being, but opinion as belonging to coming into being because of its untruth and mere subjectivity. At any rate, from Plato's point of view it follows that there is a variety of opinion as distinguished from the one truth, knowledge, science. This variety of opinion is in one respect finite—in other words, you could arrange them into types of opinions—but in another respect it is infinite. Yet also according to Plato there is not and cannot be any opinion which does not have a grain of truth in it. That is simple to understand. If someone says it is now night, he obviously says an untruth. Yet the statement obviously contains some truth. Is there not such a thing as night? Is there not such a thing as now? So without some

awareness it is absolutely impossible to put together an intelligible statement which is not based on some true events.

Now we will make a big jump to Hegel. We can state Hegel's view as
follows. Hegel also speaks of the opposition between opinion and knowledge. The opinions originate in creative acts, that is to say, the opinions
are not merely imperfect imitations of the truth. But most important,
the sequence of fundamental opinions, if that sequence is understood, is
knowledge. The variety of opinions which goes through the intellectual
history of mankind is, if properly understood, knowledge. Why is this so?
In Hegel's phrase, the substance is the subject, meaning what is truly is the
thinking subject—so much so that even a stone is intelligible as stone only
as the other of the thinking object, that is to say, only in reference to the
thinking object. There is knowledge or science, then, after the completion
of history. What produces these opinions in that sequence is reason, but
a reason which does not know itself. So in Hegel the ground of historical
change is reason, not a mixture of reason and unreason as it is in Plato.

Now let me describe an alternative which developed out of Hegel,
partly in opposition to Hegel, which is somehow presupposed by Nietzsche. History is not complete, contrary to what Hegel said. From this it
follows that the historical process is not rational, because it can be known
to be rational only if it is completed. What produces opinions is therefore
not reason but something else. The ultimate fact on the highest level is
the creativity of the individual. From this it follows that there cannot be
the knowledge, *the* science, *the* truth, but only knowledges. Therefore, we
cannot find science in the strict sense in which Plato and Hegel meant it.
What we find as the first premises of any understanding are fundamental
opinions, which have no higher status than opinions. Every knowledge or
science rests on unevident premises which only appear to be evident to
specific men. Greek science was based on certain premises which appeared
evident to the Greeks, which are no longer evident to us—similarly, our
science. But in our science, we cannot possibly know it because we are
under the spell of our prejudices. However this may be, this awareness of
the historical character of our premises is knowledge, is science. There is
no relativity about that. The highest awareness of which man is capable
is then indeed knowledge but only in the form of the self-consciousness
of the creative subject.

Nietzsche says: If this awareness is not linked to a new creative act,
nihilism inevitably follows. I remind you in this context of a distinction
which Nietzsche made in a passage we read between the knower and the

noble. What the knower knows can be interpreted basically as noble, and it must be interpreted as noble if there is to be a future. This new creative act must transform the nihilistic truth into the most life-giving truth. In other words, the true self-consciousness of history, of the fact that every human belief is condemned to perish, cannot precede the highest creative act. It must follow the highest creative act; therefore the true self-consciousness of the historical process is the recognition of the will to power. To state it differently, if the self-consciousness of the grounds of history were not a concomitant of a creative act, there would be a radical disproportion between history itself and the historian of philosophy. History means creativity. The historian and philosopher would then be a mere onlooker—a mere moon, in Nietzsche's symbolism. If there is such a disproportion, the historian or philosopher is not himself creative, whereas what he has to do to be creative is to understand it. He could do this as little as a nonmusical man can be a historian of music. To repeat, the self-consciousness of the historical process, i.e., the highest form of knowledge, must be a concomitant of a creative act, the final and highest creative act.

Now we should continue to read. We began last time the speech "On Human Prudence," on page 254. In the preceding speech, you may recall, was the first explicit statement of eternal return. Now Nietzsche returns to human problems. He speaks first of human prudence; that means the prudence which Nietzsche or Zarathustra uses in his intercourse with men.

Reader: Not the height but the precipice is terrible. That precipice where the glance plunges *down* and the hand reaches *up*. There the heart becomes giddy confronted with its double will. Alas, friends, can you guess what is my heart's double will?

This, this is *my* precipice and my danger, that my glance plunges into the height and that my hand would grasp and hold on to the depth. My will clings to man; with fetters I bind myself to man because I am swept up toward the overman; for that way my other will wants to go. And therefore I live blind among men as if I did not know them, that my hand might not wholly lose its faith in what is firm.[4]

LS: The affirmation of the past, of the fragmentariness of man, is the crucial implication of the doctrine of the eternal return. In other words, the will to the superman is inseparable from the will to man, just as the will to the future is inseparable from the will to the past. There is a double will. The danger to Zarathustra is the superman. Therefore he seeks support in men and therefore he must be blind to men, because if he were to see man as he is, he would suffer.[5] Now in the case of the precipice, the danger is to look down, and one finds support in the hand reaching up. In the case of the superman, Zarathustra looks up and finds support in his hand reaching down. He cannot possibly look down; he must be blind to men. Why does he need support? The hope for the superman rests on man, but on something given in man and from man. Zarathustra is prudent for the sake of the superman. Now let us read the sequel.

> Reader: I do not know you men: this darkness and consolation are often spread around me. I sit at the gateway, exposed to every rogue, and I ask: who wants to deceive me? That is the first instance of my human prudence, that I let myself be deceived in order not to be on guard against deceivers. Alas, if I were on guard against men, how could man then be an anchor for my ball? I should be swept up and away too easily. This providence lies over my destiny, that I must be without caution.[6]

LS: This prudence of Zarathustra has nothing whatever to do with caution, for if Zarathustra were on his guard against men, if he distrusted men, he would forsake men. Therefore, he deliberately deceives himself about men. In the sequel he speaks of a number of prudences. The second prudence is gazed by looking at the comedy played by the vain man, the third prudence by looking at evil men—the comedy of the good and the just, who are afraid of the evil men and therefore condemn the evil men. The main point, which we will perhaps take up later in a different context, is caution. The prudence of Zarathustra, whatever that may mean, has nothing to do with his caution. He does not keep anything back out of caution.

The next speech, the last of the second part, "The Stillest Hour." It appears that Zarathustra is not yet prepared to say his word, which means the doctrine of eternal return. He is still afraid of man mocking him; he is still ashamed. His hesitation is proportionate to the gravity of the doctrine.

Then we turn to the third part, which begins with the speech called "The Wanderer." Let us read on page 265.

> Reader: "You are going your way to greatness: here nobody shall sneak after you. Your own foot has effaced the path behind you, and over it there is written: impossibility.

"And if you now lack all ladders, then you must know how to climb on your own head: how else would you want to climb upward? On your own head and away over your own heart! Now what was gentlest in you must still become the hardest. He who has always spared himself much will in the end become sickly of so much consideration. Praised be what hardens! I do not praise the land where butter and honey flow.

"One must learn to *look away* from oneself in order to see *much*: this hardness is necessary to every climber of mountains."[7]

LS: Zarathustra speaks here and elsewhere of himself, and these passages are to a considerable extent untranslatable.

Now what is the meaning of these remarks? He speaks of himself, to use a slightly misleading word, as the genius. He presents not only the teaching but himself as the teacher. Those who may accept his teaching do not yet have the experience of the teacher at the moment of his inspiration. Yet that experience of the teacher, which only he has, is a part of the teaching because it is the teaching of the experiences which only the greatest men can have. Every psychology is fundamentally defective if it does not take such experiences into account. I would like to read to you a passage from *Ecce Homo*. I found this in Barrett's *Irrational Man*, page 187 and following. I read to you the introductory paragraph from this book: "Nietzsche himself describes the process of inspiration by which he wrote the *Zarathustra*,[8] and his description makes it clear beyond question that we are in the presence here of an extraordinary release of and invasion by the unconscious."[9] That can be said, provided we are perfectly open-minded as to what the unconscious is. "Can anyone at the end of the nineteenth century have any distinct notion of what poets of a more vigorous age meant by inspiration? If not, I would like to describe it. The notion of revelation describes the condition quite simply, by which I mean that something profoundly convulsive and disturbing suddenly becomes visible and audible with indescribable definiteness and exactness. There is an ecstasy whose terrific tension is sometimes released by a flood of tears."[10] Those of you who have not considered this problem should read something of what mystics say of their experience. Nietzsche's statements here remind of mystical statements — it is indeed an atheistic mysticism and a mystical experience, one might say, of life.

Let us now turn to the next speech, which is in a way the most important speech of the whole work: "On the Vision and the Riddle." The title is misleading. One would think the subject matter is vision and riddle;

the subject matter, however, is eternal return. The speech deals with what appeared to Zarathustra in a riddle and vision, namely, eternal return, but the title emphasizes the visionary and enigmatic character of Zarathustra's teaching regarding eternal return. This is a subdivided speech. The only other subdivided speech hitherto was "On the Gift-Giving Virtue," the last speech in part 1. But from now on subdivided speeches will become quite frequent. Zarathustra speaks here of the vision of the lonely. What was that? He speaks of it not to his friends and disciples, but to unknown sailors. Let us read the beginning.

Reader: When it got abroad among the sailors that Zarathustra was on board—for another man from the blessed isles had embarked with him—there was much curiosity and anticipation. But Zarathustra remained silent for two days and was cold and deaf from sadness and answered neither glances nor questions. But on the evening of the second day he opened his ears again, although he still remained silent, for there was much that was strange and dangerous to be heard on this ship, which came from far away and wanted to sail even farther. But Zarathustra was a friend of all who travel far and do not like to live without danger. And behold, eventually his own tongue was loosened as he listened, and the ice of his heart broke. Then he began to speak thus:

To you, the bold searchers, researchers, and whoever embarks with cunning sails on terrible seas—to you, drunk with riddles, glad of the twilight, whose soul flutes lure astray to every whirlpool, because you do not want to grope along a thread with cowardly hand; and where you can *guess*, you hate to *deduce*—to you alone I tell the riddle that I *saw*, the vision of the loneliest.[11]

LS: Why does he speak only to unknown sailors? He is a friend of those who do not wish to live without danger, who love riddles, who do not merely deplore that the most important things cannot be proven but rejoice on account of it. Why the joy? If the truth could be proven, it would be alien to life because life is changeable and uncertain. Wisdom would not be akin to life; wisdom must partake of the uncertainty and changeability of life.

In the sequel, Zarathustra describes his way upward.

Reader: Not long ago I walked gloomily through the deadly pallor of dusk—gloomy and hard, with lips pressed together. Not only one sun had set for me. A path that ascended defiantly through stones, malicious, lonely, not cheered by herb or shrub—a mountain path crunched under the defiance of my foot. Striding silently over the mocking clatter of pebbles, crushing the rock that made it slip, my foot forced its way upward. Upward—defying the spirit that drew it downward toward the abyss, the spirit of gravity, my devil and archenemy. Upward—although he sat on me, half dwarf, half mole, lame, making lame, dripping lead into my ear, leaden thoughts into my brain.[12]

LS: Zarathustra takes the way upward. He has therefore gravity. He overcomes the spirit of gravity or heaviness. Now is the spirit of heaviness or gravity the same as the spirit of revenge? In the sequel, the spirit of heaviness is represented by the dwarf and is overcome by courage. This is true because the spirit of heaviness is rooted in death or fear of death. The overcoming of this fear consists in really accepting death and all phases of life, once, and twice, and infinitely often, i.e., eternal return. From this it follows that the fear of death and all lesser fears are lack of courage; concern with security or certainty leads to debasement.

But is not the spirit of revenge the origin of the conjecturing of the unchangeable? Not in every respect, I believe. The spirit of revenge is compatible with the jump into faith; the spirit of heaviness as such is not. And it is also important to realize that Zarathustra presents himself as threatened by the spirit of heaviness, not by the spirit of revenge. As long as the spirit of heaviness prevails, death is the end, or else escape from death into the deathless, the eternal. Time is irreversible from birth to death. Once the spirit of heaviness is overcome, there is a circle of infinitely many deaths of each. Here, as in many other passages, the difficulty of interpreting *Zarathustra* becomes particularly clear . . .

There is a nice statement, which is unfortunately too long to read, by Heinrich Heine, in his book *Shakespeare's Maidens and Women*. At the end he gives a very famous theory by the French philosopher Guizot, from which he quotes. (I deliberately use Heine because he had a certain influence on Nietzsche regarding this lightness and heaviness.) Heine calls this man the elephant, and says the elephant is right. The soul of Shakespearean comedy is in the gay, butterfly humor, in which he flits from flower to flower, seldom touching the ground of reality. And now, after having stated this and agreed with it, Heine gives a description of the comedy in the following dream. What he means to say is that this dream truly conveys what Shakespearean comedy is, whereas the analysis is as remote from the comedy as a statement by a professor can possibly be. He has a vision of Venice somewhere on the sea in a gondola, and "A lovely lady who stood by the rudder of one of the barks cried to me in passing, 'Is it not true that you have the definition of Shakespearean comedy?' I know not whether I answered 'Yes,' but at that instant the beautiful woman dipped her hand into the water, sprinkled it into my face, so there was general laughter, and I awoke."[13] What Heine means here is this: there are experiences which as such cannot be expressed in the language of the *logos*.

Generally stated, how do we know that the element of the *logos*, of the clear and demonstrable speech, is compatible with the most important truths? Shakespearean comedy may be a minor subject that applies to the highest things. Now philosophy in the traditional sense presupposes that the element of this *logos* is compatible with the most important truths. But is this presupposition justified? This is Nietzsche's question and therefore the character of his own presentation. It is obvious that such a question is not a skeptical question, i.e., denying the possibility of knowing the truth. Compare this to a very popular view today according to which the myth in Plato appears to be distinguished from his reasoning, the *logos*, and indicates the limits of reason. Especially people say that the truth about the soul is presented by Plato in myths, and therefore Plato had a similar view that the most important truth is not susceptible of "logical presentation." But we must not forget, in Plato there is something which is always, namely, the ideas, which is beyond the soul and beyond the becoming and changing; and from Plato's point of view poetry is therefore only imitation and secondary as compared to philosophy.[14] For Nietzsche, the unchanging, the sempiternal have disappeared. Is it not therefore a necessity that poetry or something like poetry, visions, and riddles should take the place of philosophic arguments? That is what he means by the spirit of lightness as opposed to the spirit of heaviness. The spirit of heaviness tries to prevent the upward way, and the only way in which he can overcome this is through courage.

In the sequel, in the second speech,[15] he develops the vision itself. Let us read on page 269.

Reader: "Stop, dwarf!" I said. "It is I or you! But I am the stronger of us two: you do not know my abysmal thought. *That* you could not bear!"

Then something happened that made me lighter, for the dwarf jumped from my shoulder, being curious; and he crouched on a stone before me. But there was a gateway just where we had stopped.

"Behold this gateway, dwarf!" I continued. "It has two faces. Two paths meet here; no one has yet followed either to its end. This long lane stretches back for an eternity. And the long lane out there, that is another eternity. They contradict each other, these paths; they offend each other face to face; and it is here at this gateway that they come together. The name of the gateway is inscribed above: 'Moment.' But whoever would follow one of them, on and on, farther and farther—do you believe, dwarf, that these paths contradict each other eternally?"

"All that is straight lies," the dwarf murmured contemptuously. "All truth is crooked; time itself is a circle."

"You spirit of gravity," I said angrily, "do not make things too easy for yourself! Or I shall let you crouch where you are crouching, lamefoot; and it was I that carried you to this *height.*

"Behold," I continued, "this moment! From this gateway, Moment, a long eternal lane leads *backward*: behind us lies an eternity. Must not whatever *can* walk have walked on this lane before? Must not whatever *can* happen have happened, have been done, have passed by before?"[16]

LS: What is the implication of this? Infinite time, the finite number of combinations must all have been completed, and therefore there cannot be anything new. The question of course is: Why is the number of combinations finite? In infinite time there could be an infinite number of combinations. The answer is: force is necessary. Let us look at page 299.

Reader: Did my wisdom secretly urge it, my laughing, wide-awake day-wisdom which mocks all "infinite worlds"? For it speaks: "Wherever there is force, *number* will become mistress: she has more force."[17]

LS: Keep this in mind. This is the absolutely crucial premise: there is a finite number of combinations due to the fact that any force, including the force of the universe itself, must be finite.

Reader: "And if everything has been there before—what do you think, dwarf, of this moment? Must not this gateway too have been there before? And are not all things knotted together so firmly that this moment draws after it *all* that is to come? Therefore—itself too? For whatever *can* walk—in this long lane out *there* too, it *must* walk once more.

"And this slow spider, which crawls in the moonlight, and this moonlight itself, and I and you in the gateway, whispering together, whispering of eternal things—must not all of us have been there before? And return and walk in that other lane, out there, before us, in this long dreadful lane—must we not eternally return?"[18]

LS: In more concrete, cosmological language: this coming from the amoeba to the superman and beyond to the end of the human race, and then a new becoming—and this, eternally. As you see from this formulation, Nietzsche means this very literally: eternal return of the same. There were some ancient philosophers who taught eternal return, but they assumed that chance played such a role that in these specific matters there would be no eternal return of the same. The principle of Nietzsche is the finiteness of possible combinations, contrasted with the infinity of time.

Let us first conclude the discussion of this chapter. Zarathustra, after he has this vision, is afraid. Then there is a new vision: he hears the dog barking, and this dog leads him to a shepherd. A terrible snake had crawled into the mouth of the sleeping shepherd. At Zarathustra's urging, the shepherd bites off the head of the snake and then he is liberated and laughing. Zarathustra says he never heard such laughter before. This is the symbol of the emergence of the superman. Not Zarathustra, but the man who comes out of the shepherd—the shepherd being the one who guards the lower, who is about to become a superman—can bear eternal return. But there is a difficulty here. Does he, by biting off the head of the snake, destroy the cycle? Or must the cycle be headless, i.e., equality of all parts? The difference between the peak and the plain must cease to be important in the perspective of the eternal return. That is the paradox. The whole teaching of the superman, the whole teaching regarding creativity, etc., is futuristic, looking out toward completing and redeeming the future, which is the highest peak of mankind. This highest peak requires according to Nietzsche that man reaches a point where the difference between that peak and the lowest beginnings becomes indifferent. From a religious point of view, this is of course easy to understand. From the standpoint beyond history, from the standpoint of eternity, the greatest differences within the human race fade into insignificance. What Nietzsche tries to save for a nonreligious view is this ultimate transcendence beyond the historical process.

Student: Doesn't the doctrine of eternal return cause a determinism which would eliminate the choice between the last man and the superman?

LS: That depends on where you stand. If you take a stand outside, which as a knower you cannot take—let us assume Nietzsche or Zarathustra is absolutely important for the coming of the superman. But was Nietzsche free not to teach the superman? Without going into any other question regarding the status of causality which he is teaching, we simply don't know. Nietzsche is not free in the sense that he could abandon his task. He is constantly tempted to do so, but his fundamental will forces him to go on. This fundamental will is his necessity, his fate.

But let us read one more passage, page 329, paragraph 5.

Reader: "O Zarathustra," the animals said, "to those who think as we do, all things themselves are dancing: they come and offer their hands and laugh and flee—and come back. Everything goes, everything comes back; eternally rolls the wheel of being. Everything dies, everything blossoms again; eternally runs the year of being. Everything breaks, everything is joined anew; eternally the same house of being is built. Everything parts, everything greets every other thing again; eternally the ring of being remains faithful to itself. In every Now, being begins; round every Here rolls the sphere There. The center is everywhere. Bent is the path of eternity."[19]

LS: The fact that this was said in such clear form by the animals and not by man is very important. What Nietzsche has in mind is akin to what someone else called, a hundred years earlier, "the return to nature."[20] Now this living without this future and past is what distinguishes the beasts from man. In a way, men must will, from Nietzsche's point of view, the highest. But at a peak he cannot will anything more than this cycle, and from this point of view all the great historical differences, including the superman, etc., fade into insignificance.

There is the same difficulty in Rousseau. The state of nature as Rousseau describes it is a state in which man was not yet truly man because he did not yet possess reason. He only had the ability to acquire reason; therefore man in the state of nature was a stupid animal. In spite of this— Rousseau's whole doctrine, at the highest peak of Rousseau's teaching— you get again the remark "return to nature": return to the state of nature. That meant in Rousseau's practical teaching return to the state of nature on the level of humanity. This is the highest man can do. This is no longer the citizen but the man beyond civil society making communion with nature. Something similar is true of Nietzsche: a return to nature on the human level, indeed, because the man who conceives the superman, and the superman himself, is of course not a brute, though he shares something with the brutes which distinguishes both the superman and the brute from historical man, namely, the harmony and unity with the cycle of nature.

Student: . . .

LS: You must never forget this simple thing. In the first, very provisional presentation of the eternal return, the first seen were defective men. More generally, the subject was the fragmentariness of man—man's past compared with the complete man, the superman. The paradox is that the will toward the complete man requires, according to Nietzsche, in itself a "yes" to the fragmentariness, to the past, and therewith the will to eternal return—return, as he puts it, of the same. Assuming that the historical process is preceded, and not accidentally, by the evolution of the human race from other species and on to the geological process, they are linked together: if you say yes to the return of any happening here and now, which presupposes the whole past, you have to say yes to goings-on even in completely desolate deserts of which no human being ever knew anything.

May I mention one point which is mentioned in other remarks of Nietzsche. There is one very simple motive which he had in mind. Nietzsche was sure that men would use this seriousness, this earnestness, by the loss in the belief in immortality, that eternal faith, eternal bliss. . . : "If this disappears let us eat, drink, etc." Nietzsche thought of a counterweight, a counterweight which would not lead man to what he calls the afterworld but would keep him loyal to the earth and would have the same power which the belief in immortality had. And what he believes is this kind of immortality supplied by eternal return: you don't know what you did in a previous existence, but you know that any terrible thing which ruins the rest of your life you will repeat infinitely in any future life. Surely you can say this is of no interest, whereas according to the immortality doctrine, you remember your sin after life. According to Nietzsche, there is no remembering of previous sins in your future life. It is not unimportant that in the *Zarathustra* this motivation is not mentioned.

Student: . . .

LS: What Nietzsche means, and that is not peculiar to Nietzsche but to German speculation since Kant: there are two different perspectives, the perspective of the theoretician and the perspective of moral, acting man—if you look at a problem, that is, if you are confronted by it, or if you look at it from the outside. Eternal return is an end doctrine, if I may say so, not in the sense of an eschatological doctrine—it is not the highest premise from which you start and from which you deduce consequences, including moral or practical ones. The crucial point in the argument is that you must be willing to accept this most terrible perspective, you must have the courage to accept it. Differently stated, if there is a process of this kind leading to a peak, everything is meaningful.

What is the consequence of all this? In the eternal cycle, the different states are infinitely less important than they are for us now in that limited perspective, man as distinguished from that man who has that vision. Once you accept eternal return, the whole process is purposeless, whereas in the primary thesis there was purpose: the superman. Once you see that, you see that Nietzsche's final doctrine is a restoration on a higher level. Now the desperate, the paralyzing, is transformed according to Nietzsche's claim into the most life-giving thought, because it requires the highest courage to will it. The nihilist does not will it. The nihilist takes theoretical cognizance of this as a fact, and therefore his will is paralyzed. The death of God, the last man—but the possibility of the superman, and then this possibility of the superman is thought through: complete overcoming of the spirit of revenge and of the spirit of heaviness. That is positively expressed in the eternal return. You must not do what the dwarf does: he merely repeats, without understanding the human meaning of what Zarathustra says. He says of the spirit of gravity: "Don't make it too easy." Not seeing it in this perspective is making it too easy. What Nietzsche demands is that the whole dedication, enthusiasm, for the superman is preserved, and at the same time the knowledge of the perishable—the perishable character—not merely grudgingly accepted and deplored as a terrible necessity but affirmed. And this affirmation in the most extreme sense is infinite affirmation, eternal return. That is the point: Nietzsche wanted to study theoretical physics in his later years because he wanted to give the theoretical truth for that doctrine. Some critics of Nietzsche say that this was a complete misunderstanding of himself, but I don't think so. Whatever it may ultimately lead to as a theoretical doctrine, the starting point, the meaning of that doctrine, does not depend on theoretical proof because theoretical proof belongs to the spirit of gravity.

Surely the doctrine of eternal return was the doctrine of some ancient philosophers, and the question is extremely simple. If there is no omnipotent God (and no ancient philosopher admitted an omnipotent God), then the universe is eternal. That is one possibility, most clearly in Aristotle; or if the visible universe has come into being, it will also perish, and then it will infinitely come into being and perish. That one can say generally, regardless of historical evidence. The Stoics are known for that, and their doctrine is connected with Heraclitus. Heraclitus was the philosopher whom Nietzsche admired the most. What was wrong with Heraclitus from Nietzsche's point of view? Nietzsche makes two reservations regarding Heraclitus: one, he disparaged the senses; and two, he did not have a historical consciousness. As a result, Heraclitus was unaware of the phenomenon of human creativity.[21] There is a fragment of Heraclitus to the effect that all human laws are nourished by the one divine law.[22] The human law is somehow derivative from the divine law. No creativity, and then of course no will—no will to power. For Nietzsche, history and what it means is absolutely essential. What Nietzsche tries to do is to build in that modern historical consciousness into a classical framework. History will be in nature and not, as would be in Hegel, history above and beyond.

Student: . . .[23]

LS: If you take the postulate as Kant means it, that is of course not a mere fiction but only an assertion which cannot be proven theoretically, but one which we must discern if we are to live as moral beings. The existence of God according to Kant cannot be theoretically proven, but if we understand what we mean by obeying the moral law, then we assert by this very fact the existence of God. For Nietzsche, reason is derivative. Nietzsche's term for that is "the vision and the riddle." (The title means, I believe, ultimately, "Of the Vision and Enigma.") *The* vision and *the* enigma is eternal return. If you put it this way, the vision and the enigma, there is a survival in Nietzsche of the basic principle of philosophy: that you cannot leave it at the last resort at something like postulates or enigmas and visions. Nietzsche found the reconciliation of this problem only in symbols, in lightness. What he regarded as a great superiority to philosophy in the traditional sense may very well appear to others, and it appears sometimes to Nietzsche himself, as a fundamental defect which is hard to remedy. His last book, of which only fragments exist and which has not been properly edited, was meant to be a theoretical system of philosophy.

Aristotle did not have eternal return in the strict sense, but he had it in a limited way: recurrent cataclysms, new beginnings, and of course the generation of men by men never interrupted. When Aristotle set up the Academy, when he undertook a great project, he knew very well that this wouldn't last forever. They knew there would be a new barbarism, but they didn't get excited about it. There is no fundamental difference between that and what we all are supposed to do as individuals. We all know that we are mortal, and in spite of that or because of that we are supposed to do our best. Why should this not apply to societies?

Student: . . .

LS: There may be some misunderstanding regarding chance. Nietzsche does not have that strict Aristotelian view of chance which is used in contradistinction with nature. For Aristotle, chance is possible only within a whole. What Nietzsche has in mind is this. Up to now history has merely happened. Now the moment has come where men can take the helm: now man knows the mechanism, to state it very crudely, of history. Previously, things just happened to him; now he can make them happen according to his understanding. From the highest point of view, Nietzsche says, we have this process where man now takes control and becomes the ruler of the planet. From this broader point of view, this is only one phase and men must learn to live with it. He must be able to combine full dedication to a glorious future with willingness to adopt the destruction of that future. Nietzsche is aware that nothing which is not eternal can satisfy a thinking man. In Marx there is not a trace of that, and that is the great superiority of Nietzsche. But the way in which he had to do it, namely, eternity of becoming and perishing and nothing beyond the process, that creates all the difficulty. If there is an eternity beyond the process, then there is a pure mind; but if there is not, knowledge or reason can only be a so-called function of life, of the organism. Nietzsche's premises are not paradoxical at all, they are the premises of the nineteenth and twentieth centuries, but Nietzsche thought further ahead. What we can learn from him is to get out of that self-complacency and see what doctrines and what kind of doctrines we would be led to if we take these premises seriously.

According to Nietzsche, the superman, the nobility, is not possible if there is not also a nonnobility. Nobility necessarily presupposes a non-noble majority which it rules. To that extent, the acceptance of fragmentariness, even of the last man, is necessary because according to Nietzsche there is no longer a possibility of the traditional human man, either superman or last man.[24] The question is whether the last man will be the only man.

11 Survey

Nietzsche and Political Philosophy

Leo Strauss: I would like again to give a survey similar to that which I gave at the beginning of the course, because it is of no use to go on and cover additional material if we do not understand the whole. Such a survey is naturally very sweeping, and this is not without danger, but on the other hand, it is also dangerous not to make such sweeping surveys. First of all, why is it so dangerous? Because in making such a survey one naturally speaks about things one doesn't know or doesn't know well enough. Do not be fooled by those who write books about the history of man's thought. We are today confronted with alternatives to which Nietzsche himself refers: either to be specialists or to be swindlers. There is, however, a solution which can more easily be stated than properly understood and acted upon. The formula is simple: one should become a specialist in important things. But surely this is only a formula, which would need a long comment illustrated by examples in order to make sense. However, it may be necessary to make surveys because we all bring surveys with us. We all have been brought up in a certain group, say, of the history of Western thought, and there is always a great risk in accepting something of which we have not sufficient knowledge. Therefore, what is necessary is to make this explicit from time to time. The modesty not to go beyond the limits of what one is sure to understand is in fact a sham, because we always depend on things of which we do not have firsthand knowledge, and therefore this modesty means merely to pass the buck. Therefore I take this risk, but I urge you not to believe me and try to see with your own eyes: accept the statements which will stimulate your own thought but not the definite results of what I believe to be so. Even this must not be taken quite literally.

Now after this warning, let me return to the subject I discussed at the first meeting. Let us look at Nietzsche in the light of earlier thought, and earlier political thought in particular. For this purpose, it is necessary to make a distinction between classical political philosophy and modern political philosophy. In modern philosophy, I shall distinguish what I called at that time and what I shall call now the three waves: the one beginning with Machiavelli, the second beginning with Rousseau, and the third beginning with Nietzsche.

First, the classical principles, as far as they are indispensable for the understanding of our problem. Classical political philosophy is based on the view that man is a rational animal: man's perfection is determined by his nature and rationality. Behind this is the view that every being has a specific activity, a specific work—in the Greek, *ergon*. This work may be done by the individual well or ill. To take a simple example, a horse cannot possibly fly, this cannot be the work of horse. But it can run, and it can do that well or badly. Similarly, there is a human activity which is not running, and which man exercises willy-nilly all the time but not always well, probably mostly badly. Man is by nature then ordered toward his perfection because his characteristic points to this perfection, just as the characteristic of the horse points toward the characteristic perfection of the horse. Man is by nature ordered toward his perfection, excellence, his virtue. Man has a natural inclination toward virtue. The specific meaning of virtue depends on the fact that there is a hierarchy within man indicated by the distinction between body, which is lower than the soul, which in its work is lower than the mind, the intellect, *nous*. Man is a rational animal. He is the being which possesses *logos*. *Logos* means speech or reason. Man is then by nature social, which does not mean that men are by nature nice—very far from that. But even the greatest criminal and irresponsible anarchist is this only by virtue of being social, and a being which can be social in the positive sense of the word can be antisocial; he can never be asocial. Therefore, since man is by nature social, his perfection is linked up with the perfection of the society, and the developed notion of the perfect society is that of the best regime. The best regime is that which is dedicated to virtue, primarily to moral virtue, which is virtue of character, and it would be in itself the rule of the virtuous man. Now the distinction is made between the best regime in the strict sense and the best regime in the more popular sense. In the strict sense, it would be the rule of the wise without law: the rule of living intelligence. The popular view connected with this, which is more easily understood, is the rule of aristocracy: the rule of men who are good through habituation as distinguished from wisdom, the rule of gentlemen. This was in fact understood as the rule of the urban patriciate which derives its means of livelihood from farming. This much as a reminder of the more general characteristics of classical thought.

We must never forget, in thinking of the history of modern times, that there was also an alternative to classical political philosophy in classical times, and that we may loosely call classical materialism. Here, not virtue is the principle but pleasure. But, and this is decisive, the hedonists of classical antiquity were unpolitical. Political hedonism is a modern phenomenon. In other words, they don't count when we speak of political philosophy. They only gave shrewd advice on how to live pleasantly in spite of government, so to speak.

Now let us see how the problem appears in modern times, and I speak first of what I call the first wave, which begins with Machiavelli and which leads up to but not quite including Rousseau. The formula which I suggest is political hedonism: not virtue but pleasure is the primary concern. Virtue, morality, the moral law—or the natural law, as it was called—is derivative. The legal expression of that is that not man's duties but his rights are primary, and these rights are reduced to one fundamental right from which all others can be derived: the right to self-preservation. This whole view presents itself and conceives of itself as due to a lowering of the standards of classical political philosophy. They thought of course that those standards were not only lofty, but foolishly lofty and quixotic. Hence one can describe the tendency of these men—Machiavelli, Hobbes, Locke—by saying that they were, in our language, realistic to take men as they are, not as they ought to be. In this first wave, the notion of man as a rational animal is preserved. Furthermore, they preserved the orientation by nature, but here a very important change must be noticed. The relation of man to the rest of nature is, according to this first wave, not one of fundamental harmony but one of antagonism: conquest of nature or, to state it more precisely, that part of nature which is man revolts against the rest of nature and tries to dominate it. In other words, nature survives in this first wave as a standard, but rather as a negative standard. Nature is that which is to be negated or overcome but which, by its peculiar character, gives a direction to the negation, to the overcoming.

There are certain difficulties which led to the later development. Let me mention two. If man is to conquer nature, he must occupy a place outside of the whole. There must be some Archimedean point where man and man alone stands. There is no provision for that in this early teaching, and this led to the later teaching regarding freedom as developed especially in German Idealism. The question can also be stated as follows:

If nature is bad, as it must be if it is to be conquered, can it supply us with any standards? Now these questions were faced by Rousseau. In this second stage, nature ceases to be the standard: not nature but reason supplies these requirements. This appears particularly in Kant, who conceives of the moral law as the law of reason in contradistinction to a law of nature, whereas in the traditional view still preserved up to Kant, the law of reason, the moral law, was at the same time the law of nature. What about the understanding of man as a rational animal? That seems to be clearly preserved, but reason seems to no longer mean the same thing as it had up to that time. Rousseau explicitly questions the view of man as a rational animal. Not the understanding but freedom, he says, is the peculiarity of man — not understanding, but freedom of the will. In some connection with that, Kant identifies practical reason, which according to him reaches farther than theoretical reason, with the will. So Kant and even Hegel speak of reason as something different from what Plato and Aristotle meant by reason.[1]

Now with these radical changes, these men of the second wave attempt to restore classical political philosophy to give civil society, the commonwealth, back the dignity which it possessed in classical times, which it had lost by virtue of its reduction to a means for the self-preservation of the individual. In Rousseau this is perfectly clear: his whole political teaching is an attempt to restore the classical notion of the *polis*, which means to restore virtue in the classical sense. Rousseau's fight with his predecessors is a criticism of the attempt to find some substitute for virtue, for example, in trade. Take the crude formula of Mandeville, "private vice, public benefits," which means certain vices are much more conducive to the common good than virtue, a notion which was very common in the eighteenth century and part of the seventeenth century.[2] So what Rousseau and the German Idealists tried to do is a synthesis between classical political philosophy, with its elevated notion of civil society, and the first wave of modernity, with its peculiar realism.

This elaborated political doctrine stands and falls with philosophy of history, which only at this stage became essential to philosophy in general and to political philosophy in particular. What about the third wave? The third wave is characterized by the fact that now the radical break is made for the first time with rationalism, with the view that man is essentially the rational element. This break with rationalism is based on the belief in history, history understood as a nonrational process. The fundamental premises of thought are declared to be historical. They differ from historical epoch to historical epoch. The fundamental premises are contingent. Nature is indeed the basis of all history, but everything we say about nature or thought about nature is historical. There is no possibility of appeal from history to nature or to reason. What is characteristic of Nietzsche is that he is aware of this difficulty and tries to solve it by an ultimate appeal to nature, but in no way by an appeal to reason.

I must make this somewhat more specific by restating it from a slightly different point of view. I would like to bring the argument somewhat nearer now to Nietzsche's own statement. Now Nietzsche has said very clearly, perhaps most clearly in his preface to *Beyond Good and Evil*, that *the* position against which he is directed is Plato and Plato's notion of a pure mind perceiving the pure truth. From this point of view, according to Nietzsche, religion, and particularly Christianity, is only a popular Platonism. This Platonic view (with some modifications which are at the moment not important) is also that of Aristotle. There is a mind, an intellect, which perceives forms. There is such a thing as the form of things, the essence of things; there is such a thing as mental perception. This was of course by no means the view of everyone in premodern times. There was a school of thought, particularly in the Middle Ages but existing also in classical times, which is called nominalism and which denies that there is such a thing as forms, as essences, as universals. Nominalism simply says that all universals—such as tree, house, man—are mere names. Strict nominalism would say that nothing corresponds to these universals in the things. One point, however, is crucial. According to the premodern nominalists, nature operates in an occult way in the universals. These universals are not arbitrary makings of man; they are produced in us by nature. There is then, according to those nominalists both ancient and medieval, a harmony between the human mind and nature, just as it is according to Plato and Aristotle. But there was a third alternative, more extreme in classical antiquity, and that was skepticism pure and simple; and one can state the thesis of skepticism simply as follows: there is no harmony between the mind and nature, or, in other words, there is no possibility of knowledge.

Now let us look at a characteristically modern thesis, characteristically modern because all the older views survived and to some extent still survive in various ways. That characteristically modern view can be stated as follows: there is no harmony between the mind and nature, and yet there is a possibility of knowledge. In other words, it accepts the skeptical thesis but does not accept the skeptical conclusion. How is it possible that there be knowledge although there is no harmony between the mind and nature? Because knowledge is simply the harboring of given data, human understanding putting its imprint on the given. According to Locke's formulation, the abstract ideas—that is, the equivalent to universals—are the inventions and creatures of the understanding, made by it for its own use. In other words, the making of these universals is in no way a natural process.

Now connected with this view, which came into the fore in the seventeenth century, there are two other theses which we also have to consider to prepare for an understanding of Nietzsche.

The other view,[3] which I now want to mention, is this. The visible universe has come into being. There are no final causes. The genesis of the visible universe is strictly mechanical—sketched clearly by Descartes and developed in quasi-classical form by Kant. On this basis, the novel conclusion was drawn by Rousseau that if the visible universe has come into being without any final cause and is strictly mechanical, then it follows that the very understanding, the very reason, must have come into being. The peculiarity of this view becomes apparent most clearly in Rousseau's *Discourse on the Origin of Inequality*. This Second Discourse is modeled on an ancient materialistic writing, Lucretius's *On the Nature of Things*. There is no genesis of reason or understanding in Lucretius, because there are mind atoms, which as atoms could not have come into being and are always. Lucretius describes the genesis of language, but Rousseau transforms this account into an account of the genesis of reason, which is an entirely different story. Again, such men as Locke had discussed the genesis of reason, but only the genesis of reason in the individual. What concerned Rousseau was the genesis of reason in the human race. Man was originally a stupid animal, who then acquired reason. The consequence is that history from this point of view reaches much deeper than was hitherto thought. Up to that time, history meant what happened to man, i.e., what happened to an unchangeable nature of man, but now there is no such nature which is unchangeable. Man is, as man, becoming. Man has no nature to speak of.

Now I take another view which belongs to this group of teachings. In these modern doctrines of the seventeenth century, the traditional view of natural law is rewritten, so that the emphasis is rather on rights than on duties. In the traditional view, rights are derivative from duties. We have rights, e.g., the right to speak, because we have the duty to speak. That means of course a limitation of the right, because we have the duty to speak true, relevant things; therefore, we do not have the right to irrelevant lies. In this modern view, most clearly expressed in Hobbes, the fundamental fact is the natural right from which all duties are derived. This right, as I said before, is the right of self-preservation, and this doctrine is developed in a doctrine of the state of nature. Man is a rational animal prior to society—that is, the state of nature. In other words, man is by nature rational but not social: society is derivative from deliberation or calculation. Man is a being which can deliberate and calculate. Here again we see the epoch-making importance of Rousseau. Rousseau says: If man in the state of nature is presocial, then by this very fact he is prerational. How then can the state of nature supply us with any standards if it is the state of the stupid animal? The solution to this problem was found by Kant and his successors. Not nature, and particularly the state of nature, but reason—the laws of reason, in contradistinction to the laws of nature—supplies the standards. If the state of nature is what Rousseau proved it to be on the basis of the premises of Hobbes and Locke, namely, a presocial and therefore a prerational state, let's forget about the state of nature—it is meaningless for our intentions. This is the conclusion which men like Kant and Hegel drew, but not Rousseau, and here we come somewhat closer to the Nietzschean doctrine.

If self-preservation is the fundamental human, moral fact, it is implied that life itself, which self-preservation tries to preserve, is pleasant. Why do we work so hard in preserving our life, if our life itself is not thought to be pleasant or sweet? Accordingly, Rousseau says that the basis of any concern with self-preservation is the sentiment of existence, the sweet, pleasant sentiment of existence underlying all other sentiments. This sentiment of existence in his presentation is identical with the sentiment of union with nature. From this it follows that there is a contradiction between the basis of self-preservation, namely, the sentiment of existence, and what this sentiment of existence gives rise to. The sentiment of existence gives rise to concern with self-preservation. You wish to preserve that sweetest of all sweet things: existence. Now what is this that self-preservation gives rise to which is not clearly given as the sentiment of existence? In one word: civilization. The whole effort of civilization is an attempt to preserve existence, to preserve life, and there is a radical disproportion according to Rousseau between what we try to preserve and our effort, because the most fundamental fact from which we start, the sentiment of existence, the sentiment of perfect bliss, cannot be achieved by man's doing. But our activity brings it away from us, and that is the tragedy of civilization according to Rousseau. In other words, there is a disproportion between society, which is the corrective effort toward self-preservation, and the individual. There is a fundamental antagonism between everything common, be it society or science, and my own. The contradictions for which Rousseau is famous are not disgraceful contradictions; Rousseau was aware of them. The only solution, which he found as a last resort, was a return to the state of nature with its primitive simplicity—but a return on the level of humanity, for Rousseau did not think that it was possible or desirable that we should become simple brutes. This approximation to the state of nature is what we may call the solitary dreamer or artist living on the fringes of civilization.

Rousseau's greatest pupils, the German philosophers Kant and Hegel, rejected this antinomy altogether, and incidentally, Marx followed Hegel in this respect. They believed that a harmonious solution is possible, namely, the individual finding his fulfillment in the common, in the universal. Practically, the individual finds his fulfillment as a member of the rational state or the rational society. The theoretical solution of the German idealists was based on an acceptance of the fundamental dualism between nature and mind or reason. Given that dualism, no return to the submental state of nature is of course imaginable. The unfolding of the mind or of reason—that is history, from this point of view. In the vulgar version of this school, history is a rational process and a completed process.

What happened after this, as far as it is immediately relevant for our problem? It can be described as the reaction to Hegel on the basis of Hegel. Hegel had taught that the individual (including of course the individual thinker or philosopher) is the son of his time. He cannot possibly transcend the fundamental premises of his epoch or his nation. This was accepted, but against Hegel it was said that the process is not finished and not finishable. This view, that man at his highest and freest is a son of his time and that the historical process is not finished nor finishable, are the characteristics of what the Germans called the "historical consciousness," and this is the starting point of Nietzsche. Nietzsche's whole position can be described from this point of view as follows. Nietzsche turned against German Idealism, and in so doing he returns to the problem of Rousseau: the individual cannot solve his problem in and through the state or society, nor through science or rational philosophy. Nietzsche's philosophy of the future is no longer rational philosophy. Nietzsche returns to Rousseau's problem on the basis of the historical consciousness, and this explains the deviations of Nietzsche from Rousseau.

Let us see how this works out concretely. Reason or mind is derivative in Nietzsche as well as in Rousseau, but reason or mind is derivative not merely from sense perception, as quite a few British empiricists would have admitted. The whole sphere of conscious thought, including sense perception, including reason, is derivative from the self, as Nietzsche calls it; and the self, he says very enigmatically, is the body. As for the sentiment of existence, of which Rousseau had spoken, this is no longer understood by Nietzsche as an experience of fundamental bliss. It is rather an experience of anguish, exposedness, or suffering. That was the view made very popular in the middle of the last century by Schopenhauer. But Nietzsche says, against these pessimists: "Willing liberates."[4] It is absurd to deny life or to take refuge in some afterworld because of life's suffering and imperfection. One of the many formulas: "The heart of the earth is of gold."[5] In the final version, the doctrine of eternal return is understood as a most radical and comprehensive yes to life with its sufferings and imperfections.

"Willing liberates." Properly understood, that means that the acts of willing and of creation which liberate are the great views of the whole developed by creative people or creative individuals. Now these creative acts have a kind of sequence, and the totality of these acts is known to us and is history. Thought is radically historical. From this it follows that truth becomes radically problematic. Therefore it becomes necessary, in order to save the possibility of truth, to transcend history, to integrate history into a transhistorical whole which men call, and Nietzsche sometimes calls, nature. Eternal return, Nietzsche's formula for nature, comprises history, and it comprises in particular the future. This integration of history into nature takes place without restoring reason or objective knowledge to its original status.

I would like to explain this last point again. I begin again at the beginning. There is nothing eternal or sempiternal. There is no pure mind. All knowledge is perspectivity and belongs to a specific perspective. All knowledge is a function of life, i.e., of historically specified life. There is not simply the perspective of man as man as against the perspective of a dog, or an elephant as elephant. All truth, we can say, is subjective. The world as it is understood by anyone is the apparent world, and "the true world" is a meaningless term. All knowledge is interpretation and not the mere text, and therefore it is creation. There is a variety of perspectives, and this change is not a rational change, meaning a progressive development. The difficulty is this. If I say all knowledge is perspective, I have knowledge regarding knowledge. This knowledge regarding knowledge is a second-level knowledge. This knowledge regarding knowledge is knowledge of what is and not interpretation, creation, subjective thought. This leads to the great consequence that the most comprehensive knowledge of which man is capable, the highest knowledge of which man is capable, has the status of objective knowledge. Any view about men, stars, time, God, has relativity to the time of thought and is true only in that perspective, but the relation between the worldview and the specific man, this insight, is no longer perspectivity. The findings of modern science have relativity to modern man — in the first place, to modern Western man and then, by virtue of the Westernization of all men, acquire a seeming universality.

Why did Nietzsche not leave it at that? Every sociologist of knowledge leaves it at that. Why is Nietzsche more demanding? Nietzsche has stated this difficulty almost from the beginning in his second essay in *Untimely Meditations*, "The Advantage and Disadvantage of History." There he says that this doctrine of the historicity of all thought is true but deadly. Therefore this doctrine relativizes all substantive thought, because if I know that all I believe, all I cherish, is not strictly speaking true, then this formal truth is very poor and cold comfort; hence there is a fundamental conflict between truth or science and life or art. Art belongs together with life from this point of view because art is a direct expression of life. In order to live humanly, in order that there be a culture, we need closed horizons, not the open horizon of science or philosophy. We need a closed horizon, we need delusions. Or, as Nietzsche said, we need a lie: lie here does not mean what Plato means by the noble lie, which is for purely political purposes, but he meant the thing itself must be a lie. This is of course not Nietzsche's solution; no one knew better than he that it is impossible to enclose yourself in a horizon. It is not Nietzsche's solution but the statement of the problem.

A more adequate statement of the problem is this. Is it not possible to live humanly on the basis of the deadly truth of historicism or relativism? Is it not perhaps possible to live humanly on the highest level, superhumanly, precisely on the basis of relativism? Is this devastating knowledge not perhaps man's greatest opportunity, as the jumping-off place for man's highest possibility, what Nietzsche means by the superman? Nietzsche is therefore compelled to deny that the most comprehensive knowledge can have the status of objective knowledge. The highest knowledge must be itself created. It must even be created to a higher degree than all other forms of knowledge, and this must be connected with the fact that this knowledge is the first created knowledge which embodies self-knowledge of the creative character of knowledge. How is this possible? Man becomes aware that he is the creator of all categories and values. Nietzsche says, as it were, that this awareness is not truly a way to a noncreative man. He can repeat these formulae, but he cannot understand it. He talks of creativity as a blind man about colors.

Therefore the very introduction of the term creativity, if it is not a meaningless phrase, changes the picture radically. Nietzsche, however—that is, his creative act—is preceded by a kind of knowledge which is not creative, which is equally accessible to creative and noncreative men: everyone knows that God is dead. This knowledge, however equally accessible to all, is incomplete and therefore not objective. Because it is incomplete, it can be interpreted and must be interpreted in two radically different ways: it can be interpreted basely, noncreatively, as ordinary relativism; or nobly, creatively. It is merely a basic assumption of academic relativists who say that the base interpretation is more scientific than the noble interpretation. Both interpretations are not simply scientific. This mere function, formula, is neutral and therefore incomplete. I remind you in this connection of Nietzsche's distinction between the knower and the noble man. The creative interpretation of this is that all values and all categories are human creations. So the mere objective formula would be something like: merely subjective, merely historical. But to understand them as creations and to use this expression meaningfully, the individual must have some experience of creativity. He must to some extent have been a creator. The creative interpretation consists, however, in the observational assertion that all these reflections of man are human creations, and then it is developed (and that is a very simple thing) into the view that being is the will to power. The fundamental error from Nietzsche's point of view is that the notion that there is something which is always, deathless, is not a mere theoretical error but is rooted in the spirit of revenge as the spirit of gravity or heaviness, which means in a particular form of the will to power, in a particular form of the will . . .

Nietzsche gives some answer to that question in the speech "On the Vision and the Riddle." The doctrine of eternal return is based according to Nietzsche on an enigmatic vision. We may say that the very notion of an enigmatic vision is the synthesis of cognition, objective knowledge, and creation. In other words, what we call creation is also interpreted by the very poets themselves as inspiration. It is not simply their conscious production, it is also something which comes out of them without their own doing. The doctrine of eternal return is not pure awareness. The doctrine of eternal return, the touchstone of Nietzsche's doctrine, is indeed a doctrine of the transhistorical whole of nature. But it is not in itself and not meant to be a rational doctrine. It is an enigmatic vision.

I hope I have succeeded in making clear to you Nietzsche's problems. As for his answers, they are difficult to understand. At times they sound like mere assertions, of which one cannot know whether they correspond to anything.

Student: . . .

LS: Everything that is implied in this presentation, and the inductive reasoning by virtue of which he arrives at the view that Y is the function of X, surely, this is universal. That is only another way of stating: Can you avoid the universal if it is possible to conceive of it, as all historicism is trying to do, as a kind of dead and ossified antique? The natural law doctrine of the Stoics is an expression of a certain stage of classical antiquity; this stage of classical antiquity was something real and was then projected into this doctrine of natural law. That means that this universal doctrine, the doctrine of *the* natural law, is only seemingly universal because its root is a particular man, classical man.

When people today speak of "our civilization," that is of course historicism of the crudest kind, which is not even aware of its theoretical premises. Positivistic social science, even at its best, raises the question of the spirit of our age. In former times, it was very simple: philosophic questions are questions in the statement of which proper names do not occur, except incidentally. If Parmenides has a certain theory and Aristotle discusses it, he must do so by mentioning the name of Parmenides. On the basis of the historical consciousness, proper names occur in the most important passages because, if the human race is rooted in the particular, this surely must be so. This simple state of affairs shows that sooner or later we must come to the universal, and this is the great difficulty for modern thought. It is a consequence of the fact that we are rational beings and universality is an expression of our rationality.

Student: . . .

LS: . . . when I say "chipmunks are," it is presupposed that I know what it means to be. Therefore this knowledge of what it means to be precedes all possible scientific knowledge and is therefore wholly independent of any scientific knowledge. It is, in the most radical sense, *a priori*. Science therefore may be an object of philosophic study, but it cannot teach science anything . . . You can see how Nietzsche solves the problem of God. The common atheism simply says that any God or gods are simply projections of the human soul, or the relations of production, or what have you. Heidegger is aware that this is not sufficient, but on the other hand, he is unable to accept any earlier belief, as Nietzsche does. In his solution, the ground of any God or gods is not the human soul, but "to be," the highest of all grounds. This is the ground which we always presuppose, of which we always have some awareness in any speech.[6]

12 The Goodness of the Whole, Socratic and Heideggerian Critiques

Zarathustra, Part 3, 4–12

Leo Strauss: I found a statement, which Nietzsche made in his early writing on history, which might make the remarks I made last time clearer. "The doctrine of the sovereignty of becoming, of the fluidity of all concepts, types and species, of the fundamental difference between man and beast are true but deadly."[1] What he says here is that there is no being; it is therefore only a different expression of what he calls in the *Zarathustra* "the death of God." The consequence of this, as we have seen more than once, is the last man, the man who is satisfied with his situation. The premise stated here can also be stated as follows. In *The Gay Science*, aphorism 301, Nietzsche says: "Nature is always valueless."[2] Now, if the most comprehensive truth is deadly, how can we live? The first answer would be that we have to live in delusion, in the world of appearance. We have to accept fundamental lies. Science must be rejected in the name of art. These notions have been accepted by quite a few people, more in Europe than in the Anglo-Saxon countries. But Nietzsche himself was never satisfied with it, because it is impossible to live on the basis of what we know to be a delusion. Intellectual honesty asserts itself; we must accept the ugly truth, so much so that the poets themselves must become "penitents of the spirit," as he says in the speech "On Poets."[3]

But how is it possible to live on the basis of the deadly truth? I quote an aphorism from the *Dawn of Morning*, aphorism 44 (and the statement is put in italics, which Nietzsche now and then does): "*With the insight into the origin, the insignificance of the origin increases*: whereas *what is nearest* to us, around us, and within us, begins to show gradually colors and beauties and riddles and wealth of significance, of which earlier man did not dream."[4] However, we know the origins, say, evolution and things like this. We know that nature is valueless, that all values are of human origin and hence have no support from nature or God. Having discovered the emptiness of the world itself, of the objective truth, of any possible origin, of first causes, we turn more passionately to the world which is of concern to us, to our world, the world which is our work of fiction. We realize that the very concern with the origin, with the "without," with what is always, impoverishes that world and ourselves. Hence we abolish the true world. This is not merely an arbitrary act, because it is done in the first place by the positivist critique of metaphysics, by virtue of which the notion of the first cause or causes is abandoned and replaced by infinite causes and, secondly, as far as the scientist is concerned, by realizing that the scientific is only one interpretation among many.

With this abolition of every "without," namely, outside of the world in which we live and understand ourselves, there is also according to Nietzsche loyalty to the earth, being fully at home in the world. As long as we believe in any first cause or causes, this first cause has a higher dignity than the world in which we live, and therefore it impoverishes the world in which we live. So we must be fully at home in this world, yet we preserve the awareness that the world of concern to us has no support except our creativity or, in other words, the awareness that man is a rope over an abyss. But this world, with colors and values as a product of creation or interpretation, is necessarily historically determined. The expression for that is "all knowledge is perspectivity." There is not *the* objective knowledge, nor can we speak of *the* subjective knowledge because there is a variety of such subjective knowledges.

The difficulties on this level are these. In the first place, there is a variety of subjective truth or comprehensive worldviews, and the truth must be one. Secondly, there is an objective truth regarding many subjective truths. This means that the most comprehensive truth, the highest truth, is objective. Thirdly, this objective truth is deadly, so we have not solved the problem at all. Yet—and this is the last part of Nietzsche's argument that objective truth is ambiguous and incomplete—it must be interpreted and thereby completed. The interpretation is either noble or base; objectively there is no preference for the noble or base. The noble interpretation interprets the relation of these worldviews to man in terms of the creativity of man, and this creativity is defined by Nietzsche more precisely as will to power. This is the noble interpretation because it is based on the experience of creativity, whereas the base interpretation lacks this experience. And it is not a mere postulate, because it is based on an experience: the new interpretation, the final interpretation, the final philosophy, the most comprehensive perspective, is based on the self-consciousness of creativity. All earlier philosophies are interpretations and were not aware of the fundamental significance of creativity. They did not present themselves as creations or accompaniments of creations. The capstone is the doctrine of eternal return, which means an infinite affirmation of life with all sufferings and defects. The doctrine of eternal return preserves the principles: there is no without. Any concern with the without is inimical to life. Or, we can also say, the doctrine of eternal return preserves the principle that there is nothing eternal or sempiternal except individuals in their individuality: eternal return of the same. The doctrine of eternal return is based according to Nietzsche on an enigmatic vision. Perhaps all earlier interpretations of the world were also based on enigmatic visions, yet they claim to be based on objective and rational knowledge and they have been refuted by rational criticism. Nietzsche's enigmatic vision is meant to be in accordance with an objective criticism, with the deadly truth of evolution and historicism.

Now let me return to a subject to which I referred last time, the development after Nietzsche which grew out of Nietzsche. Think, for example, of the psychology of unmasking, which Nietzsche would explain as will to power in every human phenomenon, or the distinction between facts and values, which is post-Nietzschean and has its origin in certain objections of Nietzsche. But in most cases Nietzsche's influence was unavowed and perhaps even unknown. In my remarks I will limit myself to the most important existentialist, and that is Heidegger.

Heidegger's criticism of Nietzsche is very exact and according to Nietzsche's own thought. It confirms primarily the doctrine of eternal return, because if that is dropped Nietzsche's whole doctrine is finished. The doctrine of eternal return is introduced by Nietzsche, as you will remember, as the successful overcoming of the spirit of revenge. All philosophies which posit something eternal are rooted, according to Nietzsche, in the spirit of revenge, the spirit of escaping, the radical perishability of everything. The question which Heidegger raises is: Does Nietzsche overcome the spirit of revenge? Is not the very doctrine of the eternal return characterized by a revolt against the mere perishing, against the past, against time? In Heidegger's doctrine there is no eternal in any sense. His first book is entitled *Being and Time*. Being is in every sense in time, and no reference to eternity is even possible. Nietzsche himself had said when a man who suffers deeply has life under his protection, there is revenge in him.[5] Let us look at a page in *Zarathustra*, page 218, paragraph 4.

Reader: The danger of those who always give is that they lose their sense of shame: and the heart and hand of those who always mete out become callous from always meting out. My eye no longer wells over at the shame of those who beg; my hand has grown too hard for the trembling of filled hands. Where have the tears of my eyes gone and the down of my heart? Oh, the loneliness of all givers! Oh, the taciturnity of all who shine![6]

LS: We can also say that Nietzsche's emphasis on cruelty as essential to knowledge is an evasion of the presence of the spirit of revenge. And last but not least, Nietzsche, in opposition to the tarantula, or egalitarian revolution, is a counter-tarantula; and if the spirit of revenge shows itself empirically first as the spirit of the egalitarian revolution, it will also show itself in its opponent. Measured by Nietzsche's own standard, his doctrine is insufficient. He goes on to say that the doctrine of eternal return remains a riddle and that there are two ways in which people evade that riddle: the first is that the doctrine is a fantastic mysticism; the second, that it is as old as the hills. The only criticism that is of interest is that the doctrine of eternal return is a fantastic mysticism, to which Heidegger answers that our age teaches us that the doctrine of eternal return is not a fantastic mysticism. Why is that so? "What else is the essence of the modern machine except *one* form of the eternal return of the same": modern technology.[7] This is an exaggeration, because no machine produces eternally.

Given this state of affairs, we must raise these two questions. First: What is the motive of the doctrine of eternal return? And second: Why did Heidegger, or existentialism as a whole, fail to consider this? The second question is identical with the question: What is the difference between existentialism and Nietzsche? Now what is the motive of the doctrine of eternal return? I remind you of the explicit argument. The will is present, like perishability, by passing away, by time. Hence time must be so conceived that the will is not present, that the past can be willed. The only way this can be done is return of the past, eternal return. Now let us call the world of becoming and perishing the natural world. Then we have to say Nietzsche tries to preserve the natural world of becoming and perishing against any degradation by something above the natural world by willing eternal return. Let us come somewhat more closely to the conflicts in the speech on revenge.[8] The speech starts from an enumeration of human defects, generally the fragmentary character of man. This fragmentariness is to be conquered. The complete man, the perfect man, is the superman. Yet the fragmentariness is to be redeemed, and not by the completion of man but in a way in which the fragmentariness itself is to be preserved. Why is that necessary? The spirit of revenge had come to sight first as the spirit of egalitarian revolution, the tarantula. Over against this, Nietzsche asserts inequality, but on what basis? Ultimately, on the basis of nature. There is then a connection between eternal return and the concern with the integrity of the natural order.

How can this be done? Eternal return is willed before it is in any way asserted. It is willed because nature wills it. But why is nature willed? You must remember the problematic status of nature in Nietzsche's thought. Is the natural order given to man, or is it not rather created by man's will? This remains obscure. If the natural order is merely given, the will revolts; hence the natural order must be willed if it is to be accepted. The natural order is as such the object of theoretical knowledge, yet not theoretical knowledge but creative knowledge. The natural order must be somehow understood as created by man. Why does the willing of nature lead to return? Because nature is past, it essentially precedes the will. Nature, according to Nietzsche's final understanding, is the will to power; hence there is an infinite process of self-overcoming, self-overcoming being the highest form of the will to power. Yet there must be a peak, for the will to knowledge is a modification of the will to power—in a way the most spiritual form of the will to power—and the will to knowledge requires a peak. But if there is a peak, there is necessarily a descent, ultimately to the lowest forms of the will to power, what we might call inanimate matter. The will to meaning and to the highest meaning is then completely overcome and defeated by utter meaninglessness. Chance and meaninglessness defeat the meaning given the world, since there is no essential necessity that the highest human creation will last. What Nietzsche is trying to do is to transform the ultimate defeat of the will into a victory.

The third consideration: all knowledge is perspectivity. From this it follows that the highest knowledge is that related to the broadest perspective. The perspectives are rooted in the will, the fundamental will of the thinker. This fundamental will of the thinker is not merely willed, because deeper than the ego or the reason is the self. This will is fate: everything good is inherited. The unconditional, the fundamental will, is in fact conditioned. How can this be reconciled? An answer to that is the question of the eternal return.

One cannot will the peak without willing the descent. One cannot will the complete man without willing the fragmentary man. Man's conquest of nature and human nature, if completed, leads to the consequence that man manipulates everything, including himself, and this is the last man. Confronted with this situation, there is a need for a return to nature, the nonmanipulated nature: the restoration of nature. That is to say, the consequence of a return to nature is interpreted in terms of the primary process, which was the conquering process. The conqueror must conquer himself. More simply stated, in a given state of affairs the natural conditions become now the objectives of policy. Man's domestication is the result of modern civilization, but this complete domestication is incompatible with man's highest possibilities. Therefore man as a nondomesticated animal must now become the objective of policy, i.e., of will. This can be found also in, for example, Sorel.[9] The concern with the passions might become weakened, and therefore it becomes an object of policy to encourage and strengthen the passions. The doctrine of eternal return, we can say, is a theoretical expression of this state of things. Whereas in former times the passions were taken for granted as guaranteed by nature—the nature of man—and the objective of policy was to control them, now the natural conditions themselves must be willed, and in the most comprehensive form this is Nietzsche's doctrine of eternal return: eternal return is willed because nature is no longer understandable except as will.

What then is the relation between Nietzsche and existentialism? Heidegger himself has said that Nietzsche was not an existential thinker, but at the same time he says, speaking of a certain statement in Nietzsche: Here someone has cried out from the depth. Now a philosopher who cries *ex profundis* is by definition an existentialist. Aristotle never did that. From these two contradictory statements it appears that Nietzsche prepares existentialism but he transcends it or, rather, he falls back into metaphysics. How does he prepare it? The origin of all meaning is the subject, i.e., the specific subject. The decisive truth is subjective. Human life as it generally exists is a horizon-forming project. The subject is not the ego, the reason, but the self, the existing man. Theoretical concepts lead men away from the world of their concern, make men mere onlookers, prevent him from being a true self. Only the experience and not the inferred, the conjecture, can have serious meaning for man. But Nietzsche prefers the awareness, which is not in existentialism, that the question of man's origin cannot be abandoned. The cosmological problem reasserts itself in the doctrine of the eternal return. In other words, to put it in Nietzsche's own language, the question of the without cannot be abandoned. Heidegger's answer seems to be that the question of man's origin is a mystery and cannot be answered. To exist, to live as human beings, means to accept this mystery as a mystery and not try to make it a theoretical subject. But the question is whether this is feasible at all. So much for what we started last time.

Now let us continue our study of the third part of the *Zarathustra*, and if possible, to finish it.

Student: . . .

LS: There are two possibilities. According to the old-fashioned view, we would then be wiser and therefore act more wisely. This, however, is no longer possible, but it could be restated as follows: regardless of what our values are, we want to succeed, we want to get what we desire. Now the best form of knowledge regarding means for any possible ends is supplied by science; therefore, from every point of view science is required if science (and of course the most complete and comprehensive science) is available. Prudence in the older sense is superseded by science. For example, in the older days, marriage was decided by the prudent choice of the individuals concerned. Along the lines of the scientific[10] orientation, the place of prudence would be taken by a matrimonial science, which would tell everyone who is the spouse meant for him or her. In principle, this means the possibility of complete manipulation of every human being. Must one not think this through? Must one not ask whether this is in itself a good thing or a possible thing? If there is a relationship between modern science and the last man, we must ask: What is the countermovement to this development toward the last man? Nietzsche's answer to that is nature. Nietzsche, just as Plato before him, believed that the good society is a society in which the hierarchy corresponds as much as possible to the natural hierarchy.

But the conquest of nature means of course also the conquest of the natural hierarchy. I remind you of the problems with which Mr. Lasswell is concerned: the production of geniuses in a large state, which immediately affects the hierarchy as it was understood; secondly, the production of robots, that is to say, a new natural hierarchy. So nature becomes radically problematic because conquest of nature means, in the words of Marx, pushing back nature. At no point can you legitimately refer anymore to natural limits, because theoretically it is possible that these limits may be overcome. What is the limit of human power? Nature in the old sense was meant to be such a limit. Where can we take our bearings from? Kant would say the law of reason, but in Nietzsche this is excluded by the consideration that reason is derivative, derivative from the whole human being. It is a function of the organism. How can you get a moral law on this basis? Against the abstract doctrines of Hobbes and Locke, people like Montesquieu and Rousseau deny that these doctrines are of universal applicability. In the words of Rousseau, freedom is not a product of every climate: the notion that free commonwealths are to be found around the Mediterranean basin and the rest of Europe (and of course also in the Western hemisphere settled by Europeans), but in the Orient you have large empires which were not developed like the Greek cities and therefore do not have that kind of freedom. So we expect that these principles of social organization can be transplanted, that there is no natural obstacle. Does not nature become completely meaningless, since it has yielded everywhere? Nietzsche needed nature. . .

Nietzsche believed that there was a natural difference which conformed by itself to a proper order. But in spite of all the exaggerations, what he means is fundamentally the old story: there is a natural order. Now I ask: Is it not also subject to a revision in the light of the ever-increasing conquest of nature? Must one not stem this development with a view to the relations between the sexes, for example? But how can this be done as a matter of principle? That means that now, for the first time, nature must be willed.

Student: How does Heidegger maintain the importance of philosophy without any reliance on nature?

LS: One can state this very crudely as follows. Heidegger abandons everything to the complete process of energy and manipulation and seeks the principle in the following way. He raises the question: What is that which is essential and radical beyond the possibility of manipulation and human control? He answers the question with the distinction between being and to be. A being can in a certain perspective be completely manipulated,[11] but not to be. As is clear to him experientially, it is something which is radically elusive and can never be controlled. Therefore, these distinctions are absolutely decisive: there are no possible limitations as long as we are oblivious of the distinction between beings and to be.

Now let us go on with our readings. In the speech "Of Vision and Riddles," the doctrine of eternal return was propounded for the first time, though alluded to before in the section "On Redemption." Nietzsche does not take up this great theme until the speech "'The Convalescent" later on. In the meantime, he returns to some other subjects.

The speech "On Involuntary Bliss" has this meaning: Zarathustra has found fulfillment or bliss in this enigmatic vision, but only in a way. This is the meaning of the term "involuntary bliss": he has not yet willed eternal return; therefore he moves still further away from the blessed isle where his disciples are. The next speech, "Before Sunrise," is of particular importance.

> Reader: O heaven above me, pure and deep! You abyss of light! Seeing you, I tremble with godlike desire. To throw myself into your height, that is *my* depth. To hide in your purity, that is *my* innocence.
>
> Gods are shrouded by their beauty; thus you conceal your stars. You do not speak; thus you proclaim your wisdom to me. Today you rose for me silently over the roaring sea; your love and your shyness are a revelation to my roaring soul. That you came to me, beautiful, shrouded in your beauty, that you speak to me silently, revealing your wisdom—oh, how should I not guess all that is shy in your soul! *Before* the sun you came to me, the loneliest of all.[12]

LS: The sun has not yet risen and the stars no longer shine. Heaven is not visible, just as the gods are not visible. God is concealed from vision by his beauty; heaven is concealed by it, too. The beauty consists in purity and depth. Perhaps this is Nietzsche's definition of beauty. Altogether, it would not be a bad definition. Before sunrise, heaven is the abyss of light. There is the dark out of which light comes, which replaces in this context depth by height: the depth of beauty is its height. The inner world, into which we must go down, is above us.

Now this apostrophe to heaven is connected with what was said earlier about the earth: "be loyal to the earth"; "the heart of the earth is gold." Why does Zarathustra wish to ascend to heaven or to leave the earth? This was prepared by the remark about the spirit of gravity, which was represented by a mole or by a dwarf. Dwarfs live within the earth. All human beings live on the earth and beneath heaven. In the Bible, the whole is called heaven and earth and what is between them. Earth and heaven are the limits. All living beings are children of the earth. The earth can be earth only by virtue of heaven, and vice versa. Yet why must Zarathustra rise to heaven? It appears from the sequel that he needs heaven, heaven needs him. They have the most important thing in common, and that is what he calls here "unbounded yes." Now let us turn to page 277, the last sentence of the fifth paragraph.

> Reader: But this is my blessing: to stand over every single thing as its own heaven, as its round roof, its azure bell, and eternal security; and blessed is he who blesses thus.

For all things have been baptized in the well of eternity and are beyond good and evil; and good and evil themselves are but intervening shadows and damp depressions and drifting clouds.

Verily, it is a blessing and not a blasphemy when I teach: "Over all things stand the heaven Accident, the heaven Innocence, the heaven Chance, the heaven Prankishness."

"By Chance"—that is the most ancient nobility of the world, and this I restored to all things: I delivered them from their bondage under Purpose. This freedom and heavenly cheer I have placed over all things like an azure bell when I taught that over them and through them no "eternal will" wills.[13]

LS: There is a pun here in German. *Von Ohngefähr* is the oldest nobility in the world. Zarathustra imitates heaven. Only through this imitation can men become loyal to the earth and not be drawn away from the earth toward some super-heaven, as Hegel calls it. Only by such loyalty does the earth become meaningful, and hence also heaven, as an azure bell above the earth, become fully what it is. The imitation of heaven is that act by virtue of which the earth becomes truly earth. Man's primary orientation, prior to any science, is of course heaven above earth. This is so according to the biblical cosmology and philosophically confirmed in Aristotle's cosmology. What has happened to the heaven in modern times? Since Copernicus, when you look through a telescope you get an idea, and when you look through a better telescope, you see that heaven is completely disintegrated into a quasi-infinite space. This is of course bound to affect the earth: the earth becomes just one planet among many. Man loses completely his natural orientation; the whole doctrine of man must be completely rewritten so that earth appears as one planet among many and heaven as a very popular formula for extraterrestrial regions. If man is to regain his natural orientation and become again at home on the earth, somehow heaven must be restored to its ancient dignity, and the form in which Nietzsche does this will appear later. For Nietzsche, it is not merely a question of restoring a natural orientation rendered doubtful by modern science. In his view, it is not a restoration at all. For the first time, man is to become fully at home on the earth, because in premodern times there was always a principle which made men disloyal to the earth, be it the biblical God or the deathless gods of Homer who live indeed on earth. How does Nietzsche achieve this restoration of the protecting vault of heaven? Not by modern cosmology. The understanding of cosmology now means that things have no purpose — the old story of antiteleology: things don't even have an end, for the peak is not the end, it is followed by decline. Men have purposes, they set themselves purposes, but the highest purpose they can set for themselves is to be without purpose: simply to be, though to be while knowing. The highest act of creativity, we can therefore say, is the recognition . . .[14]

Reader: This prankish folly I have put in the place of that will when I taught: "In everything one thing is impossible: rationality."

A *little* reason, to be sure, a seed of wisdom scattered from star to star — this leaven is mixed in with all things: for folly's sake, wisdom is mixed in with all things. A little wisdom is possible indeed; but this blessed certainty I found in all things: that they would rather *dance* on the feet of Chance.

O heaven over me, pure and high! That is what your purity is to me now, that there is no eternal spider or spider web of reason; that you are to me a dance floor for divine accidents, that you are to me a divine table for divine dice and dice players.[15]

LS: There is no purpose but also no dominant rationality. This is the elusiveness of the whole, the enigmatic character of the whole.

A few words about the next speeches. First, "On Virtue That Makes Small." Zarathustra is the forgotten man, and the next eight speeches deal with human things as such. We may observe that from now on there are many subdivided speeches. Zarathustra has returned to the continent (as distinguished from the isle of the blessed) and finds that everything, and especially in men, has become smaller. His speech is not addressed to his disciples, but apparently it is another public speech. It is the first public speech since the one in the Prologue. Let us read on page 281, paragraph 2.

Reader: I walk among this people and I keep my eyes open: they have become smaller, and they are becoming smaller and smaller; *but this is due to their doctrine of happiness and virtue.* For they are modest in virtue, too — because they want contentment. But only a modest virtue gets along with contentment.

LS: "Contentment" is not really a good translation.[16] You see, they are not the last men, but on their way to it.

Reader: But there is much lying among the small people. Some of them will, but most of them are only willed. Some of them are genuine, but most of them are bad actors. There are unconscious actors among them and involuntary actors; the genuine are always rare, especially genuine actors.[17]

LS: What he has primarily in mind here is what has been called the other-directed man: men who do not follow their own way but imitate others. He develops this further: no dedication, no devotion; this state of mind represents itself hypocritically as resignation.

Reader: Round, righteous, and kind they are to each other, round like grains of sand, righteous and kind with grains of sand. Modestly to embrace a small happiness—that they call "resignation"—and modestly they squint the while for another small happiness. At bottom, these simpletons want a single thing most of all: that nobody should hurt them. Thus they try to please and gratify everybody. This, however, is cowardice, even if it be called virtue.[18]

LS: If we could read this speech as a whole, you would see many allusions to biblical, and especially New Testament, passages. The speech has altogether an eschatological character and expresses the expectation of the future of the superman.

The speech "Upon the Mount of Olives" has presented Zarathustra. Now he presents the ape of Zarathustra, not the disciple of Zarathustra.[19] This man who apes Zarathustra lives in a big city. His judgment of the city is the same as Zarathustra's with this decisive difference: he lives in contempt.

Reader: Here, however, Zarathustra interrupted the foaming fool and put his hand over the fool's mouth. "Stop at last!" cried Zarathustra; "your speech and your manner have long nauseated me. Why did you live near the swamps so long, until you yourself have become a frog and a toad? Does not putrid, spumy swamp-blood flow through your own veins now that you have learned to croak and revile thus? Why have you not gone into the woods? Or to plow the soil? Does not the sea abound in green islands? I despise your despising; and if you warned me, why did you not warn yourself? . . .

"But your fool's words injure me, even where you are right. And even if Zarathustra's words *were* a thousand times right, still *you* would always *do* wrong with my words."

Thus spoke Zarathustra; and he looked at the great city, sighed, and long remained silent. At last he spoke thus: "I am nauseated by this great city too, and not only by this fool. Here as there, there is nothing to better, nothing to worsen. Woe unto this great city! And I wish I already saw the pillar of fire in which it will be burned. For such pillars of fire must precede the great noon. But this has its own time and its own destiny.

"This doctrine, however, I give you, fool, as a parting present: where one can no longer love, there one should *pass by*."[20]

LS: The next speech, of the Apostates: by this Nietzsche means those who have returned to religion—apostates of the free mind, as he calls them elsewhere.

In the speech on "The Return Home," Nietzsche spoke of solitude as distinguished from forsakenness among many. In solitude you can speak freely without considering all kinds of feelings, without compassion. Now let us read on page 295 from the speech on the return home.

Reader: "Here, however, you are in your own home and house; here you can talk freely about everything and pour out all the reasons; nothing here is ashamed of obscure, obdurate feelings. Here all things come caressingly to your discourse and flatter you, for they want to ride on your back. On every parable you ride to every truth."[21]

LS: This is a very strange sentence. All things become like friendly animals or children. They will be lifted or carried by Zarathustra, and they lift and carry Zarathustra by becoming likenesses. This is very enigmatic and is taken up later on page 296, second paragraph.

Reader: For in darkness, time weighs more heavily on us than in the light. Here the words and word-shrines of all being open up before me: here all being wishes to become word, all becoming wishes to learn from me how to speak.[22]

LS: Being and becoming become word and language. The words are contained in being and becoming, and on the other hand, being and becoming learn to speak from Zarathustra. In solitude, there is a perfect transparency of being in likenesses. We have seen already that crucial character of likenesses in the section on enigmatic visions.

In the sequel, we come to more intelligible sections, first "On the Three

Evils" and later "On Old and New Tablets." Let us read the beginning of "The Three Evils."

> Reader: In a dream, in the last dream of the morning, I stood in the foot-hills today—beyond the world, held scales, and weighed the world. Alas, the jealous dawn came too early and glowed me awake! She is always jealous of my glowing morning dreams.
>
> Measurable by him who has time, weighable by a good weigher, reachable by strong wings, guessable by divine nutcrackers: thus my dream found the world—my dream, a bold sailor, half ship, half hurricane, taciturn as butterflies, impatient as falcons: how did it have the patience or the time to weigh the world? Did my wisdom secretly urge it, my laughing, wide-awake day-wisdom which mocks all "infinite worlds"? For it speaks: "Wherever there is force, *number* will become mistress: she has more force."
>
> How surely my dream looked upon this finite world, not inquisitively, not acquisitively, not afraid, not begging, as if a full apple offered itself to my hand, a ripe golden apple with cool, soft, velvet skin, thus the world offered itself to me; as if a tree waved to me, broad-branched, strong-willed, bent as a support, even as a footstool for one weary of his way, thus the world stood on my foothills; as if delicate hands carried a shrine toward me, a shrine open for the delight of bashful, adoring eyes, thus the world offered itself to me today; not riddle enough to frighten away human love, not solution enough to put to sleep human wisdom: a humanly good thing the world was to me today, though one speaks so much evil of it.[23]

LS: The world must be seen somehow as finite. Only as such can the world be good, humanly good. It is not to be completely enigmatic, but on the other hand, it must be elusive to be good. The elusiveness decides the goodness of the good. The nonelusive world, whose riddles would be completely solved or solvable, would become insignificant, shallow, unattractive. The consecration of the world follows the consecration of the earth and the consecration of the heaven. What is the basis of all that? In the case of eternal return, a vision and a riddle; now, a dream. But those visions and dreams must be interpreted.

The world which is humanly good is the apparent world, the world in which we live, in opposition to the true world, the afterworld of either revelation or science. Still, what about the true world, if only the true world of science? The true world is relative to the absolute perspective of the purely contemplative mind, and such a mind does not exist. Knowledge is a function of mind; therefore, the richest human being creates the richest world as his image, and this image is the world. From this, one would have to start to understand the statement in the speech "The Return Home" about things and their likenesses.

Now let us take the fourth paragraph on page 299.

Reader: How shall I thank my morning dream that I thus weighed the world this morning? As a humanly good thing it came to me, this dream and heart-comforter. And to imitate it by day and to learn from it what was best in it, I shall now place the three most evil things on the scales and weigh them humanly well. He that taught to bless also taught to curse; what are the three best cursed things in the world? I shall put them on the scales.

Sex, the lust to rule, selfishness: these three have so far been best cursed and worst reputed and lied about; these three I will weigh humanly well.[24]

LS: "Sex" is not a very good translation. I think lust would be much better. Zarathustra imitates his dream while awake. His clear understanding of the goodness of certain alleged evils, the three evils mentioned here, would not have been possible without a previous enigmatic vision of the goodness of the whole, although it is intelligible to some extent. What Nietzsche says about the goodness of the three alleged evils is intelligible in itself, but in Nietzsche's view this is only a consequence of a previous enigmatic vision of the whole. What he implies is this: if the world is not finite, this new morality has no basis.

Reader: Well then, here are my foothills and there the sea: *that* rolls toward me, shaggy, flattering, the faithful old hundred-headed canine monster that I love. Well then, here I will hold the scales over the rolling sea; and a witness I choose too, to look on—you, solitary tree, fragrant and broad-vaulted, that I love.

LS: What Nietzsche means is this. His weighing of these three evils takes place in the absence of man, in the presence of the sea and trees—in the absence of man, because it is from the point of view beyond man, of the superman.

Reader: On what bridge does the present pass to the future? By what compulsion does the higher compel itself to the lower? And what bids even the highest grow still higher?[25]

LS: These questions are references to the superman. The justification of these evils is made with a view to a much higher future of man, and not for the sake of laxity or convenience.

The next speech is explicitly devoted to the spirit of heaviness, a subject which has been discussed before. The spirit of heaviness or gravity is the spirit which needs support, certainty, eternal or sempiternal being, and is rooted in the fear of death. Its opposite is the spirit of lightness, which is not afraid. What is the spirit of lightness?

> Reader: And verily, this is no command for today and tomorrow, to *learn* to love oneself. Rather, it is of all arts the subtlest, the most cunning, the ultimate, and the most patient. For whatever is his own is well concealed from the owner; and of all treasures, it is our own that we dig up last: thus the spirit of gravity orders it.[26]

LS: Self-love must be learned, but love to begin with is not love at all. The good and evil in which we believe and in the light of which we are self-lovers is not our own good and evil, but we are endowed with it. It is not enough to reject, for one's own is not yet the self, which deserves to be loved.

With a view to Nietzsche's whole moral philosophy we should also read page 307, paragraphs 5 through 6.

> Reader: A trying and questioning was my every move; and verily, one must also learn to answer such questioning. That, however, is my taste—not good, not bad, but *my* taste of which I am no longer ashamed and which I have no wish to hide.
>
> "This is *my* way; where is yours?"—thus I answered those who asked me "the way." For *the* way—that does not exist.[27]

LS: Now, if you look at the heading of the next speech, "On Old and New Tablets," a difficulty becomes obvious. On the tablets are the laws, the ways, which are not merely the ways of this or that individual. And yet Nietzsche says *the* way does not exist.

Student: Is there an end to which all ways lead?

LS: That would be one solution to the problem, but it could also be that the tablets are essentially incomplete and that the completion, which is the decisive act, depends entirely on the individual.

The speech following "On Old and New Tablets," the speech "The Convalescent," is the last statement of eternal return. But let us begin on page 308, section 2.[28]

> Reader: When I came to men I found them sitting on an old conceit: the conceit that they have long known what is good and evil for man. All talk of virtue seemed an old and weary matter to man; and whoever wanted to sleep well still talked of good and evil before going to sleep.
>
> I disturbed this sleepiness when I taught: what is good and evil *no one knows yet*, unless it be he who creates. He, however, creates man's goal and gives the earth its meaning and its future. That anything at all is good and evil—that is his creation.[29]

LS: Does this statement ring a bell? All men claim to know, but this is simply a conceit: We are ignorant as to good and evil. Answer: Socrates. In a certain way, Nietzsche restores the Socratic question. In a certain way, Socrates seems to have arrived at an answer to what are good and evil. This answer, this knowledge of good and evil, was handed down from generation to generation. Nietzsche explicitly raises the question: But what is the difference? He says no one knows it yet, by which he indicates it is knowable. Nietzsche restores the question but answers it in an entirely un-Socratic way. Hitherto no one knew what was good and evil; what men believed to be good and evil were unconscious creations, primarily of peoples. Remember the speech in the first part, "On the Thousand and One Goals": this notion of good and evil is no longer possible; the people have ceased to be spiritual. Nor is the universal good and bad as revealed by God possible, but even this creation of good and evil is somehow meant to be knowledge. The creator of good and evil knows. In other words, these are not mere postulates. Let us read on page 309.

> Reader: Verily, like preachers of repentance and fools, I raised a hue and cry of wrath over what among them is great and small, and that their best is still so small. And that their greatest evil too is still so small—at that I laughed.
>
> My wise longing cried and laughed thus out of me—born in the mountains, verily, a wild wisdom—my great broad-winged longing! And often it swept me away and up and far, in the middle of my laughter; and I flew, quivering, an arrow, through sun-drunken delight, away into distant futures which no dream had yet seen, into hotter souths than artists ever dreamed of, where gods in their dances are ashamed of all clothes—to

speak in parables and to limp and stammer like poets; and verily, I am ashamed that I must still be a poet.[30]

LS: You see, the knowledge which Nietzsche has of good and evil is transmitted only by likenesses. It is a poetic knowledge, and *poiēsis* means in Greek primarily making. It is a poetic knowledge and therefore an imperfect knowledge, as you see from the end of the speech.

Let us read the next three paragraphs.

Reader: Where all becoming seemed to me the dance of gods and the prankishness of gods, and the world seemed free and frolicsome and as if fleeing back to itself—as an eternal fleeing and seeking each other again of many gods, as the happy controverting of each other, conversing again with each other, and converging again of many gods.

Where all time seemed to me a happy mockery of moments, where necessity was freedom itself playing happily with the sting of freedom.

Where I also found again my old devil and arch-enemy, the spirit of gravity, and all that he created: constraint, statute, necessity and consequence and purpose and will and good and evil.

For must there not be that *over* which one dances and dances away? For the sake of the light and the lightest, must there not be moles and grave dwarfs?[31]

LS: You see here again allusions to the eternal return and the need for the imperfect. As presented in a riddle, the vision of the eternal return is the basis of the new tablet, just as the dream of the world is the justification for the three alleged evils. Here you see the difference from Socrates most clearly. Socrates's investigation of good and evil, of human things, precedes his vision of the whole. In Nietzsche the opposite is true. From the sequel it appears that the new tablets are half-written. One reason may be that Zarathustra still has to talk in likenesses and still has to be a poet. Also, there is not *the* way; therefore the tables cannot be fully written. The second part is to be written by every man himself. This much about that long speech in general.

Let us turn to the most intelligible part, number 10, on page 314.

Reader: "Thou shalt not rob! Thou shalt not kill!" Such words were once called holy; one bent the knee and the head and took off one's shoes before them. But I ask you: where have there ever been better robbers and killers in this world than such holy words?

Is there not in all life itself robbing and killing? And that such words were called holy—was not truth itself killed thereby? Or was it the preaching of death that was called holy, which contradicted and contravened all life? O my brothers, break, break the old tablets![32]

LS: It is clear that Nietzsche does not mean we should now begin to rob and kill. What he has in mind is this. Is the simple prohibition against robbing and killing not at variance with the nature of life, and therefore with the nature of human life? This is of course an old question. I remind you only of Machiavelli and certain successors of Machiavelli. Is the world so constructed that self-preservation is not possible without the destruction of others? In Locke and Rousseau, self-preservation requires the preservation of everyone else because our lives are more endangered by other human beings, and therefore a state of peace is the demand of self-preservation. But Locke qualifies: only if this does not come into conflict with our own self-preservation. And similarly, Rousseau. One has to consider the situation of which they are always speaking: not merely war, because then one has to make the distinction between just and unjust wars, but the fundamental problem is the problem of scarcity. In situations of extreme scarcity, where all men cannot preserve themselves, what is the meaning of the unqualified prohibition against robbing and killing? Nietzsche would say such prohibitions would lead to a lowering of man. All the warlike qualities in man would disappear.

At the end of this remark, there is a close parallel to the seventh speech here, and there he develops the thesis that the good man never tells the truth. The good men are those who accept the Second Table of the Decalogue as simply valid. This kind of goodness requires a blindness to the human situation, and in that sense they never tell the truth.

Reader: This is my pity for all that is past: I see how all of it is abandoned—abandoned to the pleasure, the spirit, the madness of every generation, which comes along and reinterprets all that has been as a bridge to itself.

A great despot might come along, a shrewd monster who, according to his pleasure and displeasure, might constrain and strain all that is past till it becomes a bridge to him, a harbinger and herald and cockcrow.

This, however, is the other danger and what prompts my further pity: whoever is of the rabble, thinks back as far as the grandfather; with the grandfather, however, time ends.

Thus all that is past is abandoned: for one day the rabble might become master and drown all time in shallow waters.

Therefore, my brothers, a *new nobility* is needed to be the adversary of all rabble and of all that is despotic and to write anew upon new tablets the word "noble."

For many who are noble are needed, and noble men of many kinds, that there may be a nobility. Or as I once said in a parable: "Precisely this is godlike that there are gods, but no God."[33]

LS: We have read this passage before and tried to connect it with the problem of democracy as defended by Tocqueville. In the preceding speech, Nietzsche had demanded the breaking of the old tablets, a break with the past. He explains what breaking with the past means in his teaching: it presupposes a recollection of the past, not this rejecting of the past of which he is speaking here. The overcoming of the past is endangered by forgetting the past. Forgetting the past is mere rebarbarization, and is the result of the two new kinds of regime: tyranny and democracy. This remark about the new nobility seems to be the clearest expression of Nietzsche's political expectations, but it is questionable whether it was meant that way. We find the following statement:

The *one* movement is unconditional: the leveling of humanity, structures of ants ... the *other* movement: my movement: is on the contrary the sharpening of all opposition[s] ... removal of equality, the creation of superpowerful men. The *other* movement creates[34] the last man; *my* movement creates[35] the superman. It is *altogether not* the goal to regard the superman as the masters of the last men:[36] but: two kinds should coexist, side by side—separated as much as possible; the one[s], like [the] *Epicurean gods, not caring for the others*.[37]

That means, clearly, no political relation. This only increases the great question of the political meaning of Nietzsche's doctrine. If this new nobility does not have a political meaning proper, and if Nietzsche attacks any possibility of political organization in our age, does he not take on an infinite political responsibility which might lead to the collapse of any civilization—as, for example, of Germany in the thirties?

Let us leave it at that. Next time we shall discuss the speech "The Convalescent," the last explicit discussion of eternal return.

13 Creative Contemplation

Zarathustra, Part 3, 13

Leo Strauss: There is a great variety of opinions as to the meaning of natural right or natural law. For instance, some people, when hearing these expressions, think primarily of the precepts of the Second Table of the Decalogue, while others may think of the allegedly natural order of society as set forth in Plato's *Republic*.[1] (If you do not catch all of the little words, that doesn't make any difference, later on it will be reread.) Nietzsche may be said to have rejected entirely natural right in the first sense of the term. As for the first sense, he speaks of it in *Portable Nietzsche*— that's the edition which you use—on page 314, number 10. As for the second meaning: the same edition, pages 314–15, number 11, and pages 643–47 (the latter is paragraph 57 of *The Antichrist*). Explain, first, Nietzsche's reasoning regarding the first meaning of natural right, by which I mean regarding that passage on page 314, number 10, where he takes issue with [natural right or natural law in the sense of the Decalogue]. Second, explain Nietzsche's hesitation to set forth his doctrine of the natural hierarchy of man as an objectively true doctrine.[2]

Will you take up page 308, paragraph 2 through 3, and will you read it?

Reader: When I came to men I found them sitting on an old conceit: the conceit that they have long known what is good and evil for man. All talk of virtue seemed an old and weary matter to man; and whoever wanted to sleep well still talked of good and evil before going to sleep.

I disturbed this sleepiness when I taught: what is good and evil *no one knows yet*, unless it be he who creates. He, however, creates man's goal and gives the earth its meaning and its future. That anything at all is good and evil—that is his creation.[3]

LS: Yes, that is fine. Now you see that Nietzsche says that everyone has taken for granted the answer to the question of what is good and evil.

He makes this a question, and this was, as you know, the question raised by Socrates, who used similar formulations. Nietzsche returns to the Socratic question. Let us reflect on that for a moment. There is something in Nietzsche which reminds of Socrates. Both are not merely theoretical teachers, as the other great philosophers are. They are also, in Greek, *psychagōgoi*, "guides of the soul," fascinating as human beings as well as repelling as human beings.[4] We cannot forget them as individuals while listening to their speeches. In the case of the purely theoretical teacher— say, the mathematician—you must forget completely about them. They[5] draw their own portraits, speak about themselves. Only Rousseau has a similar character, and he had an effect similar to Nietzsche's a century or so earlier, an effect which is now spent. There is an effect of Socrates which is not spent, nor that of Nietzsche. You may contrast this with another case of a philosopher speaking of himself, and that is Descartes, who gave a kind of autobiography in his *Discourse on Method*, but the emphasis isn't entirely, as I try to indicate, on the method. Descartes uses his autobiography, a somewhat fictitious autobiography, as a device for setting forth this method. He is not interested in making us interested in him. But Socrates, in contradistinction to Nietzsche, did not write, and this contributes to Socrates's fascinating effect. So this was always "personal," in quotation marks.[6] He never addressed anonymous men, men he did not know and see, whereas every writer addresses anonymous men, men he does not know and see.

Socrates is presented in writing not by himself, but by Plato. Plato presented Socrates's life—his work or his deed, Socrates in action—as a model, but as a model which could not be imitated by everyone, and even by anyone. Socrates has a certain teacher which Plato calls, or Socrates himself may have called, his *daimonion*, his daemonic thing, which is a reality for Socrates, according to Socrates himself. As a presentation of an individual in action, Plato's work is not a philosophic work simply, but somehow poetic. Let us never forget that a philosophic reflection proper is in the form of a treatise, in which no proper names occur except accidentally. Nietzsche's work too is poetic, although in an entirely different way. To mention only the most obvious difference: Nietzsche's poetry, if you can call it that way, is not dramatic but lyrical. There is very little of the dialogue here, as you will see. In a section to which we shall turn later, in the third part, "Of the Great Longing," we find a conversation of Zarathustra with his soul. No such thing occurs in Plato. There is of course a conversation of Socrates with his soul, alluded to at the beginning of the

Banquet, but we are not told in what it consists, so that his conversations as presented by Plato are entirely conversations with other individuals. And needless to say, only the conversations with other individuals can be strictly dramatic, and not the conversation of a man with his soul.

Now, why did Nietzsche restore the Socratic question? And assuming that this question properly understood leads to the consequence that the questioner, in his individuality, becomes somehow the theme: Why is Plato's thematization of Socrates so different from Nietzsche's thematization of Nietzsche? The difference between Nietzsche and Zarathustra is not important in this context. A full answer to these questions would require a much deeper and a much more comprehensive understanding of both Socrates/Plato and Nietzsche than I possess.

Let us take a shortcut, which is sufficient for our present purposes. Let us see how Nietzsche himself viewed Socrates, and let us limit ourselves to Nietzsche's first book, *The Birth of Tragedy out of the Spirit of Music,* in which Socrates plays a central role.[7] The thesis of this early book can be reduced to the following point. The highest culture that ever was was Greek culture, and the peak of Greek culture was Greek tragedy. Socrates did not understand tragedy, and he even destroyed the tragedy. He made poetry ministerial to the city or to philosophy and therefore subordinated tragedy to the *polis* or to philosophy, and thus he did not leave tragedy as it was. As a consequence of Socrates's work, poetry in general and tragedy in particular became the subject of a discipline called poetics, of which we have the famous document in Aristotle's *Poetics.* Now this poetics is an adjunct of ethics or politics, and even perhaps a part of logic. At least in the medieval tradition, logic was divided: it consisted of a number of parts. For example, one is rhetoric, which deals with rhetorical truth; and one is poetics, which deals with poetic truth. This shows the complete subordination of poetry to philosophy. Socrates preferred the lucidity of thought and insight, the awakeness of criticism and the precision of dialectics, to instinct, divining, and creativity . . . Socrates's praise of knowledge means that the whole is intelligible and that knowledge of the whole is a remedy for all evil, or that virtue is knowledge and that the virtue which is knowledge is happiness.[8] This is optimism, and optimism on the basis of judgment. Socrates is the prototype or the first ancestor of the theoretical man, the man for whom science is not a job or a profession but a way of life, that which enables him to live and . . . Socrates is therefore not only the most problematic phenomenon of antiquity, but "the one turning point and vortex in the history of mankind,"[9] the most fateful of all men, for the first fate of men since that time is rationalism, and Socrates originated it. (This Nietzschean thesis regarding rationalism as the fate of the West was taken up in a more limited way in the sociological studies of Max Weber, as you would see if you would look at them in their context.)

Now the tradition founded by Socrates was shaken by modern science and modern philosophy. It was most visibly shaken in the nineteenth century by . . . the thought of Schopenhauer, Nietzsche's teacher. This pessimism was pessimistic also regarding reason. Not reason or science but art—and in particular, music—revealed the true character of reality. This peculiar thesis of Schopenhauer was prepared by modern science: it was modern science, trying to disclose the true world, the world as it is in itself, that led to the inevitable distinction between the true world and the world disclosed by theoretical physics, and the world in which we live, the human world. And this is the basis of all later philosophic study. It is connected with a certain phenomenon, which I can here only enumerate—the close analysis would mean relativity. It was only in the eighteenth century that a science emerged which was called at that time aesthetics. In the tradition, there was a kind of science called poetics. You know about Aristotle's *Poetics*, and that was continued throughout the ages, and there is an enormous literature on how to make poems and of how to judge poems and . . . whatever it may be. But that was a very specialized thing, of no philosophic relevance. The beautiful as beautiful was a great theme of the tradition of philosophy, but this has nothing to do with aesthetics. The beautiful as beautiful was a theme of metaphysics, not of aesthetics, for the simple reason that the beautiful in the primary sense of the tradition was much more the natural beautiful than the beautiful of human art. The enormous change, which took place around 1800, was when it was declared that the true seat of beauty is not nature but the work of art. Hegel's aesthetics is perhaps the greatest document of this change. Another change, which I can here only mention and which has something to do with what occurred also in the eighteenth century: psychology had been based throughout the ages on a bi-partition of the soul into perceiving, and deciding or willing. And now in the eighteenth century the suggestion was made that a further division is needed: perceiving, willing, and feeling—and there is a connection between the emergence of feeling as a wholly independent theme of psychology and the emergence of aesthetics as a philosophic discipline of art in general.

All this was preparatory to the emergence anew that art is superior
to science, that art is closer to reality than science. Reality related more
deeply to feeling than to detached perceiving. We all are brought up in
such a tradition to the extent to which we are not brought up in the parallel tradition of science, and therefore we all are poets in prose. Now
Nietzsche was a philosopher who can be said to have gone farther in this
respect. He tries to uproot Socrates and everything built on a Socratic
foundation, but by going to the root—to the root of the whole tradition
of rational philosophy, of rationalism in any sense of the word—he meets
Socrates again, because he goes that far. That is the secret, I think, of the
fact of this strange fascination which Socrates had for Nietzsche as . . .

I will read to you a passage which shows on the one hand the closeness
of Nietzsche to Socrates, and on the other hand, or at the same time, the
radical differences. The passage in *Beyond Good and Evil*, aphorism 295:

Genius of the heart: as it is possessed by that great Hidden One, the
Tempter-God and born Rat-Catcher of the Conscience, whose voice can
climb into the underworld of any soul,[10] who never speaks a word or looks
a look in which there is not some hind-sight, some complexity of allure
whose craftsmanship includes knowing how to be an illusion—not an illusion [or delusion—LS] of what he is, but of what constitutes one more
compulsion upon his followers to follow him ever more intimately and
thoroughly—*genius of the heart* which renders dumb all that is loud and
complaisant, teaching it how to listen, which smooths rough souls and
creates a taste in them for a new desire: to lie still like a mirror so that the
deep sky might be reflected in them—*genius of the heart* which teaches the
bungling and precipitous hand to hesitate and handle things delicately,
which guesses the hidden and forgotten treasure, the drop of goodness and
sweet intelligence beneath layers of murky thick ice; which is a divining
rod for every speck of gold that lies buried in its dungeon of deep muck
and sand—*genius of the heart*, upon whose touch everyone departs richer,
not full of grace, not surprised, not enriched and oppressed as though by
strange goods, but richer in himself, newer than before, cracked wide open,
blown upon and drawn out by a spring wind, more uncertain now perhaps,
more delicate, fragile, and broken, but full of hopes that have no names as
yet, full of new will and flow, full of new ill will and counter-flow—but
what am I doing, my friends? Of whom am I speaking? Did I forget myself
so far as not to tell you his name? Unless you yourselves have guessed who
this questionable spirit and God is; who it is that demands such praise!

For, as happens to everyone who from his early years has been a wanderer and an exile, many a strange and precarious spirit has run across my path. Foremost of all of them, and again and again, the one I was telling you about, no less a one than[11] the God *Dionysos*, the great Ambivalent One and Tempter-God, the one to whom I once, as you know, in all secrecy and all reverence, sacrificed my first-born [that means *The Spirit of Tragedy*;[12] Dionysos is the God of the dramatic art—LS] (having been the last, it seems to me, to sacrifice anything to him, for I found no one who understood what I was doing at that time). Meanwhile I learned much, all too much, of this God's philosophy by word of mouth, as I have said—I, the last disciple and initiate of the God Dionysos. It is really time, therefore, to give you, my friends, a small taste of this philosophy, insofar as I am permitted. *Sotto voce*, as is proper, for it is a matter of many things that are mysterious, new, exotic, strange, uncanny. Even that Dionysus is a philosopher and hence that Gods philosophize seems to me a piece of precarious news, designed to create suspicion among philosophers.[13]

I think that the translation is really very bad, but I would be completely unable to translate it properly from the original. Let us consider this last sentence: "Gods philosophize." That means . . . and Nietzsche refers here to a passage in Plato's *Banquet*, where Socrates says that only human beings philosophize, because to philosophize means seeking wisdom, and the Gods are wise and therefore they do not seek wisdom, they do not philosophize.[14] What does this mean, this strange expression? If the Gods are wise, then the whole is intelligible in itself. Wisdom is possible, although it is not fully intelligible, for man. But if even the Gods philosophize, if even the Gods are not wise, the whole is essentially elusive. The adequate form in which the truth must appear is an enigmatic vision, a passionate image. That is the form in which the truth appears, that is to say, the life-giving truth as distinguished from the deadly truth of science. This we have seen more than once, but here poetry or art is fundamentally insufficient nevertheless. At the end of the speech "On Poets," Nietzsche says that poets must become penitents of the spirit, that is to say, men of science—as Nietzsche means it, men of intellectual honesty. Therefore the relation is that life-giving truth is not simply opposed to the deadly truth of science: the life-giving truth is the deadly truth of science if freed from the spirit of revenge and the spirit of gratitude. The deadly truth of science: there is no being but only becoming; nature is valueless and meaningless and there is no essential difference between men and beasts,

and so on. But this deadly truth becomes life-giving truth—so the affirmation of the eternal becoming in an eternal return.

Differently stated, the deadly truth of science, objective knowledge,
is concerned with the text as distinguished from any interpretation: the
accurate truth not idealized in any way. The life-giving truth, on the other
hand, is primarily the subjective truth, the will to power's imprinting
meaning and value on the meaningless . . . Then objective knowledge is
proved as the will to power turning against itself, becoming critical of
its own intrinsic activity. But in the last stage of this process, the will to
power as the imprinting of meaning and value is at the same time the
will to the future, because there is no meaning without an ideal, without
a view of the future. As the will to the future, the will to power is necessarily a negation of the past, and therefore it is not fully positive. The
fully positive will, the will which is mere and pure yea-saying, is no longer
will simply, but acceptance. The highest form of the will to power turning
against itself is acceptance of the whole, and that means the whole is divine in its purposes and nonrationality. The peak of the will is acceptance.
You can also put it as follows: the peak of creation is contemplation or,
differently stated, true contemplation is creation. And if the theme of
contemplation is nature, nature is only, at least in its fullness, by virtue
of contemplative creation. That is the paradoxical teaching of Nietzsche.

Now to say it again: the fundamental difference between Nietzsche
and the tradition in the simplest form is explained by contrasting Nietzsche with Socrates/Plato. For Socrates/Plato, the themes of contemplation are the ideas, and they are in no way man's creation. And there is
a human relation to the ideas, and in a way, the fundamental character
of this thought is therefore *erōs*, longing for something preexistent. The
place of these ideas and *erōs* in this context is taken by Nietzsche into
the will to power as it creates any ideas or ideals; therefore there cannot
be contemplation proper in Nietzsche. But the nearest approximation
to contemplation is what we may call by the term, now common and familiar, "creative contemplation." The argument would be this. There must
be harmony between the knower and the known, but if the known, the
object, the reality, is will to power—i.e., creativity—only the creativity of
the knower can be in harmony with its object. Contemplation must be
creative contemplation. Hence Nietzsche's doctrine of the will to power is
at the same time creation and contemplation of what is. As creation, it is
incompatible with the spirit of gratitude. That means there cannot be certainty or demonstration, but only pointing to. All human activity, hence

all knowledge, is a modification of the will to power. The will to power means overcoming and it means in the highest stages self-overcoming, and the highest stage of self-overcoming is acceptance of what is. But acceptance as full acceptance in the most radical sense consists in the positing of eternal return. You accept a thing fully if you are willing to will its eternal return. The eternity of [the ideas or universals] of mental perception in the Platonic/Aristotelian sense survives somehow in the demand for enigmatic vision for eternal return. That is really the peak of Nietzsche's teaching.

I must develop it a bit more, and later on you can try to explain this in the discussion. We start again from the premise that reality is will to power and there is no essential difference between men and brutes. There is no nature of man, strictly speaking. Given this premise, the doctrine of eternal return—which means, subjectively, transformation of the will into acceptance—is the only way there can be knowledge, as acknowledging what is; and it is the only way in which there can be nature, that is to say, that which is by itself and not by being willed or posited. But precisely because acceptance is transformed will, will survives in the acceptance, in the contemplation. Contemplation is creative. Now this term is of course relatively familiar today. I thought by accident of the work of Pasternak, the author of *Doctor Zhivago*, whom you have probably read or of whom you have probably heard, when he speaks of Tolstoy:

> The chief quality of this moralist, leveller, and preacher of a system of justice that would embrace everybody without fear or favor would be an originality that distinguished him from everyone else and that verged on the paradoxical.
>
> All his life and at any given moment he possessed the faculty of seeing things in the detached finality of each separate moment, in sharp relief, as we see things only on rare occasions, in childhood, or on the crest of an all-embracing happiness, or in the triumph of a great spiritual victory.
>
> To see things like that it is necessary that one's eye should be directed by passion. For it is passion that by its flash illuminates an object, intensifying its appearance.
>
> Such a passion, the passion of creative contemplation, Tolstoy constantly carried about within himself. Indeed, it was in its light that he saw everything in its pristine freshness, in a new way, as though for the first time. The authenticity of what he saw differs so much from what we are used to that it may appear strange to us. But Tolstoy was not looking for

this strangeness, he was not pursuing it as an aim in itself and he most
certainly did not use it in his works as a literary method.[15]

But I suppose you are more familiar than I am with this kind of aes-
thetic analysis. Something of this kind must be kept in mind if one tries
to understand Nietzsche. This contemplation is meant to be creative contemplation and yet not the creative contemplation of the poet, and we
must try to understand that, because . . .
Now let us read another passage in *Zarathustra* before we go on, on
page 277, the end of the fifth paragraph, the passage which we have read
but which we will reread now.

Reader: But this is my blessing: to stand over every single thing as its own
heaven, as its round roof, its azure bell, and eternal security: and blessed
is he who blesses thus.[16]

LS: Let us stop here. To let anything be what it is, not to be distorted,
not to do violence to it—that is true perception. Every construction of
the thing, every reduction of the thing by virtue of scientific method does
not permit the thing to be what it is. Generally, knowledge is something
like this: to let everything be what it is in its fullness. But why must this
be creative? Why is this not simply taking, perceiving the thing, being
open to what the thing is? Why must it be creative? Why must Zarathustra bless these things so that they are protected by him as if he were
the heaven above him? What does it mean? Zarathustra is needed, we
can say, because the heaven is not sufficient for the purpose. Why? The
heaven itself is subject to interpretation. You can also say that heaven
has been dissolved or is dissolved by modern scientific analysis. Man, or
a certain kind of man—that is to say, the highest form of the will to
power—must do what heaven does not manifestly do. He must conse-
crate every thing, every being, so that it can be what it is. But this is not
sufficient for giving the eternal security of which Nietzsche speaks. Only
by virtue of eternal return, a human postulate, primarily can it fully be, for
every being is conditioned. It has causes: its ultimate causes are outside
of the realm of human experience. There is science applied and therefore
we have here—side by side with science, which goes beyond the realm
of human experience in order to discover the causes of things—an art
which remains strictly within the realm of human experience. Science or
metaphysics goes beyond what is within the realm of human experience.

It conjectures the ultimate causes. But this conjecture and positing of first causes is inevitable unless the will to power is converted from positing the transtemporal or the transhuman to willing eternal return. Only by being willed eternally can the thing fully be. One can state it paradoxically (we will come across a passage where Nietzsche says so later): that the thing itself cannot fully be if it is not, in a way, its own cause, so that by seeking for its causes, you do not have to go beyond the thing. You do not have to dissolve the thing in its causes, and this would be possible if the thing is its own cause by virtue of eternal return.

The other way to state it: philosophy as the most spiritual will[17] to power is the will to the *causa prima* (that is, the first cause), as Nietzsche put it in the [ninth aphorism of *Beyond Good and Evil*]. That means that philosophy is the origin of meaning and value, the fundamental will of man—either of the individual thinker or, in former ages, of the people. This will is the origin and precondition that we cannot go back behind unless we have an absolute system of mediation, which is beyond the interpretation. Otherwise there is always a relativity that each system of interpretation is as defensible as every other system, so that this will becomes the origin and precondition. Yet it is impossible to deny that this will, meaning-giving will, is at the same time conditioned. For instance, not the ego creates, but the self, and the self is a product of heritage, tradition, so that the alleged first cause is conditioned by its cause. And secondly, as will, it is directed towards the future but on the basis of the past which transforms. The past is given: imposed, not willed. If the will of an individual human being, say, of Nietzsche, is to be the origin of meaning and value, and that will manifestly has a cause, the only way out in order to save this position is to say that this will is the cause of itself: eternal return.

We should read some passages in the last statement occurring in *Zarathustra* on eternal return. That is the speech "The Convalescent," on page 327 following. We make an . . . first and then we'll turn to the questions, because I do not know whether I have made sufficiently clear what I have been trying to do for quite a few lectures: the necessity which drove Nietzsche into this, in his day absolutely paradoxical, not to say absurd, doctrine of eternal return.

Well, perhaps let us first read a few passages. On page 327, paragraph 4.

Reader: One morning, not long after his return to the cave, Zarathustra jumped up from his resting place like a madman, roared in a terrible voice, and acted as if somebody else were still lying on his resting place who refused to get up. And Zarathustra's voice resounded so that his animals approached in a fright, while out of all the caves and nooks that were near Zarathustra's cave all animals fled—flying, fluttering, crawling, jumping, according to the kind of feet or wings that were given to them. Zarathustra, however, spoke these words:

LS: Now before you go on, as for this symbolism, the doctrine of the eternal return is the condition of the superman; and that means it is the condition for the overcoming of the subhuman, of the mere animal in man.

Reader: Up, abysmal thought, out of my depth! I am your cock and dawn, sleepy worm. Up! Up! My voice shall yet crow you awake! Unfasten the fetters of your ears: listen! For I want to hear you. Up! Up! Here is thunder enough to make even tombs learn to listen. And wipe sleep and all that is purblind and blind out of your eyes! Listen to me even with your eyes: my voice cures even those born blind.[18]

LS: Yes, that is already enough. You see, the abysmal thought—that is, the thought of eternal return—is in Zarathustra. It should obey Zarathustra, but Zarathustra also obeys it. We can say that this reflects the situation that it is at the same time a creation and a contemplation. In the sequel, it appears that he cannot bear the thought. While he loses his consciousness, his animals—his eagles and his serpents—take care of him. When he has come to, his animals talk to him. Just his animals talk to him: there is a bridge between him and his animals. This of course cannot really . . . This is an image, a likeness, pointing indirectly at the impossibility of a bridge between men and brutes, and connected with that to the absence of a bridge between any man and any other man. That he develops on page 329, paragraphs 2 to 4.

Reader: "O, my animals," replied Zarathustra, "chatter on like this and let me listen. It is so refreshing for me to hear you chattering: where there is chattering, there the world lies before me like a garden. How lovely it is that there are words and sounds! Are not words and sounds rainbows and illusive bridges between things which are eternally apart?

"To every soul there belongs another world; for every soul, every other soul is an afterworld. Precisely between what is most similar, illusion lies most beautifully; for the smallest cleft is the hardest to bridge.

"For me—how should there be any outside-myself? There is no outside. But all sounds make us forget this; how lovely it is that we forget. Have not names and sounds been given to things that man might find things refreshing? Speaking is a beautiful folly: with that man dances over all things. How lovely is all talking, and all the deception of sounds! With sounds, our love dances on many-hued rainbows."[19]

LS: Yes. There is no bridge between any soul and any other soul. There is no without. All knowledge—of the highest level, at any rate—is incommunicable. There is no without, and the only communication is that indirect one by beings which are, however, always differently understood by different beings. There is no without, there is no objective knowledge, therefore an infinite variety of mediation, of interpretation. All speech is fictitious. What is, is not . . . what is, is elusive. Therefore every speech must be taken lightly, not in the spirit of heaviness with the precision of language.

Reader: "O, Zarathustra," the animals said, "to those who think as we do, all things themselves are dancing: they come and offer their hands and laugh and flee—and come back. Everything goes, everything comes back; eternally rolls the wheel of being. Everything dies, everything blossoms again; eternally runs the year of being. Everything breaks, everything is joined anew; eternally the same house of being is built. Everything parts, everything greets every other thing again; eternally the ring of being remains faithful to itself. In every Now, being begins; round every Here, rolls the sphere There. The center is everywhere. Bent is the path of eternity."[20]

LS: In other words, the animals, the beings without speech, are here represented as stating the doctrine of eternal return. There is no future. There is no future, whereas the thought of future is essential to man and obviously of the greatest importance for Nietzsche's thought of the superman. Somehow it is necessary for man, Nietzsche indicates, to return to this view which the animals, the beings not possessing speech or [reason], would take if they could speak. The animals can state the doctrine of the eternal return without any suffering. Eternal return is of course also, in this radical form, the emptiness of every moment. The center is everywhere, whereas in the scheme of history the center is not everywhere: the center is in the noon, in the moment of final truth when the will to power and the superman is seen. In the perspective of mere nature, there is no such difference in the rolling[21] of different moments. But Nietzsche tries to return to the indispensable to preserve the human perspective, which for him is a historical perspective. But this must be viewed ultimately in a transhistoric perspective, and that is what eternal return means. So in other words, there is this future: there is this moving up to a peak and then down, but this eternal return. That is the only way according to Nietzsche in which the unity of history and nature can be established.

The animals state the doctrine of the eternal return without any difficulty, without suffering. They do not suffer because, as it is said later on, they are cruel, the eagle and the serpent. But is man not cruel? The question goes on, on page 330, paragraphs 2 to 3.

> Reader: "have you already made a hurdy-gurdy song of this? But now I lie here, still weary of this biting and spewing, still sick from my own redemption. *And you watched all this?* O my animals, are even you cruel? Did you want to watch my great pain as men do? For man is the cruelest animal.
>
> "At tragedies, bullfights, and crucifixions he has so far felt best on earth; and when he invented hell for himself, behold, that was his heaven on earth."[22]

LS: And so on. Man is the cruelest animal, but he was not cruel enough. He did not dare to inflict on his most difficult things the doctrine of eternal return. He was not evil enough, for the rank of his goodness depends on the rank of his evil. Now what does this mean? It is frequently occurring to Zarathustra. You remember we spoke occasionally of the superhuman as a condition for the being of the superman. What does evil mean here? Nietzsche doesn't really suggest that some entirely still more subtle and beastly instruments of torture must be invented so that man becomes civilized. That is not what he means. Evil has here a relatively strict sense. According to Nietzsche, "good and evil" means primarily what is customary and what is against custom. "Good and evil" is primarily understood in terms of custom. Evil is then primarily a deviation from the traditional or the ancestral; hence the good ones are primarily those who know what is good and evil because they live within a tradition or within a custom. Therefore, since the superman requires the most radical break with all previous tradition, he must be evil in this sense, the most extreme form.

Let us turn now to page 331, paragraph 2 to 4 in "The Convalescent."[23]

Reader: "My torture was not the knowledge that man is evil—but I cried as no one has yet cried: 'Alas, that his greatest evil is so very small! Alas, that his best is so very small!'

"The great disgust with man—*this* choked me and had crawled into my throat; and what the soothsayer said: 'All is the same, nothing is worth while, knowledge chokes.' A long twilight limped before me, a sadness, weary to death, drunken with death, speaking with a yawning mouth. 'Eternally recurs the man of whom you are weary, the small man'—thus yawned my sadness and dragged its feet and could not go to sleep. Man's earth turned into a cave for me, its chest sunken; all that is living became human mold and bones and musty past to me. My sighing sat on all human tombs and could no longer get up; my sighing and questioning croaked and gagged and gnawed and wailed by day and night: 'Alas, man recurs eternally! The small man recurs eternally!'

"Naked I had once seen both, the greatest man and the smallest man: all-too-similar to each other, even the greatest all-too-human. All-too-small, the greatest!—that was my disgust with man. And the eternal recurrence of even the smallest—that was my disgust with all existence. Alas! Nausea! Nausea! Nausea!"[24]

LS: And so on. Now Nietzsche thinks there are two themes together: the assertion, the demand for the superman, for a man transcending greatness; man . . . everything up to now is inextricably linked to this thought, and thus with the demand for the eternal return of man as he always has been. This, paradoxically, is the essence of Nietzsche's thought. We cannot read the whole point. So in other words, the very possibility of the superman rests on the overcoming of this nausea. The greatest suffering which man can inflict upon himself is the condition for the greatest bliss possible.

We read one more passage which in a way sums up the last word which Nietzsche says on the eternal return. We have[25] only three speeches on eternal return, as we have seen: the speech "On Redemption," and "On the Vision and the Riddle," and this one, "The Convalescent." We read now only page 333, paragraph 2. The animals prophesy what Zarathustra will speak in the moment of his death; that is not by Zarathustra himself.

Reader: "'Now I die and vanish' you would say, 'and all at once I am nothing. The soul is as mortal as the body. But the knot of causes in which I am
entangled recurs and will create me again. I myself belong to the causes of
the eternal recurrence.'"[26]

LS: You see that is the point to which I referred before: that by virtue
of the eternal return it becomes possible that the condition conditions not
is a condition of this condition.

Let us stop here for a moment and try to understand that. Now when
we look at the origins of things, we refer to evolution and other things
men had unearthed at a certain moment by causes which natural science
tries to discover. Then, after man had . . . emerged, he tried to find his
bearings in the world, and he did this in greatly different ways. But I speak
of culture, of interpretation of the world, and we have here in this stage
a contrast between the objective science—natural science, social science,
whatever you may please—and the subjective interpretations of the
world. We'll take as an example—say, some tribe somewhere in central
Africa has a certain understanding of the world, and this understanding
of the world is of course wrong. We know better, we have our science
and we look at these tribes from the outside and we see, we analyze, their
patterns of life, their patterns of thought in the way in which we look at
ants or moles or life, whatever it may be. This is extremely simple, and
that is, I suppose, still the common scientific approach.

But a great difficulty arises when the scientific approach itself becomes
questioned. Let us assume that there is a difficulty in the scientific approach itself, and then this criticism is carried through to its extreme. As
we may somehow reach it, it leads to the consequence that the scientific
approach is itself such a comprehensive worldview, not necessarily and
not simply the . . . to any earlier comprehensive worldview. I have discussed on other occasions why this is not a simple [rejection], but why it
becomes necessary given certain premises. Very simply: Is science itself
not a human phenomenon? Science itself does not exist in a vacuum. Is it
not a part of the historical process of man, and therefore, as belonging to
the process of history, is it in itself not to be read as such? Now if this is
taken radically, then it means the scientific view of the world is the myth
of a certain kind of man—not in this fundamental respect different from
any other myth. Surely it is better, superior to any myth with a view to its
own standards of truth or certainty, but the question concerns precisely

whether these standards of truth and certainty are intrinsically right. This view has been made very popular, by the way, by Spengler's *Decline of the West*, which has affected present-day thought in many ways.

Now when this view is taken, how do things appear? What is the beginning of any meaning? The beginning of any meaning can then only be the individual's worldview, as it is called—be it that of some central African tribe, be it that of Western man, or any theory, with the allowance that there are within such societies at a certain stage individual differences. Say, the worldview of Nietzsche would be different from that of Hobbes . . . Now what is then the beginning, the ordinary beginning of any meaning in . . . That can only be the principle of that worldview or, in Nietzsche's language, the fundamental will of the individual thinker or the societal plan which you can adopt. But obviously, commonsensically, every such worldview, every such scheme of individuation, is not simply the beginning. It is itself somehow conditioned, and we cannot get around this fact. This is Nietzsche's formula. How is it possible? Nietzsche has first to solve this question: Given the subjectivity of every interpretation, how can there be one interpretation, one subjective interpretation which is simply superior to all others, that is different? To say that more simply: Nietzsche suggests that the solution to the riddle, the formula for the leading spirit, is power.[27]

Why is this better, superior, to other human comprehensive doctrines? We have discussed that at some length. Nietzsche tried to find the solution to this question. But let us then assume that Nietzsche has shown the possibility of one final formula, that is, the will to power. Then this doctrine of the will to power, this scheme of interpretation, is the origin of the true meaning, and obviously it is conditioned. Nietzsche was conditioned by all kinds of traditions, by the fact of his body—I don't know what. How can the origin of meaning, and in this sense the supreme condition, yet be the condition of its own conditions? This problem is solved—I mean, in words—by eternal return. He himself belongs to the causes of eternal return, and therefore to the only causes.

I would like to add a few words on the rest of the third part of the book. The next time I will state a very general theory of the fourth part. . . There are two sections that are no longer interesting, because the end of the fourth part will develop this enigmatic vision of the whole. In the fourth part it is shown how Zarathustra affects the best men of his generation long before the superman, and there are certain remarks, especially about science, which we will discuss. I would like to say only a few words about the end of the third part. These are very difficult sections.

Zarathustra's doctrine of the eternal return—and his whole doctrine—is a creation of his self, and yet at the same time an enigmatic vision of the whole of life as it is, independent of being willed. This leads to the question: What is the relation of Zarathustra's self to life? The self may also be called, with an older word, the soul. Then the question is, first, Zarathustra and his soul, and this is the theme of the next speech, "The Great Longing," and then Zarathustra and life, and this is the theme of the following speech.[28] I make only a few notes about that. The word soul is in German (as well as in Greek and Latin) of the feminine gender, so it is natural almost to consider the soul a woman, that is to say, animate. Life is explicitly presented as a woman by Nietzsche, and in the last speech of the third part[29] he has an answer: eternity is explicitly called a woman. This is the symbolism which Nietzsche uses to indicate the problem: the soul, life, eternity, female, feminine are contrasted to the will to power, which is a male principle.

Now the great longing of which he speaks is a longing for eternal return. Zarathustra addresses his soul, and as you have seen from the earlier speech, this conversation of Zarathustra with his soul is not communicable strictly speaking, therefore not susceptible of interpretation in the proper sense. Let us read only the beginning of "The Great Longing."

> Reader: O my soul, I taught you to say "today" and "one day" and "formerly" and to dance away over all Here and There and Yonder.
>
> O my soul, I delivered you from all nooks; I brushed dust, spiders, and twilight off you.
>
> O my soul, I washed the little bashfulness and the nook-virtue off you and persuaded you to stand naked before the eyes of the sun.[30]

LS: And so on. Now this goes through the whole speech. Zarathustra is the teacher of his soul, the redeemer of his soul, which means he is in an important sense superior to his soul, the master of his soul or higher than it, whereas in relation to life, in the next speech, this situation is reversed. Zarathustra is following life and not its master.

I think it is more important for our present purpose and for any purpose at this time that we try to state the problem in a more general way. [I will] start on the following point, limiting myself to the problem as it appears within political philosophy. Now in the original sense, political philosophy was concerned with the natural order as the right order of society. It was concerned therefore with a universal: the natural order of society. It didn't necessarily mean that the right order was meant to be of universal applicability; that was a very secondary question. Perhaps the right order of society was not always possible, but only under certain conditions. In that respect, there is an important difference between Plato and Aristotle and[31] modern rationalism because modern rationalism tried to achieve, tried in principle to have, an order of society which is of universal applicability, whereas Plato and Aristotle did not. But both were equally concerned with the universal, and that meant also that the individual teacher, say, Plato as individual, was absolutely irrelevant, was a mere accident . . . Strictly speaking, it was also absolutely irrelevant that it was a Greek who thought it, who taught it. The Greeks had a more fortunate position than other nations for the relevant philosophy; that had nothing to do with the substance of their philosophy . . .

Now this whole conception was based on the fundamental distinction between the universal on the one hand, and the individual or particular on the other. The universal was the authority. That was the reason why philosophy was regarded as superior to poetry, and poetry in its turn even superior to history. There isn't likely to be a split between the universal and the particular, and what is . . . between the perception of the universal—conception, as one might say—and the perception of the individual, sense perception. To give a simple example of what I mean by this primacy of the universal: rights of man would have a higher status than rights of Englishmen. The rights of Englishmen would have any claim to respect only by virtue of their agreeing with the rights of man. This orientation prevailed until the eighteenth century, generally speaking, at least among all political philosophers. The inversion of this became first visible in the reaction to the French Revolution. It had been long hidden through history, but it became open only then. I read to you two utterances from Edmund Burke, who was a leader in the fights against the French Revolution. "Our constitution," meaning the British constitution, "is a prescriptive constitution." Prescriptive means it owes its validity to the fact that it has been accepted throughout the ages. "It is a constitution, whose sole authority is, that it has existed time out of mind." The British constitution claims and asserts the liberties of the British "as an estate especially belonging to the people of this kingdom without any reference whatever to any other more general or prior right."[32]

Now these statements, made in the heat of violent political contest, had a tremendous effect in the nineteenth century and ... Let us limit ourselves to the principle. If this is accepted literally as Burke stated it, and acted upon, it means directly the opposite: the primacy of the individual, not of the individual human being, but of the individual society, for example, especially of the historical. The universal is derivative. The consequences are very common, but we usually do not reflect on the principles ... Plato ... an expression of Greekness, so the fundamental phenomenon is Greekness, an individual phenomenon, as is indicated by the fact that we have to use a proper noun to figure it. Greekness is a fundamental fact. The universal, the doctrine of Plato which is in universal terms, is derivative.

Nietzsche's philosophy is only one particular expression of this. Nietzsche would say Plato's philosophy is a projection of the deepest and most unique in Plato. It is not possible to understand it with a view to its claim to be the presentation of the truth. We have discussed this frequently. The difficulty arises very simply as follows. I come back to a point I made before. Let us say: All right, be it so that all human thought is this way. This assertion itself creates a hopeless difficulty. You remember my question: Why ... if we have here the worldviews, the ideas ... however you might call them, relative to a peculiar historical phenomenon, be it a culture, or a civilization, or a nation, or an individual—something to be described by a proper name, and this is—I mean a different value system, a different system of categories relative to a different historical unity. This whole view, the whole inference, the whole inductive process ... is outside of this relativity. We are ultimately compelled to make an assertion in universal terms, and this assertion is according to its own meaning no longer intelligible as historical in the primary sense of the term. This is the question with which all of the nineteenth and twentieth centuries is concerned in various ways. One solution, of which we have spoken on some other occasions, is to say that the problem is solved by achieving an absolute moment, so that while every doctrine is relative to a historical situation, there may be a doctrine relative to an absolute moment. And that was the solution of [Hegel]. Fundamentally, that is also the solution of Marx and Nietzsche. This modification of the ... One other way of doing the same thing, of arriving at the same thing, is the following one, which is not the way of Nietzsche: If all thought is essentially dependent on language and inseparable from language, but language is necessarily an individual language, is it possible ever to reach the universal as universal? Is universal then necessarily intelligible or accessible through the individual, through his particular language, and therefore as individual?

The original notion of political philosophy is linked up to the original notion of philosophy, and there, philosophy was understood as the most comprehensive knowledge, and as such the knowledge concerned with what is always or eternal. And what is always or eternal was understood to be in principle always equally accessible—accidentally not, but essentially always equally accessible. Over against this view came the [view] in modern times: the eternal order is not accessible. For even perhaps it is not: it is merely conjecture, as Nietzsche put it. The most comprehensive thought—that is to say, philosophy—can only concern human knowledge as such and not reality. But human knowledge as such must be conceived of as something developing, because human knowledge appears to change, for example, analysis of science as it is now with the understanding that surprising changes will occur in the future. In other words, what comes out in modern times, in our time, is this favored possibility. The most comprehensive knowledge is an analysis of knowledge, such as an analysis of science, with the understanding that this highest knowledge, scientific knowledge, is changing. We believe we can live with the notion of a changing horizon and be radically provisionalist: that is only so until further notice. But this is of course not so; the awareness of the changeability of the horizon is understood to be unchanging. That has come to stay in all changes. No one of these men regards it as possible that there might ever be a legitimate rejection of scientific method and the scientific approach. That science could collapse because people become again superstitious or maladjusted or some such thing they do not deny, but that would clearly be decay. That there could be any other legitimate or sensible rejection of the scientific approach as we understand it now is impossible. In this sense, as I [understand] it, the changeability or the awareness of the changeability of the horizon is understood as unchangeable.

One cannot leave it then at history. One cannot leave it at the primacy of the process of the individual or the particular. And Nietzsche's whole philosophy is an attempt to solve this difficulty and to give in his premises the only solution for the . . . of this: to say that on the highest level, the ground of all historical change—I mean the will to power—must transform itself into acceptance. In this very strange way, Nietzsche tried to restore something like the premodern view. But he could do it;

he did understand that this is only by understanding this acceptance as a transformed or transfigured will, therefore not simply contemplation but creative contemplation.

I leave it at this point and I want to have—perhaps you can have a brief discussion.

Student: . . .

LS: Now let me try to state it as follows. If you take earlier positions . . .

Student: . . .

LS: That is simply not true. . . They are a reaction to the nihilists as, in his way, Nietzsche was. I don't believe that this would be very helpful. I think that one could say, in the simple formula, that Nietzsche's doctrine as a whole is based on the one hand on science, both natural science and historical science—you know, evolution, the historical process, and so on—and on the other hand on what we called enigmatic vision. One could say that he's caught between those two chairs. What the men who . . . is to abandon completely the scientific support and to base their whole doctrine on a certain kind of enigmatic vision. That is, very great difficulties disappear. Very much greater clarity can come this way, but at the price of a great obscurity.

Student: . . .

LS: Yes, but the point is this. Could one not say that a complicated idea is only a concealer of the nihilistic situation. . .

Student: . . .

LS: . . .

Student: There seems to be a problem in the relationship between the last man that we've discussed earlier, and Nietzsche's ultimate superman. The last man is bad because he is simply content: he doesn't doubt, he doesn't question, he has no aspirations. He just lives contented. And yet the superman ultimately will be the same sort of man. The superman no longer doubts or questions. He has overcome wisdom with the great affirmation, and as Zarathustra does in the last section, he quietly sits and affirms. And one wonders—I mean, there is apparently a higher level of affirmation, a higher level of contentedness, and yet is there really so much difference between the superman and the last man? Both of them live in a perfect world, for them.

LS: Yes, but is there really no difference between this—is there no degree of difference between an affirmation at the end of a long process of denials, and overcomings and self-overcoming, and one which does not even begin, hasn't begun, such overcoming?

Student: There is this difference, yes. But why do we wish to deny that the point at which there are no more denials and overcoming has surpassed these? Why should not these things be viewed as a continual process, as opposed to reaching... a state of freedom or happy state, where we sit quietly?

LS: ... The last man has nothing whatever to do with the return. Nietzsche shares with the whole religious and philosophic tradition the concern with eternity, and one can say that is for him the difference between a brutish man, the last man—they are like pigs—and a truly human being, including the superhuman human being. That is ... the difference, and the sizeable difference in this: that for Nietzsche, the eternity can consist only in the eternity of the process. That, I think, makes it more simple.

Student: Then in this case, where he is willing, it is not really the superman ... What he really is willing is the process, too—I mean, a continual and eternal process to the higher man. He is not willing any given state of men, but rather the process.

LS: But now it is necessary, surely. I mean, more comprehensive than the way toward the superman is the eternal return. There are many stages—a number of stages have to be distinguished in order to answer your question. In the first place, this question: Why not an infinite process? That, I think, was an implication of your question. But an infinite process is ... That is, an infinite process means infinite relativity unless you have goals or ideals or ideas beyond the process. Now ... it is impossible to think of this; any formula of infinite progress however it might be understood is, as such a formula, final. And therefore in the decisive respect (I mean, as far as the understanding of the truth is concerned), the end has been reached. The end has been reached. That is from this modern point of view impossible, except—I mean, all these modern positions must be [final] in the sense that they must assume a peak. And Marx can say that the true history begins with the jump from the realm of necessity to the realm of freedom, but that is a wholly unsupported assertion. The decisive point is that the character of human history up to the time of the jump, as well as the outline of what is afterward, appears as it appears now ... before Marx. There is no possibility for Marx that, viewed from the postrevolutionary moment—I mean strictly postrevolutionary, not ... final transition, that in some way Marx's whole doctrine will appear to be absolutely uncertain. I remember ... non-Russian Marxist, Georg Lukács, who writes in German ... he tried, under the influence of Max

Weber and such people, to apply Marxism to himself. That was the famous formula of Max Weber and his study on the sociology of religion
that seemed to be so plausible. Of course it was absolutely un-Marxist . . .
and in a weak moment Georg Lukács said, I expect that . . . the Marxist
doctrine . . . i.e., the best hitherto . . . this philosophy is the best hitherto,
not the best since.[33] Now what does this in practice mean? Take this example. The theorists of the French Revolution were the most progressive
thinkers of the eighteenth century. Of course they were wrong, as we
know now, but at that time, that was the best you could have. Now apply
it to Marxism. Marxism is the best now, but it may have basic defects
which will appear only a hundred years from now. Now, looking at it from
a practical point of view, it means this: the suggestion is made to us to
undergo infinite sufferings and commit atrocious deeds with the certainty
that the whole thing will look like a very defective thing in retrospect, and
therefore either it is the truth, the final truth, or it is not.

And later on we came back to—it was stricken from the record; I don't
know what that would do—we come back to a very simplistic doctrine,
which merely professing this scheme, you know . . . is advancing, and so
our knowledge now is better than it was a hundred years ago, and so on
and so on, but which of course evades the problem of finality in the decisive respect. You see, you can have infinite progress as much as you like
in secondary matters. For example, you can make an infinite progress of
medicine or many kinds of techniques, that's no problem. But the comprehensive knowledge which we all presuppose and which we all claim to
profess—even if we are extremely modest, we all claim to profess that, we
all have opinions—then of course in this respect, we are surely doubting
from time to time, quite naturally. But here that cannot be avoided. It
can be avoided only in one way, this is . . . by modern thought, and that is
something about Socrates and Plato. But that is a long story.

Student: You said earlier in this course that prior to the first wave of
modernism the assumption was that nature is good; if we can show something to be natural, it is good; and the objection from the moderns was
that we cannot be sure of this, because nature can . . . Now in essence it
seems to me that what Nietzsche does in the doctrine of eternal return
is show that although in one sense this meant an enigmatic vision, in another sense it is the inescapable nature . . . Now doesn't Nietzsche need
this necessity, given the premises of modernism, to affirm that it is true?
But because the fact it is true doesn't make it good. Now perhaps Nietzsche would admit this, but I'm not sure.

LS: Nietzsche returns, in his way, to the assertion that nature is good. What does it mean when he says the earth is a half of the whole . . . he starts not from the historical solution, which was very powerful in Germany . . . and sensing the difficulties and the nihilistic consequences, attempts to transcend it, and he returns to nature while avoiding . . .

Student: To get back to the problem of the deadly truth and the true and general statements, other than the nihilistic ones, and this negated kind of Nietzsche's own: Is there any claim to objectivity as regards not necessarily what creates and makes—you know, eternal return, something like this—but the fact that this deadly truth must be interpreted creatively—

LS: . . .

Student: Then in what standard? Or how can he say that the necessity of interpreting this creatively, you know, and not nihilistically, that this is true? I mean, he has to make a true statement. What is his standard?

LS: You have to see there are various levels of that, and I tried to give you a kind of location. . . "Enigmatic vision" means of course the experience of something as true, and if this is not relevant, one can simply say then that I don't care now how this is related to truth, accessible to science or scientists. . .

On Wednesday I will speak of the fourth part of *Zarathustra*, and I will limit myself to the section dealing with science—that is nearest to our hearts or to our minds—and then you can have another discussion. . .

14 Restoring the Sacred and the Final Question

Zarathustra, Part 4

Leo Strauss: . . . but I give a very brief survey of the fourth part of *Zara-thustra*, and then I summarize the argument again, and then we'll have a kind of final discussion—final for the time being.

Now the fourth part of *Zarathustra* is in a way an anticlimax. The whole substance of Nietzsche's, Zarathustra's, teaching has been devel-oped in the first three parts, and in the fourth part he plans to return to the question of Zarathustra and present-day man. He is waiting for fishes, for the human beings who became fish, for men who wouldn't have been following the quest of present-day man, men who cannot possibly be super yet. There are altogether nine individuals who come up. The first is a soothsayer, in the second speech, who announces to Zarathustra the cry of distress of the higher man, of the superior man. The soothsayer is always a bringer of bad news, as we know from earlier occasions. After the soothsayer, two kings come up, who are radically displeased with modern life, being kings. . . and they also seek the higher man.

Now our special problems come in the next speech, "The Leech," to which we will turn immediately, and let us first read on page 362, para-graph 3, following.

Reader: "I am *the conscientious in spirit*," replied the man.

LS: Yes, we have heard of this conscientiousness of the spirit before. You will recognize that. Go on.

Reader: "and in matters of the spirit there may well be none stricter, nar-rower, and harder than I, except he from whom I have learned it, Zara-thustra himself.

"Rather know nothing than half-know much! . . . In the conscience of science there is nothing great and nothing small."

"Then perhaps you are the man who knows the leech?" Zarathustra asked. "And do you pursue the leech to its ultimate grounds, my conscientious friend?"

"O Zarathustra," replied the man who had been stepped on, "that would be an immensity; how could I presume so much! That of which I am the master and expert is the *brain* of the leech: that is *my* world. And it really is a world too. Forgive me that here my pride speaks up, for I have no equal here. That is why I said, 'Here is my home.' How long have I been pursuing this one thing, the brain of the leech, lest the slippery truth slip away from me here again! Here is *my* realm. For its sake I have thrown away everything else; for its sake everything else has become indifferent to me; and close to my knowledge lies my black ignorance."[1]

LS: In other words, he was his own leech; therefore it is called "The Leech." Now that means the man of science in the highest sense of the term, in Nietzsche's opinion: the man who is absolutely dedicated to the truth, to scientific truth, and that means to truth for its own sake, the truth which has no attraction whatever except that it is the truth. The ugly truth, the nonedifying, and its inspiration is intellectual honesty at all costs. This is, as Nietzsche also says in other [places] of this,[2] in a way the highest of which man of the nineteenth century is capable. It requires a complete lack of any outlook, of any hope, of any prospect, except [science] as the greatest sacrifice — not a certain sacrifice, but the sacrifice of every feeling, of every . . . of the heart, to do that.

It is an old theoretical idea that for those choosing to pursue this,[3] there is no longer any question of the knowledge of the whole, however depressing it may be. Generally speaking, we can say that the tradition, the philosophic tradition, consisted of an idealistic tradition, the teaching of which was manifestly edifying. And then there was an entirely unidealistic tradition, the materialistic tradition of classical antiquity, which is manifestly unedifying but which presented itself as edifying insofar as it liberated man from superstitious fears. That was the Epicurean tradition. The greatest document of that is Lucretius's poem, *On the Nature of Things*. If one reads Lucretius more carefully, one sees that this promise of liberation from fears is only a provisional recommendation. The demand is in one respect comparable to that of the nineteenth century, of this man of intellectual honesty. One must learn that the only true liberation consists in seeing the truth in its fallible character. But nothing to which we can be attached, which we can love, can be eternal. What is eternal are the atoms and the void, and Lucretius's poetry said it clearly by presenting, at the beginning of his poem, nature in its pleasing aspect: generation, love—it begins to approach the topic of Venus—and in the end is the description of the plague, nature in all its horrors. And the education which the reader is supposed to undergo while studying it is that it accepts the plague and all the horrors, and greater ones than the plague, I mean, the infinite eternity of atoms and the void with . . .

But in this nineteenth-century sense of science which Nietzsche describes here, there is infinitely less science than in Lucretius's poem. There is no view of the whole anymore: the [brain] of the leech, that's all. And he knows everything about it; he can write what they call the definitive book or the definitive article on the [brain] of the leech. And the absurdity of course is this, that by the very nature of this kind of scientific study, definitiveness is altogether impossible. He has a small island of knowledge surrounded, as it would be, by the black and dark eternity. But the black and dark universe of course affects the life which he has on the small sphere. Any change, any [alteration] in human knowledge will relativize what he . . . of the leech, and that means the great heroism involved in this dedication.

One can of course look at the same thing somewhat differently, but perhaps also somewhat more superficially. I don't know if you remember Sinclair Lewis's *Arrowsmith*, which was one of the few presentations of the scientist as a human problem in modern literature. And there you have also the real specialist—in other language, a medical man who [labors over] an extremely limited problem to which he dedicates [all his] gifts, while excluding everything else—his whole human life, that is, especially his relation to woman and . . . and other human relations deeply burned up in this process. And the man lives entirely for nothing but the quest of truth in this really limited sense, which can therefore no longer have any human meaning. It must be for its own sake alone.

We will come back to the question of science later on. Nietzsche will take up the subject again in this part. Next we read "The Magician." The magician, he is a man who pretends to be religious, in other words, just the opposite of the man of intellectual honesty, who pretends to suffer from God's cruel and savage attack on him. The suffering consists in the fact that his is not simply edifying, and pleasing, and redeeming knowledge, but precisely the terror of religion, and he opens himself to the terror of religion, and accents now a very long problem . . . But we read only page 368, paragraphs 1 to 2.

Reader: "Don't flatter!" replied Zarathustra, still excited and angry, "you actor from the bottom! You are false; why do you talk of truth? You peacock of peacocks, you sea of vanity, *what* were you playing before me, you wicked magician? In *whom* was I to believe when you were moaning this way?"

"*The ascetic of the spirit*," said the old man, "I played *him*—you your-self once coined this word—the poet and magician who at last turns his spirit against himself, the changed man who freezes to death from his evil science and conscience. And you may as well confess it: it took a long time, O Zarathustra, before you saw through my art and lie. You *believed* in my distress when you held my head with both your hands; I heard you moan, 'He has been loved too little, loved too little.' That I deceived you to that extent made my malice jubilate inside me."[4]

LS: . . . In other words, what the leech is, is played in pseudoreligious garb by the magician. He is, we can also say, the poet who has lost his naïveté and would wish to be a *homo religiosus*, a religious man. Nietzsche has thought without any question of Richard Wagner in his writing on the question. Now then the next of the higher men is the last pope. In the last chapter, "The Magician," the last pope seeks Zarathustra as the most pious among those who do not believe in God. Then the next of the higher men is the ugliest man. The ugliest man is the murderer of god. He is afraid, not of persecution but of compassion and pity, and this fear of compassion and pity is the motive of his terrible deed. Let us read page 377, paragraph 3.

Reader: "But that you passed me by, silent; that you blushed, I saw it well: that is how I recognized you as Zarathustra. Everyone else would have thrown his alms to me, his pity, with his eyes and words. But for that I am not beggar enough, as you guessed; for that I am too rich, rich in what is great, in what is terrible, in what is ugliest, in what is most inex-pressible. Your shame, Zarathustra, honored me! With difficulty I escaped the throng of the pitying, to find the only one today who teaches, 'Pity is obtrusive'—you, O Zarathustra. Whether it be a god's pity or man's—pity offends the sense of shame. And to be unwilling to help can be nobler than that virtue which jumps to help."[5]

LS: Now turn to page 378, paragraph 4.

Reader: "But he *had to* die: he saw with eyes that saw everything; he saw man's depths and ultimate grounds, all his concealed disgrace and ugliness. His pity knew no shame: he crawled into my dirtiest nooks. This most curious, overobtrusive, overpitying one had to die. He always saw me: on such a witness I wanted to have revenge or not live myself. The god who saw everything, *even man*—this god had to die! Man cannot bear it that such a witness should live."[6]

LS: Now one can perhaps state this thought as follows. If there is a simply perfect being, man reveals himself necessarily as imperfect and he stands naked in his imperfection before God. He cannot be proud. Human existence cannot be inner. This is the problem of rebellion. It is rebellion in the action of the ugliest man because it is an act of revenge and revenge degrades, and therefore Zarathustra is not the ugliest man according to Nietzsche. Since the positing of God is itself an act of the spirit of revenge, the action of the ugliest man is the revenge on the spirit of revenge. It is therefore an imperfect form of Zarathustra's own teaching.

The next higher man is the voluntary beggar. This is a parody on the. . . "The Voluntary Beggar" presents the cows as models of man. You may remember the speech "On the Chairs of Virtue" at the beginning of *Zarathustra*, where sleep is presented as the end of virtue and there is also a very [brief] reference to cows.[7] Now this speech, "The Voluntary Beggar," is also a travesty on Zarathustra's return to nature, but for Zarathustra the place of the cows is taken by the eagle and serpent. Then we come to "The Shadow." That means the shadow of Zarathustra, and this is the nihilist. . . We read only one section on page 386, paragraph 2.

Reader: "'Nothing is true, all is permitted': thus I spoke to myself. Into the coldest waters I plunged, with head and heart. Alas, how often have I stood there afterward, naked as a red crab! Alas, where has all that is good gone from me—and all shame, and all faith in those who are good? Alas, where is that mendacious innocence that I once possessed, the innocence of the good and their noble lies?"[8]

LS: This and the following speech are the centers of the fourth part of *Zarathustra*. This follows immediately the section on nihilism, as you can see; and its theme is also in a way a description of the solution as seen at noon, where Zarathustra is almost prepared to sleep because the world has become perfect just now. A strange tranquility goes over. No activity beyond the activity of the will . . . That is to say, he insists upon denying that the world has now become perfect. His will is directed not to this noon, the natural noon of every day, especially of every summer day, but to the great noon in the future. In accordance with that is the next speech. Zarathustra hears again, in the moment where he begins to regard the world as perfect, the cry of distress of the higher man. This time the cry comes from his cave. It is a common cry of all his visitors, the higher men. Zarathustra tells them that he is waiting for men superior to them. These highest men at this time are not the bridge to the superman.

The speech on "The Last Supper" follows immediately. We read here only one passage, on page 397, paragraphs 3 and 4.

Reader: "Be of good cheer," Zarathustra answered him, "as I am. Stick to your custom, my excellent friend, crush your grains, drink your water, praise your fare; as long as it makes you gay!

"I am a law only for my kind, I am no law for all. But whoever belongs with me must have strong bones and light feet, be eager for war and festivals, not gloomy, no dreamer, as ready for what is most difficult as for his festival, healthy and wholesome. The best belongs to my kind and to me; and when one does not give it to us, we take it: the best food, the purest sky, the strongest thoughts, the most beautiful women."[9]

LS: Let us stop here. This will raise a certain difficulty. Remember we read on an earlier occasion a passage "the way does not exist," at the end of the speech "On the Spirit of Gravity": "'This is *my* way; where is yours?' — thus I answered those who asked me 'the way.' For *the* way — that does not exist."[10] Now here we have a somewhat different statement. Zarathustra's love. . . It is not merely for him, it is for him and those who are his life. His love is not a love for everyone. This also has to be considered for the understanding of the title[11] of the whole work, "A Book for All and None." Now this love of Zarathustra, toward which he's striving, is not a love for all. His love is not for everyone. But how can this be recognized, incidentally? How can the love of Zarathustra only be for some, and yet for Zarathustra it would be a love for all? How can we reconcile this?

Student: . . .

LS: Yes, but still, if it is meant only for some, how can we call it a love for all?

Student: . . .

LS: Yes, but still, he says it's a book for all, and in a way it is addressed to all men. Well, the others, those who do not belong to him, who cannot accept his love, are also given advice as to what they should do. In some cases, advice to commit suicide—very extreme for some.

Now the next speech of higher man, that is Zarathustra's table talk on the occasion of the last supper. We have no time to discuss that. The next three speeches are for us especially important.[12] These form a unit among themselves, and the speech "On Science" is the center. In a way, science is the center; in a way, science is the problem for him.

Now I mention only the most obviously important points. Zarathustra is dissatisfied with his superior men. He escapes from the cave into fresh air. In Zarathustra's absence, the old magician sings his song of melancholy. It is an expression of sheer despair, and there occurs the formula—page 410, paragraph 2, beginning.

Reader: "Suitor of truth?" they mocked me; "you?
No! Only poet!"[13]

LS: And let us turn then to the bottom of page 412.

Reader: Thus I myself once sank
Out of my truth-madness
Out of my day-longings,
Weary of day, sick from the light—
Sank downward, eveningward, shadowward,
Burned by one truth,
And thirsty:
Do you remember still, remember, hot heart,
How you thirsted?
That I be banished
From all truth,
Only fool!
Only poet![14]

LS: Yes. It is not difficult to understand how that is, why one could ascribe this to Zarathustra or to Nietzsche himself. If you think of the problem of an objective and subjective truth, by virtue of the conditioning which is subjective truth, it is in a way separated forever from conjecture and therefore only. . . This speech is made partly in Zarathustra's absence. The man of science is disgusted by this insincere, clever magician's song of melancholy. But then, while the scientist develops his view, Zarathustra reappears and replies to the man of science. The man of science was the only one who was completely unimpressed by the magician's song, say, for example, by Richard Wagner, but you can replace him by any other figure of the same kind.

Now what the scientist says about his science—you remember the speech about the leech, you know, the specialist [in the brain] of the leech, [and the brain] exclusively, whose sole inspiration is intellectual honesty cut off from all possibilities of hope and edification. Now this is presented here from a somewhat different point of view, on page 414, paragraph 2.

Reader: "And verily, we talked and thought together enough before Zarathustra returned home to his cave for me to know that we *are* different. We also seek different things up here, you and I. For I seek more *security*, that is why I came to Zarathustra. For he is the firmest tower and will today, when everything is tottering and all the earth is quaking. But you—when I see the eyes you make, it almost seems to me that you are seeking *more insecurity*: more thrills, more danger, more earthquakes. You desire, I should almost presume—forgive my presumption, you higher men—you desire the most wicked, most dangerous life, of which *I* am most afraid: the life of wild animals, woods, caves, steep mountains, and labyrinthian gorges. And it is not the leaders *out* of danger who appeal to you most, but those who induce you to leave all ways, the seducers. But even if such desire in you is real, it still seems impossible to me."[15]

LS: Do you understand that? Although it's real, it seems to him[16] to be impossible. Must not what is the real or actual necessarily be possible? What does Nietzsche deny with this seeming absurdity? Well, obviously he does not mean logical impossibility. . .

Reader: "For fear is the original and basic feeling of man; from fear everything is explicable, original sin and original virtue. From fear my own virtue too has grown, and it is called: science. For the fear of wild animals, that was bred in man longest of all—including the animal he harbors inside himself and fears: Zarathustra calls it 'the inner beast.' Such long old fear, finally refined, spiritualized, spiritual—today, it seems to me, this is called *science.*"[17]

LS: Yes. That is the vision of the scientist. What science means is the most individualized fear, but it is no longer fear of wild beasts and such—you may not even perhaps be afraid—but there is fear of intellectual uncertainty. The essence of science is certainty: concern with certainty, with support, with control. That science seems to be greatly different from what we said originally about science as animated by the spirit of intellectual honesty. It seems to be something entirely different. We must see how this is worked out.

Now let me first see Zarathustra's reply, "Thus spoke the conscientious man."

Reader: Thus spoke the conscientious man; but Zarathustra, who was just coming back into his cave and had heard and guessed this last speech, threw a handful of roses at the conscientious man and laughed at his "truths." "What?" he cried. "What did I hear just now? Verily, it seems to me that you are a fool, or that I am one myself; and your 'truth' I simply reverse. For *fear*—that is our exception. But courage and adventure and pleasure in the uncertain, in the undared—*courage* seems to me man's whole prehistory. He envied the wildest, most courageous animals and robbed all their virtues: only thus did he become man. *This* courage, finally refined, spiritualized, spiritual, this human courage with eagles' wings and serpents' wisdom—*that*, it seems to me, is today called—"[18]

LS: Let us stop here. So you see, the expectation from the earlier speech would be that this is the essence of science: the spirit of courage, of daring, and not concern with certainty. But this answer is not given. The answer given is that this deritualized daring or courage is Zarathustra. Science is replaced by Zarathustra. Now what does this mean? Science is impersonal. It is meant to arrive at the truth valid for all men, universally valid. Zarathustra is an individual. How must the truth be understood if it becomes incarnate as it were, even individual, as distinguished from the anonymity of a thing called science? Yet this is not so personal . . . The truth in the highest sense, the elusive truth, belongs to the individual creative contemplator, so this truth is in a sense Zarathustra's truth and not the truth simply.

Zarathustra wants to leave the cave again, but he is kept back by the wanderer, Zarathustra's shadow, that is to say, nihilism incarnate. The next speech, or rather song, is "Among the Daughters of the Wilderness." The relation is this. In the magician's song of melancholy, Zarathustra is altogether absent. When the scientist makes his speech, Zarathustra is partly present. At the nihilist's speech or song, he is completely present. That indicates the relative nearness of emotions of these three kinds of men to Zarathustra. Now we cannot read this poem, if it is a poem, if it deserves to be called a poem. We read only the speech, the verse with which it begins, on page 417, the second section of that speech.

Reader: *Wilderness grows: woe unto him that harbors wildernesses!*[19]

LS: Yes, let us stop here. The theme is fighting. Now what does it mean, this growth of the desert, of the wilderness? That is not explained here or anywhere, but it should be perfectly clear by now. What could this growing wilderness possibly mean? I'm surprised. After all, it is the song of the nihilist—
Student: The growth of the nihilist.
LS: Yes, of the nihilist, the growth of nihilism, the growth of despair, which of course can very well grow together with the growth of certain delusions. You know that book . . . contradictory, of course: the devastation of man is increasing, but then he says this devastation is terrible only to those who harbor themselves, not to the self-complacent. They simply don't notice anything. That is the theme. But if this terrible theme of the future of man, especially of the . . . man, is treated with utmost . . . here. Let us see only on page 419, paragraph one, end.

Reader: I, being a doubter, however, should
Doubt it; after all, I come
From Europe
Which is more doubt-addicted than all
Elderly married women.
May God improve it!
Amen.[20]

LS: On page 421, paragraph 2, second half.

Reader: As a moral lion
Roar before the daughters of the wilderness!
For virtuous howling,
My most charming girls,
Is more than anything else

European fervor, European ravenous hunger.
And there I stand even now
As a European;
I cannot do else; God help me!
Amen.[21]

LS: Do you see the allusion in the last sentence? Do you remember that?

Student: . . .

LS: Now if we begin first with this: there are two references to Europe. Europe is a continent of doubt and a continent of moral indignation, of moralists. This fits in with what was said before. The intellectual honesty of the leech is the unity of doubt and morals. The moralist is honest. The doubt, an indication of these high [pursuits] of truth, which has no attraction other than that of truth. Now the story here in that speech is that this despairing European is in the African desert, confronted with a continent completely free from doubt and the moralist.[22] That's the idea: there are two girls in the desert, and these girls are presented as particularly free from morality and doubt. But these two girls . . . and they stand there insufficiently dressed and there are some remarks about their legs. But even that is not satisfactory, because one leg is not visible. She is a dancing girl, but then closer inspection shows that one leg is missing because an inhabitant of the desert, a lion, had nibbled it away. In other words, even this comfort—to see some beings free from European diseases and European despair—is replaced because of this unfortunate action of the lion. The nihilist presents his theme of despair in a spirit of . . . and these daughters of the desert are a kind of caricature of that which Europe needs and by which it could be redeemed: the superman.

Now the book does not finish here by any means. In the sequel, "The Awakening" and "The Ass Festival," what happens is this. In Zarathustra's absence, all the higher men worship the donkey as a God, and then they of course also have breached relations. The donkey's sound is in German. I repeat it, transcribed. The sounds of animals differ in different languages a little, and in German it is said to be "y-ah," which can be read as *Ja*—I mean "yes." So the donkey, as it were, a *Ja*-sayer, is again a comical prefiguration of the true "yes" of eternal return.

Now this much about this fourth part of *Zarathustra*. We do not have the time, and I believe it is also not necessary for our purposes, to go into this other teaching. Now, I would like first to give you all a summary, and then we will have the discussion.

I spoke last time of the relation of Nietzsche to Socrates, and I remind you of only one point here. Ultimately, the opposition of Nietzsche to Socrates turns around the Socratic or Platonic thesis that the highest form of awareness is mental perception of ideas, of unchanging things. The whole of rationalism from Socrates on until the nineteenth century has truth in its vision. Nietzsche tries to uproot Socratism, rationalism in all its forms, and that means in a way a return to human thought as it was prior to Socrates, or it means a return to pre-Socratic thought. The pre-Socratics are a number of Greek thinkers prior to Socrates, and there is especially one who was of the greatest importance to Nietzsche, and that was Heraclitus. One can state the doctrine of Nietzsche in a simplified way as follows. Why did he not simply accept the teaching of Heraclitus, of which his . . . we only know through [fragments]? But that was not the reason why Nietzsche deviated from Heraclitus. I mentioned this on a former occasion. Nietzsche had two reservations against Heraclitus: first, Heraclitus too distrusted the senses, against which Nietzsche says the senses do not deceive us; and the second reason, that Heraclitus as well as other philosophers did not think historically, they lacked the historical conscience. To summarize these two points: Heraclitus too made the distinction between the true world and the apparent world. The apparent world is the sensibly perceived world interpreted in the light of an authoritative opinion, in the light of a *nomos*, a convention, a merely human creation. Against this, Nietzsche asserts that the apparent world, that is to say, valueless nature interpreted by human creation, is the true world. The true world has to be abolished, in Nietzsche's sweeping formula. One can describe this step of Nietzsche as follows: that nature is completely replaced, or at least overlapped, by history. This is the meaning of historical consciousness. But Nietzsche cannot leave it at this, and this is the great difficulty.

But to come back to the previous formulation, the apparent world is the valueless nature interpreted by human creation, and this is the true world. From this, there follows the famous formula Nietzsche [supplies]: "loyalty to the earth," to be entirely at home in the world, this sensible world. There is no without, any without of the human world. The world that concerns us, the world in which we live, leads into the mere void. The things are what they are as experienced by man in his fullness, and not by merely perceiving or comprehending man. The things are what they are as experienced by creative man.

I will explain this, partly repeating remarks I have made earlier. The question concerns, we can say, the thing, any thing. The most elaborate analysis of the thing is the Aristotelian analysis, of which I mention here only the most fundamental one. Every thing is covered by the fact that it is a thing possessing quality. The table is round, but the roundness is not the thing; it is only a quality of it. The table is the bearer of this quality, but we use the traditional term: the substance. Now the question concerns the different status of the quality. Somebody might say the table is round and the table is good. These two qualities, round and good, have entirely different statuses, according to Aristotle. Its roundness belongs to the table; its goodness is essentially relative to something different from the table— obviously, in this case, to man, or even to a specific man. A table for a child would be lower, for example. But there is another point which we must not forget. When I say of a dog, for example, that it is complete, entire, whole, perfect, I mean the dog as it is in itself; there is no relativity to man implied in that. So not every good is relative to man; there is a goodness, a perfection in the things themselves. For example, a certain dog is blind. He has this privation, this defect; this belongs to this particular dog as much of course as its color, so a certain kind of goodness, or perfection, or beauty belongs to the thing as much as the merely sensitive quality and a great deal more. There is another kind of quality, which we usually forget but which we do not quite forget, in a way, thanks to one of the models of anthropology, and that is the quality of which I give this example (I'm sorry I'm so unimaginative that I always give examples . . .): the sacred cow. The cow is white, the cow is female, the cow is healthy, the cow is ten years old, whatever it may be. These are all qualities which belong to the cow. Then there is a certain reference to usefulness, which is ordinarily when we say the cow is good and have it in mind not its state of the body, its entireness, but its good with a view to its goodness in milk, and so on. This is relative to man because . . . but what about its station as viewed by the Hindus, for example? Aristotle would say that is entirely alien to the cow itself. It is imputed or ascribed to the cow on the basis of a *nomos*, of a convention, of a law, of a merely human creation. This was, sufficiently for our present purposes, the most elaborate classical doctrine of the thing.

Now this was radically modified at the beginning of modern times, and that affects us up to the present day, and that was the distinction between the primary and the secondary qualities. And this meant that all qualities other than extension and solidity are merely subjective. The table in itself is not round; that is only relative to our organization of our human senses. But when it itself has a certain weight, a certain measurement and so on, again, they are objective. So in a way, that leads to a dissolution of the thing. It becomes something like a parcel of matter, however matter might be analyzed, into molecules, atoms, and so on. But here, in the process of this modern development, the following difficulty arose: that the primary qualities themselves proved, in a different way than the secondary qualities (the sensible way), to be subjective.

In the present-day language, the thing, as distinct from the sensible quality, is a logical construct; and all the contents of science, like atoms and so on, have of course logical constructs. By virtue of this, the thing evaporates completely. On the contrary, the valid [inference] is made[23] that the only thing which is not man-made entirely are the mere sensations. They are given, but what we make of them by interpreting them in terms of things and qualities is [also a] logical construction [of man]. The thing evaporates unless we cease to regard such activity or creativity, human creativity, as entirely alien to the thing. And if we take this crucial step, we arrive at the conclusion that it is precisely the fullest and the richest subjectivity which constitutes the thing in its fullness. It is only a very poor creativity and subjectivity which goes into constituting the thing as merely perceived thing, the table or whatever it may be. As a consequence of that, such qualities as the graciousness of the deer, the majestic character of the river, all these qualities which we apply to things—and especially the poets apply to things—are as real as the qualities which we ascribe to them in a merely cognitive detachment. If I say there is as much subjectivity involved in the merely cognitive things, then in this fullest sense only—and even then there is no reason why we should leave it as a most impoverished subjectivity and not [richer] subjectivity.

This may work very well up to a certain point... We may be able to restore to the thing in its fullness even much beyond what Aristotle himself did. For example, Aristotle would absolutely deny that these poetically described qualities belonged to the thing itself. What he ascribed to the thing affectedly—that is, when we are affected by the thing and not really detached from it—did not belong to the thing in Aristotle's sense. But once we go much beyond Aristotle and when we come much closer to our... understanding of things in prescientific life. But there is one absolute limit to this [path]. We can never arrive again at the sacredness

ZARATHUSTRA, PART 4   243

of the cow. You know, the cow may affect us in infinitely many ways very deeply, but it can never affect us in the way that we regard it as sacred. The [difficulty] is this: the problem of history remains, the problem of the historical variety of human creation—in other words, the variety of historical worlds as distinguished from the one world in which we live, in which all humans live. In the world of the Hindus, the cow is sacred, and its sacredness belongs as much to the cow as its whiteness or any other quality, but not in other historical worlds. All knowledge, as Nietzsche's formula says, is perspectivity, and the highest form of that perspectivity (or the most interesting form, at any rate) is the historical perspectivity, that men in different historical worlds conceive of things in radically different ways. The consequence is historical relativism, which is nihilism in the sense that nothing is true because on the highest level nothing is true, and this absence of truth on the highest level casts its shadow on limited truth, which common sense would naturally impose upon it. The deadly truth of which Nietzsche speaks is objective truth. This is in a way the starting point of Nietzsche, this nihilism as most clearly revealed in historical relativism. All values, all categories of understanding and identification are historically variable and owe their validity entirely to man's creative act, not to themselves.

I remind you again of this simple formula, which I . . . read the modern social scientists or modern Christians—our point of view is not relative to a specific humanity and therefore cannot be relative. But that of course is not posited among them and no one thought that it was posited in Nietzsche. Nietzsche tried to overcome nihilism by a new creation, but this new creation had to be in harmony with intellectual honesty. Intellectual honesty was a necessary but not a sufficient condition. Intellectual honesty means not to deny the deadly truth of nihilism but to create on the basis of it. Now one formula is this: the distinction between the knower and the noble man. It means this. The objective truth is incomplete, but you cannot possibly leave it at that. You must interpret it, and there are fundamentally only two ways of interpreting it: it's understood either basely, or else nobly. Basely means uncreatively, and nobly means creatively. So the base interpretation, the uncreative interpretation, is really the self . . . in nihilism; whether it is aware, we don't know. Nietzsche's creation expresses itself in the doctrines of the will to power and eternal return. At this point, this doctrine or complex of doctrines comes first to sight as relative to the most comprehensive perspective on the truth, measured by all known perspectives. Nietzsche claims that his perspective takes in everything which has become noble under the narrower perspectives, and therefore is more comprehensive.

But Nietzsche could not leave it at that because he had to assert [finality], and in the [end that meant] that in the decisive respect there was nothing provisional about his doctrine of the moment. In the decisive respect, his doctrine was final, and this finality is expressed in the formula "God is dead." In the most important respect, man has radically changed. Nietzsche's perspective must have been the final perspective, and this can also be explained as follows. The doctrine of the will to power. . . is primarily an attempt to understand history. The doctrine of the will to power is an attempt to state, particularly, the ground of historical knowledge, the ground of history. This ground is found in human creativity, and we can provisionally say will to power is primarily human creativity. Nietzsche's doctrine of the will to power is then the self-consciousness of human creativity and, with good reason, final. Up to now men created all views, all new existence, without knowing it. They regarded them as given, as objectively valid, but now it is realized that these were all human creations. And so Nietzsche's creation is one made [into] the cause, in knowing what he has done, knowing that he was not simply finding something different but putting his imprint on the judgment.

Now as self-consciousness is the ground of history, Nietzsche's doctrine seems to be purely contemplative, looking at creativity as completed, and that is the situation in Hegel's doctrine. In Hegel's doctrine it is not meant to be creative, but only the final consciousness of creation. Nietzsche rather said [awareness] of this self-consciousness of creativity as the ground of history accompanies the final creative act. Nietzsche's self-consciousness of creativity is understood by him somehow as itself creative. There is a [version] of this argument, if you can call it that way, in which the simplest or the best expressions of how Nietzsche used the truth would be to say the truth appears to him in an enigmatic vision or creative contemplation. There is a kinship here between Nietzsche's understanding of philosophic truth and poetry, and his awareness of it is underlying "The Song of Melancholy" in the fourth part of the *Zarathustra*. This doubt, even if it is not mere poetry, hasn't anything to do with that being the truth which is philosophy as distinct from poetry.[24] Nietzsche called himself the poet of the *Zarathustra*, incidentally.

Now the transition from the second to the third step. By the first step, I meant the most comprehensive perspective hitherto. The second step, the final creation, to the third, enigmatic vision, corresponds to the transition from will to acceptance. Will belongs to whatever is creation—will to the future, to history—and acceptance belongs together with the eternal return and this paradoxical reassertion of nature as comprehending history within itself. The affirmation of nature: that is [the end to] which Nietzsche is tending. That means in somewhat more practical terms that there is no possibility of an infinite pushing back of the natural limit to human expression, [as proposed] by Marx. There are absolute limits, assignable limits, to what men can sensibly wish to do with regard to nature, and especially his own nature. One example is what Nietzsche understands by the natural relation of the two sexes. Most importantly, the natural hierarchy of men, which means there is a need for all kinds of men, however defective, low, or base. No redemption of the whole human race, no transformation of every human being. Again, in opposition to Marx, no realm of freedom because the realm of freedom in the Marxian sense means of course a transformation of every human being and in a way the redemption of every human being.

From this point of view, Nietzsche, looking at the modern development especially in Europe, demanded a restoration of the natural hierarchy and the formula for that was, as we have seen in *Zarathustra*, a new nobility over against the coming democracy. Nietzsche was not for one moment deceived by the powers of the Hohenzollern monarchy in Germany, for example, whereas the *London Times* wrote in 1898, I happen to know, after the death of Bismarck, that however uncertain the future may be, one thing can safely be said: "the work of Bismarck will last." Except that twenty years later the work of Bismarck had been completely destroyed or practically completely destroyed—and that is, incidentally, a good example of what political foresight means in practice: [no one] should be impressed by any foresight.

At any rate, Nietzsche saw that this will not last and ultimately socialism would come, and he saw the only hope in a new nobility which would no longer be national but the rulers of the planet. The notion of the superman is linked to this political problem. In very simplistic language, one part of Nietzsche's tendency regarding the superman is the looking out for planetary rulers, for men sufficiently large, sufficiently strong, sufficiently good, and sufficiently evil for becoming planetary rulers. We cannot conceive for one moment the following fact regarding the political meaning of Nietzsche's doctrine. Nietzsche, we can say, originated the atheism of the political right. Up to Nietzsche's time, the simple thing that I believe is not considered is that the atheism was political. The only

true atheism was an atheism[25] of the left in the various communist, socialist, and radical democratic movements. The right was conservative and
therefore, whether sincerely or insincerely, theistic. The alliance of Rome
and [throne] was the formula for conservatism in the nineteenth century
in Europe.

Now this atheism of the right: the first famous conservative thinker
in this situation to openly proclaim atheism was Nietzsche's teacher,
Schopenhauer. But it is quite characteristic: Schopenhauer was merely a
conservative, and nothing is poorer than Schopenhauer's doctrine of politics. It's a very crude version of [Nietzsche's] doctrine. Schopenhauer was
a conservative, which means in practice that in 1848—in the famous revolution, democratic revolution which was then crushed—Schopenhauer,
living in Frankfurt-am-Main, gave his class, or his three classes, to an
Austrian battalion commander so that he could more conveniently
shoot at the democrats, and he was entirely proud of it. That was the
sole political action of Schopenhauer, either in deed or in speech. But
Schopenhauer was politically nonexistent. Nietzsche created on the right
a political radicalism and let it be opposed to the political radicalism of
the extreme left, especially the communists; and one cannot for one moment overlook the fact, or minimize it, that Nietzsche's doctrine was with
a kind of inevitability corrupted into fascism. You could say that anyone
who tries to understand this phenomenon does not fall back to Nietzsche's nobler form. . .

In making these remarks, I am loyal to the principles of interpretation
of Nietzsche himself, and aphorism 6 of *Beyond Good and Evil*, the beginning. I read the following remarks:

> Gradually I have come to realize what every great philosophy up to now
> has been: the personal confession of its originator, a type of involuntary
> and unaware memoirs; also that the moral (or amoral) intentions of
> each philosophy constitute the protoplasm from which each entire plant
> [meaning the whole system—LS] has grown. Indeed, one will do well
> (and wisely), if one wishes to explain to himself how on earth the more
> remote metaphysical assertions of a philosopher ever arose, to ask each
> time: What sort of morality is this (is *he*) aiming at?[26]

In a later passage, in aphorism 211, Nietzsche uses the expression "*the
political* (moral)."[27] So moral and political are for Nietzsche not separable
in the last resort. Therefore, applying to Nietzsche his own principles of

interpretation and therefore proceeding in a perfectly fair way, one must look at the perverse and by no means negligible sort of interpretation: What does Nietzsche's doctrine—his metaphysics, if you want to call it that—mean politically? But since you are infinitely more sensible, then you try to understand Nietzsche's doctrine in psychological terms— although no one, perhaps, was more guilty of popularizing the psychological explanation of philosophic doctrines than Nietzsche himself. And you know the character of these psychological interpretations: Nietzsche was a very sick man; he was very miserably sick, and no women, and so on and so on, and that is taken as a clue to his meditation. It is barely possible that certain otherwise wholly inexplicable passages . . . symbols could be illuminated by reference to Nietzsche's private life. There are some points where I believe it is impossible—the significance of which are. . . but in the main, we don't know Nietzsche's . . . and it is, I would say, both more intelligent and more decent—somehow, the two things are, I believe, not in such a . . . to start from . . . of natural and . . . facts, which are matters of . . . rather than from . . .

I leave it at that. I could have made some more points, but I leave it at that. Otherwise we will not have time for our discussion. Are there some questions which you would like to get . . .

Student: . . .

LS: His animals, the eagle and the serpent, are closer to Zarathustra than any human being. . . What does it mean? It means that his animals are already and eternally, so to speak, what man should only become. And that meant what man would become by becoming his true [self] or, in other words, would become by becoming reconciled with the doctrine of eternal return and by the new [nobility]. There is a formal parallelism—I think I mentioned this before—between the end of [Nietzsche's doctrine] and that of Rousseau. You know, in Rousseau's return to the state of nature, sometimes Rousseau also uses very extreme remarks about the return to the state of nature. Of course, Rousseau knew that we cannot make ourselves into stupid animals again; even if we tried, we couldn't and . . . What Rousseau means, and what Nietzsche too means, is a return to nature from the . . . of humanity. This paradoxical formula is the only one which [makes sense], and now of course the question: Why not [other animals]? Why a serpent and eagle, and not a cow or a ram? But because . . .

Student: . . .

LS: Yes, but of course it presupposes the . . . that there is a radical difference between man and the beasts. And if this whole notion is confronted with the problem of its future, the future of its species as man is concerned. That is one of the massive difficulties of Nietzsche's doctrine: that on the one hand it denies and on the other hand it asserts all the time that there is an essential difference between men and beasts. It's always somehow connected with the denial of the independent stages of the intellect. The intellect as specifically human . . . is derivative, and if it is derivative, derivative from what? From the subrational.

Student: . . .

LS: Yes, but in this sense, surely, and that is what Nietzsche implies by will to power. The will to power means creation, and creation is of course the . . . brother to mutation. There is something new that could not be predicted on the basis of . . .

Student: . . .

LS: Yes, that is a long, long story, but when there is a creative act by virtue of which the human species came to be, and then, on the basis of the existence of man, we have a series of creative acts, not successive necessarily, but . . . by virtue of which individual tribes or nations created an image of goodness under which they lived . . . And then there is a still later step in which the creative tribe, the creative nation, is replaced by the creative individual; and an important part of that is by virtue of which the nation becomes . . . ceases to be the highest unit. The whole human race, understood . . . and the goal or ideal is now to be universal. The ideal of the universal state, according to this interpretation, is [achieved], and now by virtue of this universal ideal the nation ceases to be [creative], and this gives the possibility of the liberation of the individual as individual. And then, therefore, in the post-Christian or even the Christian world, the individual creator becomes of decided importance . . .

Student: Why is the doctrine of eternal return so necessary to Nietzsche?

LS: Well, we have discussed this. It is an absolutely necessary and legitimate question, but I do not know whether I can now extend that and set it forth really . . . Well, I will try to answer this question superficially. Nietzsche's doctrine of will to power and creativeness is at variance with what we understand by knowledge. Knowledge means to perceive what is, and not the group's stamp or imprint on mere matter. Nietzsche is compelled, in spite of everything he says about the creative activity, to combine to this receptive character of knowledge, and therefore it can be . . . in stages. Only one stage could be called creation, yes, but creative contemplation. And when there is an enigmatic vision, there the element of putting the imprint seems to be wholly absent, and only the . . . Now if you start from the assumption—from which I believe one shouldn't start, but from which Nietzsche in fact started—that the fundamental phenomenon is the will to power, it becomes necessary to understand the phenomenon of more . . . modification of the will to power, but a modification of such a nature that the will to power—putting the imprint on things—turns against itself, meaning it prevents itself from putting the imprint. Now an acceptance as radical acceptance, infinite acceptance, means an infinite "yes" to what is and was: eternal return. Well, you can also start from nature. Nietzsche's whole doctrine presupposes that there is such a thing as nature, not merely in the sense of an inarticulate, mere matter which is interpreted, articulated, by man but, for example, in this paragraph 57 of the *Antichrist* to which I have referred, there is by nature a hierarchy of men. Now, but again: if he starts from will as the funda- mental phenomenon, nature cannot be except as will as a possible . . . and I think again it is this . . . which . . . The other point I mentioned: the only thing about creation and meaning is [that they are from] this man, but there is a variety of human perspectives. And therefore it comes down ultimately to this: that there must be a hierarchy of perspectives, and Nietzsche of course admits that as part of that hierarchy. Now that means that this doctrine, the will to power and everything that goes with that— the origin of all articulation and meaning, and of true articulation and meaning—is Zarathustra's will. Everything else is conditioned by, depen- dent on, this creative act. But common sense tells us, and told Nietzsche, that this first cause—I use a Nietzschean term—one could have even . . . mind, that this first cause is obviously caused. This ultimate condition is obviously conditioned. How can this contradiction be avoided? If the conditions of the condition are themselves the work of the condition in a theory on life, that is a remarkable section on the . . . I myself belong to the causes of my return. I think if you trace it back to the fundamental problem, you will always come to that: that condition, understanding, perception is regarded as derivative.

It is very easy to transform Nietzsche's thesis into such [views] which are in no way paradoxical, and call as trivial and elementary the truth, you know, and their causes. What is knowledge? On the basis of the . . . It can only be a function of the human organism and it must be understood as a function of the human organism. And what does this mean? Knowledge is derivative. Knowledge can only be understood in terms of the function it has for human life. In a very popular view, which is still usually honored, although it is slowly perhaps . . . man needs science for living, or at least for living well, for survival on the lowest level. Today that has almost disappeared . . . But if this justification of science is impossible, because if man needs science for living or living well, then you have an objectively valid value judgment: then you say in effect that science is good, and that can be demonstrated because man needs science for living and for living well. Now as you all know, today it is said there cannot be objectively valid value judgments, and that means in the complete case it is impossible to prove that man needs science for living or living well. Now what then is the meaning of science? One way to answer the question is this: that you can put any construction on science as you please. It is a human activity which has built-in rules of procedure, and so on and so on. Better, it has a function, but which function depends entirely on the actual case. The question of the goodness of science cannot be answered.

In other words, the only question which we can address ourselves to is the question of the criteria of validity of scientific constructs, the logic of science. The psychological question regarding the genesis of statements, theories, and so on is of no importance. That is very common today, this view, but one cannot say it is a satisfactory account of what science is. It may be barely sufficient for intrascientific, say, for intralaboratory use. It is not sufficient for giving an account of science as a human . . . It is a very strange thing that the phrase "the sovereignty of reason" is still very frequently used. I have seen a book with the title *Sovereignty of Reason* . . . but one wonders what this sovereignty means if reason—or science in particular, and logically the highest form of it—is unable to answer the question of its own meaning.[28] One can say that this kind of difficulty, which in this particular form is surely post-Nietzsche, that Nietzsche begins to raise questions where it is fashionable . . .

Student: . . .

LS: I do not quite understand what you mean, and if I do understand, there are a number of questions involved in your simple question. First, I did not try to show the origin of the thesis, unless you mean in this way: Which substantive necessities led Nietzsche to posit eternal return, given his premises? . . . But that, I think, is a necessary question . . .[29] Surely it is not sufficient, because the question arises—granted that starting from the will to power, there is no choice but to teach eternal return. This first is the premise, though, and assuming for a moment this fundamental premise, is the confusion sensible? I would like to make only one remark on this point, and that is very gratifying to people like me. In *Zarathustra*, Nietzsche is . . . this fact of enigmatic vision of eternal return and its moral meanings. But later on, and partly even at the same time, he found it necessary to go either to Paris or to Vienna to study physics in order to get some proof of the doctrine of eternal return, which is of course deplored by those who radicalize Nietzsche's criticism of reason but which, I think, can only be understood from the opposite point of view. But I think in your question there was some other element.

Student: Well, I asked how could he rest with the doctrine, and you sort of pointed out that he couldn't, but even if he could prove that, say, the will to power is the fundamental phenomenon, it would still be a necessity in nature and would not be dependent upon Nietzsche's will, or Zarathustra's.

LS: Yes, now it's true; that is exactly the ambiguity of the doctrine of eternal return, that it becomes undistinguishable whether it is the will or acceptance. There is another difficulty connected with that. You know, that is what Nietzsche says in one place, which I quote—it's not a . . . quotation . . . will, by eternal return, turns out to be will . . . That is what you mean. In other words, this is connected with another question which I continually discussed: Is there no simple contradiction between Nietzsche's futurism, his historical conscience, his concern with the superman, and the doctrine of the will to power—which is the basis for that on the one hand, and the eternal return, with its complete transhistorical meaning on the other hand? That I am not so sure is the case. I mean, the Nietzschean formulation may be contradictory at some point—that I do not know, and it's not particularly important—but I see no contradiction in this assertion itself: that man, individually or socially, living at any time, thinks and must think in terms of the future, [at least] privately, on twelve hundred levels if man and, in a way, society still figures that perhaps it is necessary there are some people who think even of the future of mankind. That means a certain condition. Then it is no longer possible to look at mere individuals . . . by itself because of the highest interconnections. This seems to me to be perfectly compatible with admitting that no future, however perfect—no future of human society, however perfect—will last forever, just as in our own time we know that we are going to die, and therefore this questions arises. If there will be an end of any perfect society, which I might . . . let us assume it is of . . . beauty and brawn, even that society will perish. And then the question arises. Compare then the whole process, beginning before the beginning of man and ending after the disappearance of the final man, is this a singular, unique process—as it is, according to the biblical doctrine on very good ground, but according to the modern secularized consciousness, on no good ground—very simply, an unsupported heritage from the biblical tradition? And Nietzsche [took] his rejection of the biblical tradition seriously. He said: Must we not question the dogmatic assumption of the uniqueness of the process of human civilization? And that of course does not necessarily mean eternal return of every human ... but is it not much more rational that the infinity of such costly processes...

Student: ...

LS: Is it not on the most common level a way out of despair to become rigorous, impudent... Now why should this not be possible on the most comprehensive level if man becomes disappointed of the true self, the possibility of truth, that he belongs to the possibility? Nietzsche discusses that partly in the speech "On the Tree on the Mountainside," the first part, where the young man speaks the poem and the will is in danger of becoming just trivial, uninteresting. That is possible. In a way he is superior... That is, all his nine men in their thought are individually somehow aware of the crisis of modern life, but not sufficiently aware.

Student: ...

LS: Yes. Nietzsche simply rejected this altogether, from the very beginning ...[30]

Notes

EDITOR'S INTRODUCTION

1. Leo Strauss to Karl Löwith, 23 June 1935, *Gesammelte Schriften*, ed. H. Meier and W. Meier, 3 vols. (Stuttgart and Weimar: J. B. Metzler, 1996–2001), 3: 648. Hereafter cited as GS. An English translation of this letter appears in "Correspondence, Karl Löwith and Leo Strauss," *Independent Journal of Philosophy* 5–6 (1988): 182–84.

2. "Religiöse Lage der Gegenwart," GS, 2: 389. For an English translation, see "Religious Situation of the Present," in *Reorientation: Leo Strauss in the 1930s*, ed. Martin D. Yaffe and Richard S. Ruderman (New York: Palgrave Macmillan, 2014), 234.

3. Strauss to Gerhard Krüger, 17 November 1932, GS, 3: 406.

4. Strauss to Krüger, 12 December 1932, GS, 3: 415.

5. Strauss to Löwith, 2 February 1933, GS, 3: 620–21.

6. Preface to the English Translation, *Spinoza's Critique of Religion*, trans. E. Sinclair (New York: Schocken, 1965), 31.

7. *Thoughts on Machiavelli* (Glencoe, IL: Free Press, 1958), 296.

8. See *Socrates and Aristophanes* (New York: Basic Books, 1966), 6–8; "The Problem of Socrates," *Interpretation* 22 (1995): 322–24 (1970 lecture); and "The Origins of Political Science and the Problem of Socrates," *Interpretation* 23 (1996): 136–39 (1958 lecture).

9. "What Is Political Philosophy?," in *What Is Political Philosophy? and Other Studies* (Chicago: University of Chicago Press, 1988), 54–55; also "The Three Waves of Modernity," in *An Introduction to Political Philosophy: Ten Essays by Leo Strauss*, ed. Hilail Gildin (Detroit, MI: Wayne State University Press, 1989), 81–98, and chapter 11 below.

10. See "Note on the Plan of Nietzsche's *Beyond Good and Evil*," first published in *Interpretation* in 1973 and reprinted in *Studies in Platonic Political Philosophy* (Chicago: University of Chicago Press, 1983; henceforth SPPP). Significantly, this essay appears as the central chapter of SPPP, according to Strauss's plan for the book, and just after the essay "Jerusalem and Athens: Some Preliminary Reflections." The Nietzsche seminars of 1959 and 1967 shed much light on this enigmatic essay. Robert Pippin exposes some enigmas in "Leo Strauss's Nietzsche," *Principle and Prudence in Western Political Thought*, ed. C. Lynch and J. Marks (Albany: State University of New York Press, 2016); Laurence Lampert offers a detailed commentary on the essay in *Leo Strauss and Nietzsche* (Chicago: University of Chicago Press, 1996).

11. *Beyond Good and Evil*, no. 23, "On the Prejudices of Philosophers." See the remark

254 NOTES TO PAGES XIV–XVII

of Seth Benardete: "Plato's psychology was Strauss's way to Plato's ideas: and Strauss's way was the way of the *Republic*." Seth Benardete, "Memorial Speech for Leo Strauss," in S. Benardete, *The Archaeology of the Soul: Platonic Readings of Ancient Poetry and Philosophy*, ed. Ronna Burger and Michael Davis (South Bend, IN: St. Augustine's Press, 2012), 376.

12. It should be noted that Strauss regards natural right in this sense as a "problem" not susceptible of a doctrinal solution. See *Natural Right and History* (Chicago: University of Chicago Press, 1953), 7–8, 29–30, 125–26; *What Is Political Philosophy?*, 38–39. Famously he proposes an ironic reading of the rule of philosopher-kings in Plato's *Republic*. Indeed, it could be said that for Strauss the view that nature is a problem links, rather than divides, Plato and Nietzsche, although they have differing formulations of the problem. Strauss counters Heidegger's reading of Nietzsche's philosophy as the completion of Platonic metaphysics with a reading of it as the renewal of Platonic political philosophy.

13. *SPPP*, 174–75.

14. The problem might be restated as follows: If the contemplative life is not supported by an enduring, intelligible cosmic order (as Strauss more than once states is the case), then is the modern turn to the primacy of will, lawgiving, and creation justified? Nietzsche would be a very instructive case, for he undertakes a recovery of contemplation but on the basis of will, and perhaps reveals a deeper necessity for that grounding of philosophy than one finds in the tradition between Machiavelli and Marx. Be that as it may, Strauss is not Nietzschean, and his recovery of Socratic political philosophy takes another path.

15. This is also the case in "Note on the Plan" in *SPPP*.

16. *Nietzsche* (Pfullingen: Neske Verlag, 1961). For an English translation, see *Nietzsche*, trans. David Farrell Krell, 4 vols. (New York: Harper & Row, 1979–87). See also Strauss, "Problem of Socrates," 324: "The profoundest interpreter and at the same time the profoundest *critic* of Nietzsche is Heidegger. He is Nietzsche's profoundest interpreter *because* he is his profoundest critic." Strauss's correspondence discloses his serious engagement with all the writings of Heidegger appearing after the end of the Second World War. See letter to Jacob Klein, 1 August 1949, *GS*, 3: 598–99, and the following letters to Karl Löwith: 23 February 1950, *GS*, 3: 674; 21 December 1951, *GS*, 3: 676–77; 13 December 1960, *GS*, 3: 684–85; 15 March 1962, *GS*, 3: 685–87; 12 March 1970, *GS*, 3: 695–96. Some of Heidegger's pre-1961 writings already contain important accounts of Nietzsche's thought, notably *Holzwege* (1950), *Was heisst Denken?* (1952), and *Vorträge und Aufsätze* (1954).

17. This point is reinforced by study of the correspondence, especially with Karl Löwith.

18. See the lecture of 1956, "Existentialism," in *Interpretation* 22 (1995): 303–20, and "Philosophy as Rigorous Science and Political Philosophy" in *SPPP*, 29–37. More generally, Strauss regards the humanitarianism of modern rationalism (of which Nietzsche and Heidegger are, in Strauss's estimation, the heirs in differing yet related ways) as coming about through a fusion of philosophy and religion, or of Athens and Jerusalem.

INTRODUCTION: NIETZSCHE'S PHILOSOPHY, EXISTENTIALISM, AND THE PROBLEM OF OUR AGE

1. William Barrett, *Irrational Man: A Study in Existential Philosophy* (Garden City, NY: Doubleday Anchor Books, 1958).

2. David Riesman, Nathan Glazer, and Reuel Denney, *The Lonely Crowd* (New Haven: Yale University Press, 1950).

3. *The Portable Nietzsche*, ed. and trans. Walter Kaufmann (New York: Viking Penguin, 1954).

4. In *SPPP*, 138–40, Strauss identifies these as *Gorgias* 483e and *Timaeus* 83e, and notes a passage in Aristotle's *Rhetoric* 1373b4 on the law according to nature.

5. For Strauss's account, published posthumously, see "Three Waves of Modernity."

6. Thomas Hobbes, *Leviathan*, chapter 13.

7. The transcriber notes that there was a change of tape here.

8. "Of the Advantage and Disadvantage of History for Life," the second of four *Thoughts out of Season* (*Untimely Meditations*) (1874).

9. In original transcript: "characteristically"; "theoretically" is suggested by the editor.

RESTORING NATURE AS ETHICAL PRINCIPLE: *ZARATHUSTRA*, PROLOGUE

1. *Ecce Homo*, "Why I Am a Destiny," 3.

2. *On the Genealogy of Morals*, second essay, 25.

3. *Ecce Homo*, "Genealogy of Morals."

4. Strauss has in mind the more literal translation of "rope-dancer" for the German word *Seiltänser*, which Kaufmann translates as "tightrope walker."

5. *Zarathustra*, 1, Zarathustra's Prologue, 5.

6. *Zarathustra*, 1, Zarathustra's Prologue, 6.

7. *Zarathustra*, 1, Zarathustra's Prologue, 2. Presumably Strauss's translation.

8. *Zarathustra*, 1, Zarathustra's Prologue, 5. Though the full passage was read aloud, here it has been abridged.

9. *Zarathustra*, 1, Zarathustra's Prologue, 3.

10. There was a change of tape at this point.

11. *Zarathustra*, 1, Zarathustra's Prologue, 4. *Portable Nietzsche*, 126–27.

12. Cf. Plato, *Phaedrus* 244a.

13. Matthew 10:16: "Behold I send you forth as sheep in the midst of wolves: be ye therefore wise as serpents, and harmless as doves."

14. *The Will to Power*, 983.

15. *Zarathustra*, Zarathustra's Prologue, 5. *Portable Nietzsche*, 129.

16. Auguste Comte (1798–1857), the father of positivism, presents his theory of the three stages of human knowledge in his *Course on Positivist Philosophy* (1830–42).

17. *Zarathustra*, 1.1, "On the Three Metamorphoses." *Portable Nietzsche*, 137–38.

18. Strauss's reference is uncertain, as Nietzsche never seems directly to refer to mind (presumably *Geist*) as nihilistic. He may, however, have the preface and section 10 of *Beyond Good and Evil* in mind.

19. *Zarathustra*, 1.1, "On the Three Metamorphoses." *Portable Nietzsche*, 139.

20. The Tenth Commandment is not discussed during the Sermon on the Mount, though the Sixth, "Thou shalt not commit adultery," is in Matthew 5:27–30. Strauss may have this passage in mind, where Christianity's otherworldly orientation and rejection of this world as sinful are especially pronounced.

21. *Zarathustra*, 1, Zarathustra's Prologue, 5. *Portable Nietzsche*, 130.

22. *The Protestant Ethic and the Spirit of Capitalism* (1905).

23. Strauss appears to be translating from the German original of a fragment from the *Nachlass* (spring 1880, no. 19). The first sentence of the quotation in fact occurs at the end of the quotation. The minor changes made to Strauss's translation have been noted. The original text can be found in Friedrich Nietzsche, *Sämtliche Werke: Kritische Studienausgabe in 15 Bänden* (Berlin: de Gruyter, 1967–77), 9: 52.

THE CREATIVE SELF: *ZARATHUSTRA*, PART 1, 1-8

1. Strauss quotes from Eric Havelock's *The Liberal Temper in Greek Politics* (New Haven: Yale University Press, 1957). Strauss reviews this work at length in "The Liberalism of Classical Political Philosophy," in Leo Strauss, *Liberalism Ancient and Modern* (Chicago: University of Chicago Press, 1968). The quotation appears on page 64.

2. *On the Genealogy of Morality*, third essay, 1 and 28.

3. *Zarathustra*, 1.2, "On the Teachers of Virtue."

4. Plato, *Apology of Socrates* 40d–e.

5. *Zarathustra*, 1.2, "On the Teachers of Virtue."

6. *Zarathustra*, 1.3, "On the Afterworldly."

7. *Untimely Meditations*, "Schopenhauer as Educator," 3.

8. *Zarathustra*, 1.4, "On the Despisers of the Body."

9. *Twilight of the Idols*, "Raids of an Untimely One," 32.

10. *Beyond Good and Evil*, 62.

11. The socialist doctrines of Josip Broz Tito (1892–1980), president of the Socialist Federal Republic of Yugoslavia, 1953–80.

12. Strauss translates a fragment from the *Nachlass* (spring 1880), no. 19, in *Sämtliche Werke: Kritische Studienausgabe im 15 Bänden*, 9: 52.

13. There may have been a change of tape at this point.

14. *Beyond Good and Evil*, 75.

15. *Phaedrus* 253c ff.

16. *Zarathustra*, 1.5, "On Enjoying and Suffering the Passions."

17. *Zarathustra*, 1.5, "On Enjoying and Suffering the Passions." *Portable Nietzsche*, 148.

18. *Zarathustra*, 1.7, "On Reading and Writing."

19. Strauss discusses this point in *Thoughts on Machiavelli*, 40; he provides a citation on page 303, note 46, which reads: "Cf. letter to Vettori of January 13, 1514 with *Florentine Histories* VIII 36." As Strauss elaborates, he makes reference to *The Gay Science*, 1.

20. *Zarathustra*, 1.8, "On the Tree on the Mountainside."

21. *Zarathustra*, 1.8, "On the Tree on the Mountainside." *Portable Nietzsche*, 156.

22. See *On the Genealogy of Morality*, first essay.

THE TRUE INDIVIDUAL AS THE HIGHEST GOAL: *ZARATHUSTRA*, PART 1, 9-15

1. *Zarathustra*, 1.9, "On the Preachers of Death."

2. *Zarathustra*, 1.9, "On the Preachers of Death.

3. *Zarathustra*, 1.10, "On War and Warriors."

4. *Zarathustra*, 1.10, "On War and Warriors."

5. This may not be a direct quotation, but in Strauss's view an implication of "Schopenhauer as Educator," which has an extended critique of the state. Or see *Will to Power*, 725.

6. *Zarathustra*, 1.12, "On the Flies of the Market Place."

7. *Zarathustra*, 1.12, "On the Flies of the Market Place."

8. Strauss refers to sociologist William H. Whyte's 1956 best-seller, which addressed the effects that mass organization through corporations had on America.

9. Herbert McClosky, "Conservatism and Personality," *American Political Science Review* 52 (1958): 27–45.

10. *Zarathustra*, 1.12, "On the Flies of the Market Place."

11. *Zarathustra*, 1.13, "On Chastity." *Portable Nietzsche*, 166.

12. *On the Genealogy of Morals*, third essay, sec. 2.

13. *Zarathustra*, 1.14, "On the Friend." *Portable Nietzsche*, 168.

14. *Republic* 571b–2b.

15. *Zarathustra*, 1.14, "On the Friend." *Portable Nietzsche*, 169.

16. The German *Mitleiden* could be rendered as either "compassion" or "pity"; hence Strauss's vacillation between the two terms.

17. There was a change of tape at this point.

18. *Zarathustra*, 1.15, "On the Thousand and One Goals."

19. After the quotation, the transcript reads "[Homer]," where the translation does not. It is not clear whether the insertion is Strauss's or the transcriber's. The reference is to Homer, *Iliad* 6.208, 19.321ff.

20. Just as with the previous quotation, the transcript here reads "[Herodotus]." The reference is to Herodotus, *Histories* 1.136.2. Cf. *Ecce Homo*, "Why I Am a Destiny," sec. 3.

21. *Zarathustra*, 1.15, "On the Thousand and One Goals."

22. *Zarathustra*, 1.15, "On the Thousand and One Goals." *Portable Nietzsche*, 170.

23. "Considerations on the Government of Poland" (1772).

24. "Considerations on the Government of Poland," chapters 2–3.

25. *Zarathustra*, 1.15, "On the Thousand and One Goals."

26. *Zarathustra*, 1.15, "On the Thousand and One Goals." *Portable Nietzsche*, 170.

27. *Zarathustra*, 1.15, "On the Thousand and One Goals." *Portable Nietzsche*, 171–72.

28. Sec. 249.

29. The transcript does not include Mr. Dannhauser's question.

30. *Zarathustra*, 1.15, "On the Thousand and One Goals." *Portable Nietzsche*, 172.

31. *Twilight of the Idols*, "Raids," sec. 12. Thomas Carlyle (1795–1881) was a Scottish historian, essayist, and critic. Among his best-known works are *The French Revolution* (3 vols.) (1837); *On Heroes, Hero-Worship & the Heroic in History* (1841); and *Past and Present* (1843).

32. *The Lonely Crowd*, by David Riesman, Nathan Glazer, and Reuel Denney (1950), is

a sociological work which presents different types of characters found in society and uses these types as an instrument to analyze changes in society over time. In *The Organization Man* (1956), William Whyte coined the term "groupthink" to describe tendencies he saw in society and especially in the workplace.

33. There was a change of tape at this point. When the recording resumed, a portion of the tape was inaudible.

POSTULATED NATURE AND FINAL TRUTH: *ZARATHUSTRA*, PART 1, 16-22

1. In this aphorism, Nietzsche discusses the implications of loving man for God's sake.

2. In "On the *Euthydemus*," Strauss notes that Crito imposes the external conversation on Socrates, while Socrates's *daimonion* imposes the internal conversation on him. Cf. *SPPP*, 68–69.

3. The question is in parentheses in the transcript; presumably the transcriber paraphrased a question that was largely inaudible.

4. Cf. *Zarathustra*, 4.7, "The Ugliest Man." *Portable Nietzsche*, 375–9.

5. Soviet biologist Trofim Lysenko (1898–1976) was appointed by Stalin as the director of the Institute of Genetics at the USSR's Academy of Sciences, a position he occupied at the time Strauss's course met in 1959. By the middle of the 1950s, however, Lysenko's theory that acquired characteristics were inherited was largely rejected even in the Soviet Union, where he played a prominent political role. Because of his prominence, his slow loss of power—from being challenged in the early to middle 1950s to losing his position as director in 1965—received significant media attention in the United States.

6. "But whosoever shall deny me before men, him will I also deny before my Father which is in heaven" (Matthew 10:33). "Whosoever therefore shall be ashamed of me and of my words in this adulterous and sinful generation; of him also shall the Son of man be ashamed, when he cometh in the glory of his Father with the holy angels" (Mark 8:38).

7. Harold D. Lasswell (1902–78), professor of political science and law at Yale University, raised questions about the ethical implications of increasingly intelligent machines. See, for example, "The Political Science of Science: An Inquiry into the Possible Reconciliation of Mastery and Freedom," *American Political Science Review* 50 (1956): 975–76.

TRUTH, INTERPRETATION, AND INTELLIGIBILITY: *ZARATHUSTRA*, PART 2, 1-12

1. *Zarathustra*, 2.2, "Upon the Blessed Isles." *Portable Nietzsche*, 198.

2. *Zarathustra*, 2.2, "Upon the Blessed Isles." *Portable Nietzsche*, 198–99.

3. *Zarathustra*, 2.2, "Upon the Blessed Isles."

4. *Zarathustra*, 2.2, "Upon the Blessed Isles." *Portable Nietzsche*, 199.

5. *Zarathustra*, 2.2, "On the Pitying." *Portable Nietzsche*, 200.

6. Strauss refers to Henri Bergson's *Creative Evolution* (1907).

7. *Zarathustra*, 2.3, "On the Pitying."

8. *Zarathustra*, 2.3, "On the Pitying."

9. *Zarathustra*, 2.4, "On Priests."

10. The transcript does not provide the text of the aphorism. The translation supplied is that of Marianne Cowan (Chicago: Gateway-Henry Regnery, 1955), since Strauss uses it elsewhere in the lectures and presumably does so here, as well.

11. *Zarathustra*, 2.5, "On the Virtuous."

12. From "The Wanderer and His Shadow" (first published as the final sequel to *Human, All-Too-Human*, aphorism 261). *Portable Nietzsche*, 70.

13. Alexis de Tocqueville, Author's Introduction, *Democracy in America* (1835).

14. *Zarathustra*, 2.7, "On the Tarantulas."

15. *Zarathustra*, 2.7, "On the Tarantulas."

16. Cowan translation.

17. *Zarathustra*, 2.8, "On the Famous Wise Men." *Portable Nietzsche*, 214–15.

18. Strauss refers to *Sophist* 231a–b, where the Stranger compares the philosopher and the sophist to a dog and a wolf (see Strauss's comments on the lover of knowledge just below).

19. *Zarathustra*, 2.8, "On the Famous Wise Men." *Portable Nietzsche*, 216.

20. The transcript shows a set of empty brackets, as though the text of the aphorism was to be inserted. It is not known whether the aphorism was read aloud in class. The translation provided here is from *Beyond Good and Evil*, trans. Cowan.

21. *Zarathustra*, 2.8, "On the Famous Wise Men." *Portable Nietzsche*, 216.

22. Dante, *Inferno*, canto 4.

23. Strauss refers to the very first line of the preface to *Beyond Good and Evil*.

24. *Zarathustra*, 2.11, "The Tomb Song." *Portable Nietzsche*, 224.

25. From *Nietzsche Contra Wagner*, epilogue, section 2. Originally from section 4 of the preface to the second edition of *The Gay Science*. Though the full passage was read aloud, here it is abridged.

26. "On Self-Overcoming."

27. *Zarathustra*, 2.12, "On Self-Overcoming." *Portable Nietzsche*, 225.

28. *Zarathustra*, 2.2, "Upon the Blessed Isles." Strauss's translation or paraphrase.

29. Strauss refers to Harold Lasswell's works *Psychopathology and Politics* (1930) and *Power and Personality* (1948).

30. Cf. Walter Kaufmann, *Nietzsche: Philosopher, Psychologist, Antichrist*, 4th ed. (Princeton: Princeton University Press, 1974), chap. 10; Strauss, "The Three Waves of Modernity," 97–98.

31. The transcriber notes that the student's question had to do with "infinite delicacy."

WILL TO POWER AND SELF-OVERCOMING: *ZARATHUSTRA*, PART 2, 15-20

1. Seneca, *Epistles*, 49.

2. Strauss refers to Henry Adams's (1838–1918) *The Education of Henry Adams*, which chronicles the failures of his formal education in light of the rapid industrial progress of late-nineteenth-century America, and his subsequent attempt at self-education.

3. Strauss's translation. Kaufmann has "perception."

4. *Zarathustra*, 2.15, "On Immaculate Perception."

5. George H. Sabine (1880–1961), political scientist, was best known for his work *A History of Political Theory* (1937), a standard text in courses on political philosophy at the time.

6. *Zarathustra*, 2.15, "On Immaculate Perception." Though the full passage was read aloud, here it has been abridged.

7. Strauss refers to the end of Marx's short note that has come to be known as the "Theses on Feuerbach" (1845). Strauss's translation or paraphrase.

8. *Zarathustra*, 2.16, "On Scholars." *Portable Nietzsche*, 237.

9. *Zarathustra*, 2.16, "On Scholars." *Portable Nietzsche*, 237–38.

10. *Zarathustra*, 2.16, "On Scholars." *Portable Nietzsche*, 238.

11. *Faust* II, ll. 12104–5.

12. *Zarathustra*, 2.17, "On Poets." *Portable Nietzsche*, 238–39.

13. *Twilight of the Idols*, "The Problem of Socrates."

14. *Twilight of the Idols*, "The Problem of Socrates," 5.

15. *Beyond Good and Evil*, 231, trans. Cowan.

16. The meaning of this phrase is unclear; perhaps a word or phrase is missing.

17. *Faust* II, ll. 12108–9.

18. *Zarathustra*, 2.17, "On Poets." *Portable Nietzsche*, 239–40.

19. *Zarathustra*, 2.17, "On Poets."

20. Cowan translation.

21. *Zarathustra*, 2.18, "On Great Events." *Portable Nietzsche*, 241–42. Though the full passage was read aloud, here it has been abridged.

22. "Schopenhauer as Educator."

23. *Zarathustra*, 2.18, "On Great Events."

24. *Zarathustra*, 2.18, "On Great Events."

25. *Zarathustra*, 2.18, "On Great Events." *Portable Nietzsche*, 245.

26. *Zarathustra*, 2.19, "The Soothsayer." *Portable Nietzsche*, 245.

27. Cf. *Untimely Meditations*, "Schopenhauer as Educator," sec. 4.

28. *Zarathustra*, 2.19, "The Soothsayer."

29. The transcriber indicated that the student's question addressed the relation between reason and the will to power.

30. "On Redemption."

31. *Zarathustra*, 2.20, "On Redemption." *Portable Nietzsche*, 249.

32. *Zarathustra*, 2.20, "On Redemption." *Portable Nietzsche*, 249–50.

33. *Zarathustra*, 2.6, "On the Rabble."

34. The phrase in German reads, "Wie soll er uns heissen?"

35. *Zarathustra*, 2.20, "On Redemption."

36. *Zarathustra*, 1.22, "On the Gift-Giving Virtue."

37. In "On Free Death."

38. In original: "That."

39. "jenes Zuviel"

40. In original: "the Dionysian condition."

41. *Ecce Homo*, "Birth of Tragedy," sec. 4.

42. *Beyond Good and Evil*, 62.

43. *Zarathustra*, 2.20, "On Redemption." *Portable Nietzsche*, 251.

44. *Zarathustra*, 2.20, "On Redemption." *Portable Nietzsche*, 251.

45. Sec. 1.

46. *Zarathustra*, 2.20, "On Redemption." *Portable Nietzsche*, 251–52.

47. It is possible that the obscurity of this sentence is due to transcription errors, but it is impossible to know.

48. The transcript indicates that the student's question addressed the role of chance in Nietzsche's teaching.

SUMMARY AND REVIEW: FUSING PLATO AND THE CREATIVE SELF

1. Strauss makes much the same point in "Relativism," which is reprinted in *The Rebirth of Classical Political Rationalism* (Chicago: University of Chicago Press, 1989), 24.

2. *Zarathustra*, Zarathustra's Prologue, 5. *Portable Nietzsche*, 130. Strauss's translation or paraphrase.

3. See, e.g., John Dewey, *Experience and Education* (1938).

4. Sec. 575.

5. *Beyond Good and Evil*, 9.

6. Cowan translation.

7. In the original transcript: "higher in line."

8. Friedrich Heinrich Jacobi (1743–1819).

9. The exchanges can be found in Gotthold Lessing, *Philosophical and Theological Writings*, ed. H. B. Nisbet (Cambridge: Cambridge University Press, 2005), 241–56.

10. *Beyond Good and Evil*, 9. Cowan translation.

11. *Beyond Good and Evil*, 230. Cowan translation.

12. *Beyond Good and Evil*, 188. Cowan translation.

GREEK PHILOSOPHY AND THE BIBLE; NATURE AND HISTORY: *ZARATHUSTRA*, PART 2, 20-22

1. Herbert McClosky, "Conservatism and Personality," *American Political Science Review* 52 (1958): 27–45.

2. Cf. *Beyond Good and Evil*, 42.

3. *Zarathustra*, 1.22, "On the Gift-Giving Virtue," 3. *Portable Nietzsche*, 190–91.

4. Spinoza, *Ethics*, 4, prop. 67.

5. *Zarathustra*, 2.20, "On Redemption."

6. *Zarathustra*, 2.20, "On Redemption." *Portable Nietzsche*, 253–54.

ETERNAL RECURRENCE: *ZARATHUSTRA*, PART 2, 21; PART 3, 1-13

1. *Zarathustra*, 3.12, "On Old and New Tablets," 11.

2. David Riesman, Nathan Glazer, and Reuel Denney, *The Lonely Crowd* (1950).

3. *Beyond Good and Evil*, 9. Cowan translation.

4. *Zarathustra*, 2.21, "On Human Prudence."

5. In the transcript: "he would suspect."

6. *Zarathustra*, 2.21, "On Human Prudence." *Portable Nietzsche*, 254.

7. *Zarathustra*, 3.1, "The Wanderer."

8. In original: "this book."

9. The quoted text is found only on pages 187–88 of *Irrational Man* (Garden City, NY: Anchor Books/Doubleday, 1958), but is immediately followed by the bulk of section 3 of "*Thus Spoke Zarathustra: A Book for All and None*," in *Ecce Homo*, which extends onto page 188.

10. Strauss is reading Barrett, who quotes Nietzsche. No translator is cited in Barrett's *Irrational Man*, and the translation may be Barrett's own. *Irrational Man*, 187–88.

11. *Zarathustra*, 3.2, "On the Vision and the Riddle." *Portable Nietzsche*, 267–68.

12. *Zarathustra*, 3.2, "On the Vision and the Riddle." *Portable Nietzsche*, 268.

13. Heinrich Heine, *Florentine Nights, The Memoirs of Herr von Schnabelewopski, The Rabbi of Bacharach, and Shakespeare's Maidens and Women* (New York: John H. Lovell Company, 1891), 432–38 (from Heine's quotation of Guizot to the dream Strauss quotes). The transcript does not indicate that Strauss quotes this volume, though this may be the case because of the use of the first person, and the similarity of the quotation to the translation in the above edition. Nonetheless, the translation may be Strauss's.

14. Strauss refers to the discussion of poetry in *Republic* 10.

15. That is, the second division of the speech.

16. *Zarathustra*, 3.2, "On the Vision and the Riddle," 2.

17. *Zarathustra*, 3.2, "On the Three Evils," 1.

18. *Zarathustra*, 3.2, "On the Vision and the Riddle," 2. *Portable Nietzsche*, 270.

19. *Zarathustra*, 3.13, "The Convalescent," 2.

20. Strauss seems to have Rousseau in mind, as becomes apparent in what follows and in later sessions.

21. *Twilight of the Idols*, "'Reason' in Philosophy," sec. 2.

22. Fragment B114, according to the Diels-Kranz numbering.

23. The transcriber indicates that the question concerned the status of reason in Nietzsche's thought.

24. The original transcript reads: "even of the last man, because according to Nietzsche there is no longer a possibility of the traditional man, either or."

SURVEY: NIETZSCHE AND POLITICAL PHILOSOPHY

1. Cf. Leo Strauss, "On the Intention of Rousseau," *Social Research* 14 (1947): 462–63; *Natural Right and History*, 254–55, esp. 255 n. 4.

2. Strauss refers to the subtitle of Bernard Mandeville's (1670–1733) *The Fable of the Bees; or, Private Vices, Public Benefits* (1714).

3. That is, the first of "the two other theses."

4. *Zarathustra*, 2.20, "On Redemption," *Portable Nietzsche*, 251ff.

5. *Zarathustra*, 2.18, "On Great Events," *Portable Nietzsche*, 244.

6. The transcriber notes that the remainder of the tape is inaudible.

THE GOODNESS OF THE WHOLE, SOCRATIC AND HEIDEGGERIAN CRITIQUES: ZARATHUSTRA, PART 3, 4-12

1. Apparently Strauss's translation of a passage from "Of the Advantage and Disadvantage of History for Life" from *Untimely Meditations*. Strauss uses a very similar translation in his posthumously published essay "Note on the Plan of Nietzsche's *Beyond Good and Evil*," which can be found in *SPPP*, 177.

2. Presumably Strauss's translation.

3. *Zarathustra*, 2.17, "On Poets." *Portable Nietzsche*, 238–41.

4. Apparently Strauss's translation.

5. Here Strauss appears to paraphrase and, in the paragraph after the quotation from *Zarathustra*, directly to quote from Heidegger's essay "Who Is Nietzsche's Zarathustra?," which was published in *Vorträge und Aufsätze* in 1954. The present reference is from a draft of *The Gay Science* preserved in Nietzsche's *Nachlass* and can be found in *Vorträge und Aufsätze, Gesamtausgabe* (Frankfurt am Main: Vittorio Klostermann, 2000), 7: 120.

6. *Zarathustra*, 2.9, "The Night Song."

7. Heidegger, *Vorträge und Aufsätze*, 124 (emphasis added from the original). The volume also contains "The Question concerning Technology," to which Strauss appears to make reference in his interpretation of the quotation.

8. "On the Tarantulas."

9. Georges Sorel (1847–1922), a French thinker known for his work on syndicalism and violence, author of *Reflections on Violence* (1914). Strauss seems to be referring to his writings on the political role of myth, which influenced the political ideas of figures like Benito Mussolini.

10. It is possible that Strauss said "scientistic" here; the word "scientism" originated in the nineteenth century.

11. The original transcript reads: "A being can in a certain perspective completely manipulate . . ."

12. *Zarathustra*, 3.4, "Before Sunrise." *Portable Nietzsche*, 276.

13. *Zarathustra*, 3.4, "Before Sunrise."

14. There was a change of tape at this point.

15. *Zarathustra*, 3.4, "Before Sunrise." *Portable Nietzsche*, 278.

16. The German reads *Behagen*, which might better be translated as "comfort" or "pleasure," not in the strong sense, but in the weaker sense of being pleased with something or finding something pleasant.

17. *Zarathustra*, 3.5, "On Virtue That Makes Small," 2. *Portable Nietzsche*, 281.

18. *Zarathustra*, 3.5, "On Virtue That Makes Small," 2. *Portable Nietzsche*, 281–82.

19. That is, in "On Passing By."

20. *Zarathustra*, 3.7, "On Passing By." *Portable Nietzsche*, 289–90. Though the full passage is likely to have been read aloud, here it has been abridged.

21. *Zarathustra*, 3.9, "The Return Home."

22. *Zarathustra*, 3.9, "The Return Home."

23. *Zarathustra*, 3.10, "On the Three Evils," 1. *Portable Nietzsche*, 298–99.

24. *Zarathustra*, 3.10, "On the Three Evils," 1.

25. *Zarathustra*, 3.10, "On the Three Evils," 1. *Portable Nietzsche*, 300.

26. *Zarathustra*, 3.11, "On the Spirit of Gravity," 2. *Portable Nietzsche*, 305.

27. *Zarathustra*, 3.11, "On the Spirit of Gravity," 2.

28. That is, section 2 of "On Old and New Tablets."

29. *Zarathustra*, 3.12, "On Old and New Tablets."

30. *Zarathustra*, 3.12, "On Old and New Tablets," 2.

31. *Zarathustra*, 3.12, "On Old and New Tablets," 2. *Portable Nietzsche*, 309.

32. *Zarathustra*, 3.12, "On Old and New Tablets," 10.

33. *Zarathustra*, 3.12, "On Old and New Tablets," 11. *Portable Nietzsche*, 314–15.

34. In original: "the other movements create."

35. "Creates" is Strauss's insertion.

36. The text reads: "die letzteren als die Herren der Ersteren aufzufassen."

37. Strauss appears to give his own translation of a fragment from Nietzsche's *Nachlass*. In support of this interpretation is the awkward translation of *Ameisen-Bauten* as "structures of ants," where we would expect "anthills." Since the punctuation was the choice of the transcriber, that has been changed in accordance with the German text, from which Strauss appears to read directly. Where Strauss skips over text, ellipses have been introduced. Any changes to the quotation itself have been noted. The original text can be found in Friedrich Nietzsche, *Sämtliche Werke: Kritische Studienausgabe in 15 Bänden*, 10: 244.

CREATIVE CONTEMPLATION: *ZARATHUSTRA*, PART 3, 13

1. Strauss refers to the founding of the just city in speech by Socrates and his interlocutors in *Republic*, books 2–5 (368d–484a).

2. Strauss begins the session by explaining how the final exam will be administered. He dictates the exam question, so that the students will have time to prepare "properly."

3. *Zarathustra*, 3.12, "On Old and New Tablets," 2.

4. Cf. *Twilight of the Idols*, "The Problem of Socrates," sec. 8.

5. That is, Nietzsche and Socrates.

6. Cf. *Twilight of the Idols*, "The Problem of Socrates," sec. 8.

7. Cf. sections 1–18.

8. Cf. *Twilight of the Idols*, "The Problem of Socrates," sec. 4.

9. Cf. *The Birth of Tragedy*, 15.

10. The transcript here provides the aphorism in Cowan's translation as read by Strauss. Cowan's translation reads "psyche." The substitution of "soul" appears to be Strauss's.

11. Here the transcript has "than" where the Cowan translation has "that." "Than" is correct; the German is *als*.

12. That is, *The Birth of Tragedy out of the Spirit of Music*.

13. Cowan's translation.

14. Plato, *Symposium* 203e–204a.

15. Strauss reads from Boris Pasternak, *I Remember: Sketch for an Autobiography*, trans. David Magarshack (New York: Pantheon, 1959), 69.

16. *Zarathustra*, 3.4, "Before Sunrise."

17. In transcript: "the most political way."

18. *Zarathustra*, 3.13, "The Convalescent." *Portable Nietzsche*, 327.

19. *Zarathustra*, 3.13, "The Convalescent," 2.

20. *Zarathustra*, 3.13, "The Convalescent," 2. *Portable Nietzsche*, 329–30.

21. In transcript: "writing"; "the rolling" is an editorial insertion.

22. *Zarathustra*, 3.13, "The Convalescent," 2.

23. A change of tape was made at this point. The portion of the text that was lost has been reinstated.

24. *Zarathustra*, 3.13, "The Convalescent," 2.

25. The transcript has a blank space here; it may have indicated a pause or an inaudible word.

26. *Zarathustra*, 3.13, "The Convalescent," 2.

27. In original transcript: "the leading spiritual power."

28. "The Other Dancing Song."

29. "The Seven Seals."

30. *Zarathustra*, 3.14, "On the Great Longing." *Portable Nietzsche*, 333–34.

31. The transcript indicates that there was a "tape difficulty" here and shows two sets of ellipses, which have been deleted. "And" was supplied by the editor.

32. The first quotation is from Burke's *Speech on the Representation of the Commons in Parliament*, while the second is from his *Reflections on the French Revolution*. Strauss cites these same lines together in *Natural Right and History*, 319. For Burke's text, see *The Works of the Right Honourable Edmund Burke* (London: Bohn's British Classics, 1855), 6: 146, 2: 306.

33. Strauss addresses this point in his essay "Relativism," reprinted in *The Rebirth of Classical Political Rationalism*, 19–20.

RESTORING THE SACRED AND THE FINAL QUESTION: *ZARATHUSTRA*, PART 4

1. *Zarathustra*, 4.4, "The Leech." *Portable Nietzsche*, 362–63. Though the full passage is likely to have been read aloud, here it has been abridged.

2. There appears to be a word or phrase missing here, but the transcript does not indicate it.

3. In the transcript: "It is an old theoretical idea that the Jews to — an absolute meaning of it — there is no longer any question of the knowledge of the whole . . ." This may be a mistranscription.

4. *Zarathustra*, 4.5, "The Magician," 2.

5. *Zarathustra*, 4.7, "The Ugliest Man."

6. *Zarathustra*, 4.7, "The Ugliest Man."

7. *Zarathustra*, 1.2, "On the Teachers of Virtue." *Portable Nietzsche*, 141.

8. *Zarathustra*, 4.9, "The Shadow."

9. *Zarathustra*, 4.12, "The Last Supper."

10. *Zarathustra*, 3.11, "On the Spirit of Gravity," 2. *Portable Nietzsche*, 307.

11. That is, the subtitle.

12. These speeches are "The Song of Melancholy," "On Science," and "Among Daughters of the Wilderness."

13. *Zarathustra*, 4.14, "The Song of Melancholy," 3.

14. *Zarathustra*, 4.14, "The Song of Melancholy," 3.

15. *Zarathustra*, 4.15, "On Science."

16. In transcript: "me" instead of "him."

17. *Zarathustra*, 4.15, "On Science." *Portable Nietzsche*, 414.

18. *Zarathustra*, 4.15, "On Science." *Portable Nietzsche*, 414–15.

19. *Zarathustra*, 4.16, "Among Daughters of the Wilderness," 2.

20. *Zarathustra*, 4.16, "Among Daughters of the Wilderness," 2.

21. *Zarathustra*, 4.16, "Among Daughters of the Wilderness," 2.

22. In original transcript: "moralism."

23. In the transcript: "created."

24. It is difficult to follow Strauss's point here.

25. In original transcript: "Up to Nietzsche's time, the simple thing I believe is not considered: atheism was political; only an atheism of the left . . ."

26. Cowan translation.

27. Both translation and emphasis are presumably Strauss's.

28. Strauss may be referring to Ernst Nagel, *Sovereign Reason* (Chicago: Free Press, 1954).

29. The rest of this passage is difficult to follow.

30. The remainder of the tape was not sufficiently audible to transcribe.

Index

Goethe, Johann Wolfgang von, 38, 109, 111, 113, 116
growth, 85–86, 130–31

happiness (*eudaimonia*), 4, 11–12, 23–24, 36
Havelock, Eric, 256n1
heaviness, 45–46, 86–87, 163–64, 169, 216, 234–35. *See also* death; revenge (spirit of); spirit of gravity
Hegel, G. W. F., xiii, 106; aesthetics of, 208; epistemology of, 158; history and, 12–13, 16, 73, 100, 121–22, 134, 140, 147, 156–57, 170, 179, 194, 223, 244; Marx on, 106; reason and, 6–7, 12; Rousseau and, xiii; on the state, 53; temporality and, 12–13
Heidegger, Martin, xi, xiii, xiv, xvii–xviii, 128, 184, 187–88, 190, 192, 254n12, 254n16
height, 46, 88–89, 106, 158, 201–2, 217
Heine, Heinrich, 113, 163–64, 262n13
Heraclitus, 170, 240
herd, the, 23–24, 31–34, 43, 61–62, 129. *See also* communism; egalitarianism
higher men, 229–30, 233–36
high noon, 73, 79–80, 114, 133, 140, 147–48, 234
history: as conflict, 59–61; creativity and, 158; death of God and, xvi, 10–11, 22–24; end of, 73, 106, 124, 134, 140–41, 147, 156–57, 179, 223, 244; eternal return and, 74–75, 166, 216–17; evolution and, 9–10, 24–25, 185–87, 225; Heraclitus and, 179–80, 240; nature and, xiv–xv, 3, 7–11, 216–17; Nietzsche on, 13–14, 17; progress and, xii–xiii, 2, 12, 39–41, 67–68, 74, 82–83, 88–89, 132, 140, 144–48; Rousseau and, 10–12; science and, 32–33, 67–68, 100; unity vs. plurality of, 73–74; values and, 3–4, 90–91, 144–46, 155–56, 174–76, 179–80, 200–201, 204, 241–44. *See also* Hegel, G. W. F.; Marx, Karl; morality; nature; reason
Hitler, Adolf, 130
Hobbes, Thomas, 5–6, 8, 11, 129, 174, 178, 191–92, 220

honor, 22, 34, 43
human, the: all-too-human and, 68, 201–2; animals and, 20–21, 24–26, 39, 50, 67, 79, 83, 122, 127–28, 141, 144–45, 166–67, 212, 215, 248; fragmentation and, 120, 149, 151, 168, 188–90; the last man and, 23–24, 27–29, 31–34, 67, 70, 73, 83, 98, 124, 129, 171, 190, 204, 226; perfectionism and, 4, 11–12, 18, 26, 36–37, 173–74, 188–89; projects of, 14, 17–18, 49–66; reason and, 177–78; rule of the earth by, 66, 171, 174–75, 248; scientific study of, 26–27; sociality of, 173, 196; the superman and, 24–25, 33–35, 51–52, 101, 129–30, 147–49, 154, 188–89
Human, All Too Human (Nietzsche), 18–19
Hume, David, 42

id, the, 38, 66, 69
idealism, 41, 157, 174–76, 179, 222, 240–41
ideologies, 126–27
indifference, 135–37, 166
individualism, 131–32; art and, 76; death of God and, 21–22; democracy and, 153; historical relativism and, 13–14; horizon-creation and, xiii, 131–32; Rousseau's, xiii, 6, 59, 70–71; society and, 56–59, 61, 64–65, 68, 71–72; universality and, 179; as virtue, 49–66
insights, 133–34
inspiration, 91, 182–83
intellectual honesty, 13, 48, 95–96, 112–13, 185, 231–32, 238–39
interpretation, 83–84, 92–100, 106, 131–34, 155, 213–14, 220–22, 228, 243, 246–47
Irrational Man (Barrett), 1–2, 161, 262n10

Jacobi, Friedrich Heinrich, 134
Jacobins, 101
Jefferson, Thomas, 87
Jerusalem, xvi–xvii. *See also* Bible, the; modern philosophy; religion
"Jerusalem and Athens" (Strauss), 253n10, 254n18

jump, the, 134, 163
juvenile delinquency, 77, 101–2, 154

Kant, Immanuel: the categories and, 155–56;
historicism and, 121–22; moral law and,
6–9, 49–50, 70–71, 91–92, 138–39, 170;
reason's edification and, 6, 9, 12, 37, 41–
42, 175, 178, 191; scholarship on, 108–9
Kaufmann, Walter, 3, 100–101
Kierkegaard, Søren, 3, 128, 134
knowledge: of Being, 40–42, 95–96;
contemplation and, 205–28; creativity as
opposed to, 40–43, 78, 92, 104, 137–38,
181–82, 189; of God, 79–80; Hegel
and, 158; historicism and, 155–56, 244;
of history, 10; of the human, 26–27;
interpretation and, 131–32, 135–36, 155,
213–14, 220, 228, 243, 246–47; morality
and, 82, 168–69; objective vs. subjective
truth and, 14–15, 17, 127, 180, 186; peaks
of, 73, 79–80, 133–34, 148, 166, 189, 217;
Plato on, 157, 164; progress narratives
and, xii–xiii, 12, 39–41, 67–68, 74, 82–83,
88–89, 132, 140, 144–48; saints of, 52;
scholarship and, 107–9; skepticism
and, 7–8, 83–84, 128–29, 164, 176–77,
238–39; social sciences' pursuit of, 1, 27;
solipsism and, 215–16; will to power and,
xv, xvi–xvii, 92, 103–7, 131–32, 137–38,
142–43, 211–12, 248–50

Lampert, Laurence, 253n10
La Rochefoucauld, François de, 84–85
Lasswell, Harold D., 75, 99, 191, 258n7
last man, the: death of God and, 23–24, 33;
democracy and, 204; moralism and, 31–
34; psychoanalysis and, 129; science and,
67, 83, 98; social sciences and, 27; the
superman and, 27–29, 73, 124, 171, 226;
Zarathustra passages on, 23–24
"Last Supper, The" (*Z.* section), 234
law, the: morality and, 60–62; nature and,
5–6, 128, 174, 183, 205, 254n12; reason
and, 7–9

leap, the, 134, 163
"Leech, The" (*Z.* section), 229–31
Lenin, V. I., 130
Lessing, Gotthold Ephraim, xiv, 134
Lewis, Sinclair, 231
liberalism, 54–55, 70, 78, 86, 144–45. *See
also* democracy; egalitarianism
"Liberalism of Classical Political Philosophy,
The" (Strauss), 256n1
Liberal Temper in Greek Politics, The (Havelock), 256n1
life: art and, 78–79; belief in, 51–53; as
doctrinal test, 146; eternal return and,
148–49; horizon-forming projects and,
133; the last man and, 23–27; revenge
against, 91; self-consciousness and,
142–43; value of, 11; will to power and,
145–46; wisdom and, 131–32, 136. *See also*
affirmation; creativity; death; defective,
the; democracy; revenge (spirit of);
self-preservation; spirit of gravity; will
to power
lightness, 45–46, 86–87, 93, 163–64, 193–94,
200, 216
likenesses, 197–99, 202
Lincoln, Abraham, 108
lion, the, 29–30, 34, 118
Locke, John, 5–6, 9, 11, 174, 177–78, 191–92,
203
logos, 164, 173
London Times, 245
Lonely Crowd, The (Riesman, Glazer, and
Denney), 2, 65
love, 55–56, 70–71, 93, 105, 147, 162–63, 200,
234–35
loyalty to the earth, 25, 31–32, 36–37, 68, 99–
100, 117–19, 180, 186–99, 240–42
Lucretius Carus, Titus, 177, 230–31
Lukács, Georg, 226–27
Lysenko, Trofim, 71, 258n5

Machiavelli, Niccolo, xii, 46, 99, 173–74, 203,
254n14
"Magician, The" (*Z.* section), 231

Mandeville, Bernard, 175
Manu (code of), 139
Marx, Karl, 12, 73–74, 89, 97, 100, 106,
    121–30, 134, 140, 156, 171, 179, 191, 223,
    226, 254n14
masks, xiv, 187
mass culture, 2
materialism, 100, 106, 143, 156, 174. *See also*
    Marx, Karl
McClosky, Herbert, 144
Michelangelo, 14–15
Milton, John, 70
moderation, 79
modern philosophy: Being question and,
    xi, xiii; contemplation and, 104–5, 142;
    death of God and, xvi; egalitarianism
    and, xiv; epistemology vs. metaphysics
    in, 40–42; fact-value divide and, 1–4, 14,
    59, 67, 77–79, 127–28, 144–45, 249–50;
    historical consciousness and, xiii, 1–4,
    10–11, 22–25, 73, 106, 124, 134, 140–41,
    147, 156–57, 179, 223, 244; inherited
    doctrines of, 126–27; mode of, 142, 170;
    natural right and, 1–8, 16–33, 128–29,
    174, 203–5, 222–23, 254n12; political phi-
    losophy and, 172–73, 175–76; positivism
    and, 1–2, 18, 29, 94, 127–28, 143–45,
    176–83, 219; progress mythos and, xii–
    xiii, 12, 39–41, 67–68, 74, 82–83, 88–89,
    132, 140, 144–48; religion and, 30–32;
    things in themselves and, 69–70. *See also*
    Descartes, René; Hegel, G. W. F.; Kant,
    Immanuel; Rousseau, Jean-Jacques
Montesquieu, Charles-Louis de Secondat,
    191–92
moralism, 31–32, 82–85, 140, 238–39
morality: becoming and, 200–201; creativity
    and, 200–204; eternal return and, 74,
    168–69; Greek philosophy and, 146;
    happiness and, 4, 11–12, 23–24, 36; the
    herd and, 61–62; historicism and, 9–10,
    16–17, 90–91; individualism and, 49–66;
    Kant on, 6, 60–62, 64–65; knowledge

and, 168–69; natural right and, 11, 16–33,
    138–39, 203, 222–23; political science
    and, 153–54, 246–47; religion and, 6, 29,
    85–86, 146; spirit of gravity and, 86–87;
    the superman's emergence and, 24–25,
    47–48; utilitarianism and, 17, 61; virtues
    and, 34–35, 43–44; the will and, 49–50
Mussolini, Benito, 130, 263n9

Napoleon Bonaparte, 73
nations, 59, 61–63, 68–69, 146–47, 222
natural right, xiv–xv, 1–6, 8, 11, 16–33, 128–
    29, 174, 203, 205, 222–23, 254n12
Natural Right and History (Strauss), 3
nature: chance and, 171; conquest of, 89,
    174–75, 190; creativity and, 124–25,
    129–30, 137; eternal return and, xvi,
    141, 182–83; evolution and, 9–10, 140,
    188–89; goodness of, xv, xvi, 11, 128–29,
    227–28; hierarchies and, xiv–xv, 87–88,
    108–9, 124–25, 139, 149, 171, 189–90,
    204–5; history and, xiv–xv, 7–11, 16,
    32–33, 67–68, 175–76, 216–17; human
    nature and, 26, 67–68, 173, 190–91, 245;
    knowledge and, xv, 134–37, 176–77; laws
    of, 5–6, 205; morality and, 138–39, 203;
    obedience to, 137–39; reason and, 7–12,
    16, 175, 178; rebellions against, 149–50;
    relativism and, 75–76; Rousseau on,
    8–9, 11, 20, 84–85, 167, 175, 179, 247;
    self-preservation and, 4; skepticism and,
    7, 16, 174–75; as standard, 8, 15, 61, 137,
    173–74, 178; state of, 5, 8, 129, 167, 178;
    universality of, 5; the will and, 190; will
    to power and, 139–41
nausea, 196–97, 218
Nazism, 45, 100–101, 153
necessity, 7–8, 15, 24, 27, 51, 60, 69, 115, 124–
    25, 142–43, 166–67, 169, 189, 202
neo-communism, 128
Nietzsche (Heidegger), 254n16
Nietzsche, Friedrich: existentialism and,
    2–3, 14–15, 188–89; Heidegger and,

243; human nature and, 26; nature and, 75–76; perspectivism and, 132–33; science and, 32–33, 67–68; truth and, 13, 155–56, 233–34
"Relativism" (Strauss), 261n1
religion, xi, xv; atheism and, 22–23, 28, 68, 183–84; death of God and, 21–22, 33, 65, 71–72; Greek thought and, xvi, xvii, 176; historicism and, 10–11, 29–30; intellectual honesty and, 48; the jump and, 134, 163; Kierkegaard and, 128; moral imperatives and, 6, 29–31, 36–37, 63–64, 85–86, 203, 205, 256n20; natural law and, 5–6; revenge spirit and, 87–88; science and, 77; subjectivity and, 36–39; temporality and, 123–24, 251–52
Republic (Plato), 26, 205, 254n12
resentment, 123–24. *See also* revenge (spirit of)
"Return Home, The" (Z. section), 197–99
revenge (spirit of), 87–88, 123, 149–50, 155, 163, 169, 187–89
Riesman, David, 2, 65
rights of man, 6, 124, 149, 177–78, 222
romanticism, 10–11, 63
Rousseau, Jean-Jacques: French Revolution and, 101; historicism and, 10–12; individualism of, xiii, 59, 70–71, 84–85; morality and, 31; nature and, 8–9, 11, 20, 167, 175, 179, 192, 203, 247; Nietzsche on, 179–80; political philosophy and, xiv, 173–76, 178–79; subjectivity and, 6

scholarship, 106–9, 172
Schopenhauer, Arthur, 31–32, 115–16, 180, 208, 246
science: art and, 76, 78–79, 94–95, 185, 208–9, 213–14; atheism and, 77–78; criteria of, 145; deadly truth and, 13, 32, 40–41, 69, 101–2, 133, 137, 143–44, 181, 185–86, 194–95, 210–11, 229–30; definitions of, 97–98; evolution and, 9, 77, 79, 82–83, 185–86, 215; fear and, 236–37; histori-

cism and, 32–33, 67–68; infinite progress and, 39–40; the last man and, 67, 83, 98, 191; "The Leech" and, 229–30; objective knowledge and, 14, 17; philosophy and, 91, 127–28, 136–37, 180–81, 219, 249–50
self, the: the body and, 37–41, 45, 49–50, 180; creativity and, 40–48, 69–70, 93, 106, 181–82; definitions of, xvii, 131; the ego and, 37–40, 44–45, 52–53, 61, 64, 74, 129, 131, 189–90; overcoming of, 117, 137, 139, 143–44, 211–12, 225–26; the passions and, 43–44; subjectivity and, 4–5
self-preservation, 4, 11–12, 27, 48, 85, 97, 174, 178–79, 203
Seneca, Lucius Annaeus, 103
sense data, 7–8, 179–80, 240
serpent, the, 151–52
sexuality, 42–43, 55–56, 71, 199
"Shadow, The" (Z. section), 233
Shakespeare, William, 38
Shakespeare's Maidens and Women (Heine), 163–64
shame, 82–84, 97, 232–34
sincerity, 56, 65
skepticism, 7, 18–19, 41, 65, 128–29, 164, 177, 238–39
social sciences, 1, 26–27, 59–60, 67, 77–78, 98–99, 101–2, 144–45, 183, 243
Socrates, xiii; modern philosophy and, xi; Nietzsche and, xiv, 109, 201, 205–11, 240; philosophical project of, 58; Plato's writings and, 206–7; religion and, xvi, xvii; Strauss and, xiii
solipsism, 215–16
"Song of Melancholy, The" (Z. section), 244
"Soothsayer, The" (Z. section), 112–16
sophists, 91
Sorel, Georges, 190, 263n9
souls, 39–40
Speech on the Representation of the Commons in Parliament (Burke), 265n32
Spengler, Oswald, 76, 116, 220